Five Years That Shook the World

Five Years That Shook the World

Gorbachev's Unfinished Revolution

EDITED BY

Harley D. Balzer

GEORGETOWN UNIVERSITY

Westview Press
BOULDER • SAN FRANCISCO • OXFORD

Copyright © 1991 by Westview Press, Inc.

Published in 1991 in the United States of America by Westview Press, Inc., 5500 Central Avenue, Boulder, Colorado 80301, and in the United Kingdom by Westview Press, 36 Lonsdale Road, Summertown, Oxford OX2 7EW

Library of Congress Cataloging-in-Publication Data
Five years that shook the world : Gorbachev's unfinished revolution / edited by
  Harley D. Balzer.
    p. cm.
  Includes index.
  ISBN 0-8133-1196-9—ISBN 0-8133-1197-7 (pbk.)
  1. Soviet Union—Politics and government—1985–   .
    2. Perestroika.
3. Gorbachev, Mikhail Sergeevich, 1931–   . I. Balzer, Harley D.
DK288.F58 1991
947.085′4—dc20   90-24880
                                                                                          CIP

Printed and bound in the United States of America

  The paper used in this publication meets the requirements
  of the American National Standard for Permanence of Paper
  for Printed Library Materials Z39.48-1984.

10   9   8   7   6   5   4   3   2

Half measures can kill when on the brink of precipices,
chafing in terror at the bit,
we strain and sweat and foam because we cannot
jump just halfway across.

Blind is the one who but half sees the chasm,
and half recoils because he lost his way...

—Yevgeny Yevtushenko

(Translated by Alexis Obolensky
and Victor H. Winston)

... we are in the midst of a yet unfinished revolution... The birth pains of
modern industrial society, which Marx often mistook for the death throes of
capitalism, are being enacted before our eyes.

—Adam Ulam

Contents

Preface and Acknowledgments

Whatever the fate of his attempt to restructure the Soviet Union's economy and political system, Mikhail Gorbachev has changed the world. The political landscape of Central and Eastern Europe has been altered in ways that seemed unimaginable even in 1987 or 1988. The role of communism in the Third World will never again be the same. Yet the domestic revolution remains unfinished, and its direction uncertain. By early 1991 many analysts shifted their focus from Gorbachev's chances for "success" to the possibility of a return to Stalinism. Neither the revolution nor the debate is finished.

The goal of this volume is to present a balanced analysis of perestroika with an eye to the ongoing political, social and cultural changes. In assessing the first five years, the contributors have sought to treat the period as a coherent historical episode, despite the lack of perspective that is so important to historians. I have already written about the effects of perestroika and glasnost on Sovietology ("Can We Survive Glasnost?" *AAASS Newsletter*, Vol. 20, No. 1 [January 1989] pp. 1-2). Virtually every contributor to this volume would undoubtedly want a chance to revise what has been written by the time the book is published. We have discussed semi-seriously the comparative advantages of issuing the volume in loose-leaf binders to permit periodic updating, or perhaps publishing "on line" with regular emendations.

Sovietology may indeed come to that. But it smacks of Orwell. Instead, we have made an effort at reasoned judgments of Gorbachev's first five years, with some additions based on events up to the end of January 1991. All of the contributors completed work on their chapters by that date.

The chapters published here are based on papers prepared for a conference on "The First Five Years of Perestroika: What Have We Learned? What Has Gorbachev Learned?" held at Georgetown University March 8-9, 1990 in conjunction with the celebration of the 30th Anniversary of Georgetown's Russian Area Studies Program.

The conference was sponsored by the Georgetown University Russian Area Studies Program. Additional financial support was provided by the Social Science Research Council and by the Georgetown University Graduate School.

In addition to these chapters, a number of other scholars presented papers at the conference which, for various reasons, could not be included in the volume. Alfred J. Rieber, Vladimir Voinovich, Karen Dawisha, Robert Campbell, Herbert Levine, Yaacov Ro'i, Gail Lapidus, Mark Zlotnik, Rose Gottemoeller, Dale Herspring and Ted Warner all provided insights that were of benefit in completing this volume. The panel chairs, David Ransel, Marjorie Mandelstam Balzer, Valery Petrochenkov, Stuart Brown, Thane Gustafson, Richard Scribner and Robert Lieber contributed comments and expertise.

The conference would not have been possible without the work of Jill Roese, the Russian Area Studies Program Administrative Assistant.

In preparing the manuscript for publication, compiling the appendixes and preparing the index, I was fortunate to have the assistance of Susan Brent, Laura Guinn, Eric Johnson, Elizabeth Kirkwood, Jennifer Long, Elizabeth O'Shea, Ann Rubin, Valerie Sperling, and Valerye Strochak.

Susan McEachern of Westview Press has been involved in this project from its inception, and her enthusiasm was a major factor in bringing it to fruition. Chris Arden, Diana Luykx, and Bev LeSeur were of tremendous help in processing the manuscript.

Marjorie Mandelstam Balzer has made an intellectual and personal commitment to this project far beyond what mere mention in a preface can acknowledge. Her support, in all its forms, is gratefully appreciated.

Harley D. Balzer
Cabin John, MD

In preparing the volume for a second printing, we have corrected typographical errors, added some items to the bibliography, and extended the "Chronology" to December 1991. The text of the chapters has not been modified. Laura Guinn and Eric Johnson were of tremendous assistance in making these revisions.

USSR Population By Republic

According to the 1989 Census

Republic	Population	Titular Nationality
Russian Republic	147,021,869	81.5%
Ukraine	51,471,499	72.7%
Belorussia	10,151,806	77.9%
Moldova	4,335,360	64.5%
Armenia	3,304,776	93.3%
Azerbaidzhan	7,021,178	75.6%
Georgia	5,409,841	70.0%
Estonia	1,565,662	61.5%
Latvia	2,666,567	52.0%
Lithuania	3,674,802	79.6%
Kazakhstan	16,464,464	39.7%
Kirghizia	4,257,755	52.4%
Tadzhikistan	5,092,603	62.3%
Turkmenistan	3,522,717	72.0%
Uzbekistan	19,810,077	71.4%
TOTAL	285,761,976	

Total as of January 1, 1990: 288,623,600

Source: *Soiuz*, No. 32, August 1990, pp. 12-13.

Republics of the
Soviet Union

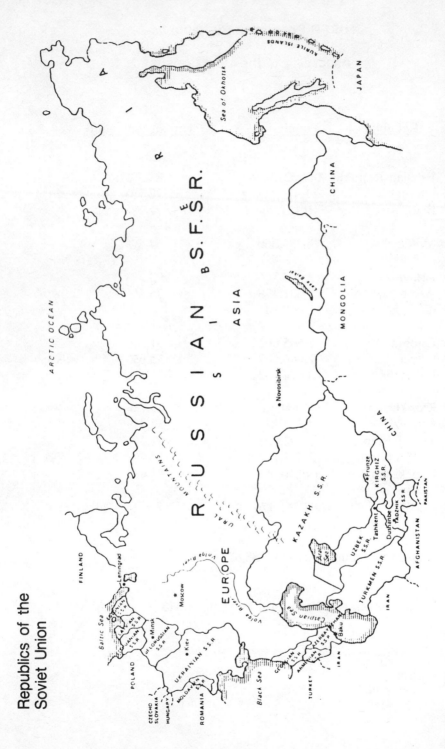

Reproduced with permission from Carl Haub. "The Population of the Soviet Union." *Population Profiles.* Second Series. Unit 4 (Washington, Conn.: Center for Information on America, 1981).

Introduction

No one should have been expected to predict the extent of the changes in the USSR in the second half of the 1980s. To have anticipated the accession of a younger leader who would not only succeed in consolidating political power but also sustain a major assault on the inevitable resistance to reform demanded too much foresight. More than a few of Mikhail Gorbachev's closest supporters have stated that had Gorbachev himself known in 1985 just how far he would be drawn along the path of perestroika, he might not have taken the first steps. The five years from 1985 to 1990 were a time of learning for the participants as well as for the outside observers.

To have failed to predict the sweeping changes is not the same as to be taken totally by surprise when they happened or to misunderstand their character. By 1985 there already existed a substantial body of scholarship that pointed to the *possibility* of serious change in the Soviet Union.[1] Few scholars were willing to go so far as to state that dramatic change was inevitable—that sort of prognosticating is best left to mystics. But scholars who were tracking the social processes in Soviet society—particularly the ones with a comparative bent—had come to the conclusion that major changes were at least possible and perhaps even likely.

The scholars contributing to this volume do not represent a single academic school or approach to the study of the Soviet Union. Their contributions cover a range of important topics and do not conform to a single orientation. Nevertheless, all were inclined to believe that the changes that took place in the USSR during 1985–1990 were "for real." Scholars who maintain that the entire enterprise of perestroika amounted to nothing more than *pokazuka* (a facade) or *maskirovka* (deception to veil an impending attack), or that glasnost was nothing but another clever trick of Communist propaganda, are not represented here. Also absent are those who pronounced that Gorbachev was doomed to fail from the

1

outset.[2] The scholars represented here would regard the successful evolution of the Soviet Union into a non-Communist state with a less restrictive political system as possible, though they would undoubtedly differ in their assessments of the likelihood of such a transition.[3]

The theme of the plausibility of systemic reform emerges clearly in the first chapter. Blair Ruble's contribution effectively summarizes the argument that Mikhail Gorbachev is as much the product as the initiator of change in the USSR. Previous articles by Ruble and others have detailed the changes in education, employment, urbanization and other elements of "civil society."[4] Here, Ruble discusses these changes in the context of what he calls a "revolution of the mind," by which he means a cognitive shift that has produced conditions that could make successful perestroika possible. Critics have argued that civil society analyses are overly determinist, resembling the errors of modernization theorists in the 1960s and 1970s.[5] Yet few of the partisans of civil society argue that democratization is inevitable or irreversible. They assert that it is possible, and should not be dismissed *a priori* on the basis of autocratic traditions or national character.

From their titles, one might conclude that Ruble's presentation directly contradicts Gertrude Schroeder's analysis of the Soviet economy as being on yet another treadmill of unpromising reforms. Yet both authors are guardedly optimistic. Both are aware of the tremendous problems confronting Soviet reformers, but they also detect something new in perestroika that makes it qualitatively different from previous Soviet efforts at reform. That something is the participation of civil society. Involvement of society in the reform effort rests on two reciprocal processes: a willingness on the part of the government to drop its pose of omnipotence according a legitimate place to input from "below," and a willingness by at least some elements of society to participate in the process. Ruble frames it as a solution to the twin dilemmas of hyperinstitutionalization and underinstitutionalization—a syndrome combining excessive centralization with inadequate capacity to mediate the needs of the system in any but the crudest terms.

If the lesson of the impossibility of maintaining the hyperinstitutionalized state with the resources available has finally been learned, the future does indeed look more promising. But the promise is not of a new era free from conflict. One of the important lessons of the late twentieth century is that basic political questions of power and resource distribution are constantly being reconfigured. The crucial issue is not a final allocation of power or rewards, but rather the mechanism by which reallocation takes place—the legitimate political behavior in the system. What has happened in the Soviet Union since 1985 is a profound redefinition of legitimate political behavior. It may take some time for a balance to be struck, and we should remember that there is never a "final" version of such relationships. They are always subject to change.

Most Soviet scholars, politicians, and intellectuals would begin an analysis of perestroika by focusing on the economy. Even those who boast of their rejection of Marxist concepts often turn out to have been influenced significantly by decades of materialist ideology. At a time when Gorbachev himself has recognized that fixing the economic mess requires social, psychological, and even spiritual renewal, many of his close collaborators, not to mention the old guard, still believe that the economic situation is the key to everything else.

In chapter 2, Gertrude Schroeder details the false starts and grievous errors in Soviet economic policy during Gorbachev's first five years. But the success of perestroika will not be evaluated on economic grounds alone. It was perhaps inevitable that economic change would be halting and inconsistent. To get to serious economic reform, Gorbachev himself needed to learn a great deal and the political situation had to be altered quite radically. Rather than "losing" or "wasting" five years, Gorbachev might have been using the time not only to figure out for himself what needs to be done, but also to create a political framework in which it could be accomplished. Whether he will be granted the additional time in which to implement what he has learned remains to be seen. There are few successes to report, and merely adding to the learning curve can no longer be hailed as an achievement. Most people now know what must be done, in terms of price reform and marketization, but no one has yet produced a plausible prescription for how to actually accomplish it.[6]

Western observers of the USSR are frequently struck by the contrast between dismal performance and tremendous potential. Dr. Schroeder ends on a relatively optimistic note, stressing precisely that potential. So does Alec Nove in an essay written for another collection.[7] The natural and human resources available in the USSR and the absurd obstacles placed in the path of rational economic behavior lead many to believe that impressive results could be achieved relatively quickly if the proper formula were adopted. But not all sectors of the economy are amenable to rapid transformation: in many crucial areas, such as the energy sector, serious restructuring will require a generation.[8]

Schroeder has been one of the most consistent critics of flawed Soviet economic reforms.[9] She may part company with the most pessimistic analysts in her conclusion that the economic problems of the USSR are still susceptible to remedy. Although there is little basis for optimism in what has been accomplished thus far, the steps that must be taken to initiate improvements in economic performance are not a secret. What such changes require is political will combined with enough public faith or acquiescence to ride out the transition period. One of the tragedies of perestroika is that failure to carry through the economic reforms has made any future efforts even more difficult.

Among the most serious considerations in any economic program will be the nation's desperate ecological situation. A half-century of extensive development has left the USSR with myriad environmental difficulties that will require much time and money to correct. In Chapter 3, Murray Feshbach not only chronicles the ecological crisis, but also points to its consequences for the population's health and broader demographic trends. His conclusion, not so much stated as allowed to emerge from the weight of the evidence he cites, is that the costs of the remedies far exceed what even a vibrant reformed economy would be capable of generating. Resource constraints will indeed force some very difficult choices on the Soviet political system, whatever its form.

In Chapter 4, Harley Balzer focuses on the evolving political system, providing not so much a narrative as an impressionistic evaluation of developments. Drawing on his training as a historian and his experience in the U.S. political system, he seeks to place perestroika in the context of Russian and Soviet political development.[10] Balzer concludes by noting the contradictions in Gorbachev's political approach. These contradictions were a source of strength when Gorbachev had to strike a balance between the Party apparat and radical reformers, but they could increasingly become a liability if an electoral system continues to develop.

National and ethnic tensions will continue to present Gorbachev with some of his most difficult political problems. In chapter 5, Paul Goble discusses the nationalities issue. His treatment can be placed in the context of three major lessons about the Soviet nationalities problem. First, comparative study reminds us that the Soviet Union is hardly the only country facing serious ethnic and national difficulties. Yet it is dangerous to assume that events must unfold in similar patterns just because some of the conditions are similar. Second, many of the ethnic problems confronting the USSR result from relative success in raising the educational levels, increasing the economic complexity, and expanding the role of the media in national areas. New elites in these regions, rather than expressing gratitude to Moscow, have become increasingly assertive. Again, however, the trend is hardly unique to the USSR. Third, national tensions were exacerbated because Gorbachev had to learn a great deal about ethnic identity after he became Soviet leader—lessons most Western politicians learn in the process of gaining office.

The breathtaking political and foreign policy changes in 1989—1990 made it difficult to remember that during 1986—1988 glasnost appeared to far outpace perestroika. Initially, almost everyone was caught up in the exhilaration of being able to make statements, mention names, and print materials that had been taboo for sixty years. But the novelty of breaking taboos must inevitably wear thin. Many observers of the cultural scene have shifted from emphasizing the unprecedented character of things that were said and published to bemoaning the lack of truly new and stimulating cultural products.

In Chapter 6, Josephine Woll, a close observer of the panoply of changes in literature and culture, offers a concise survey of the way the cultural landscape has altered in the course of the five years under study.[11] Woll's overview is complemented by Helena Goscilo's in-depth analysis of developments in Russian literature in Chapter 7. Both find that the main body of glasnost literature, which Dr. Goscilo terms "alternative prose," has emphasized political alternatives more often than artistic ones. Many Soviet editors use political rather than aesthetic standards when selecting works for publication. Their journalistic emphasis, while understandable, is also regrettable. It inevitably gives much Soviet literary work of the perestroika era a time-bound rather than timeless quality.

The experience of literature shows that the traditions of censorship and imposition of limits die hard. Merely removing the most blatant mechanisms of censorship does not guarantee extirpation of all controls, especially those internalized by individuals who are products of the Soviet cultural system. By the same token, it may be quite difficult to reimpose censorship on writers and journalists who have become accustomed to freer expression.[12]

If the political, social, and cultural changes constituting perestroika are contradictory and still inconclusive, it is much more difficult to discount the results of changes in foreign and defense policy. Historians often suggest that would-be reformist Russian rulers such as Catherine the Great and Alexander II generally found it easier to expand the empire than to reform it. Mikhail Gorbachev has found it much easier to shrink the Soviet empire than to restructure it.

Soviet withdrawal from Eastern Europe constitutes a solution more advantageous to the NATO allies than any outcome that might have been hoped for from a military victory. If the cold war is over, the chief question facing the United States and its allies concerns the nature of the "postwar settlement." A choice exists between the model from World War

I or that from World War II—the "Carthaginian Peace" of reparations and penitence or the Marshall Plan variant of succor for the defeated. Those who oppose the latter—the "soft" peace—have noted that the Soviet military-industrial complex continues to turn out modern weapons at a rate far exceeding that necessary for defense requirements. Some of the ongoing Soviet weapons production can be explained by inertia, and some of it by common sense: No country is going to scrap its newest, most expensive hardware when it has lots of old, obsolete equipment in its inventory. The process of defining the legitimate security needs of both sides will be protracted and difficult. No one should expect either side to unilaterally sacrifice opportunities to shore up its position. At the same time, it would be irresponsible to ignore the extent of the Soviet military effort, particularly in light of Ministry of Defense criticism of the arms control treaties and other agreements negotiated by the Ministry of Foreign Affairs during Eduard Shevardnadze's tenure.[13]

The magnitude of change in superpower relations emerges clearly from the three contributions to this volume dealing with international affairs and security. In Chapter 8, Angela Stent focuses on Central and Eastern Europe, using her detailed knowledge of the German situation to evaluate developments related to the "common European home." German unification has clearly been the most dramatic symbol and most rapid result of the 1989-1990 Eastern European revolution.[14]

In Chapter 9 Robert Huber draws on his decade of experience in the U.S. congressional policy process as well as on his academic training to provide both a summary of lessons learned in U.S.-Soviet relations and a prescription for integrating those lessons into scholarship and policy.[15] His major themes are the unplanned character of the changes that have taken place and the need to respond by formulating a view that puts an end to the "uniqueness" of the Soviet Union in Western conceptions of foreign policy. It is time to regard the USSR as one very important state in an international state system, rather than as some sort of exceptional entity. The lessons about both internal politics and foreign policy learned from other transitions to democracy should be examined for clues to the Soviet situation.

The final chapter, by Jerry Hough, is even more directly concerned with the policy process. Hough expands on arguments he has made elsewhere regarding the common interests of the USSR and the NATO nations.[16] In this connection, he would extend the borders of the "common European home" to encompass everything from Vladivostok to California. Hough argues that U.S.-Soviet cooperation is crucial to any future world order. His warning that the major threat to the United States and Europe was likely to come from another Khomeini in the Third World was written in mid-1989. It would appear to have been borne out by the Iraqi invasion of Kuwait in 1990.

Hough's chapter emphasizes that the enterprise of perestroika cannot be divorced from the outside world. Indeed, the United States has an important role to play in the developments. Even though it cannot be decisive, it can have a major influence. One of the tragedies of the late twentieth century may be that at a time when the mounting of another Marshall Plan could finish the work of rebuilding a peaceful, democratic, unified Europe, the United States is too saddled with debt and too distracted by other problems to undertake the effort.

Gorbachev and perestroika constitute a no-lose proposition for the United States. If Gorbachev fails, if his reforms really lead nowhere, then the Soviet Union will continue to be the economic and technological "basket case" that its leaders now freely admit it had become in the era of stagnation. Conversely, success is possible only if Gorbachev takes steps that make the Soviet Union much more a part of the world community, more integrated into international economic relationships, more *interdependent* with other nations. Interdependence is not a guarantee of peace, brotherhood, friendship and a security alliance between the USSR and the United States. But it is a formula that makes the Soviet Union much less threatening, much less dangerous, and much more amenable to reasonable settlement of disputes in the world. That is probably the best we can hope for.

In addition to noting what this volume contains, mention should be made of what has not been included. Despite our desire to be comprehensive, space and time limitations inevitably precluded the coverage of many important subjects. A partial list of the topics to which we would have liked to devote chapters includes religion, informal groups, gender issues, youth, the military, and science and technology.

1. As communism has lost even its formal standing as a belief system, religion has grown in importance in Soviet society. What it lacks in its capacity to serve as a basis for unity or to legitimate imperial expansion may be compensated by the genuine strength of religious feelings. As Balzer notes in Chapter 4, Gorbachev has extended his appeal for public involvement in perestroika by sanctioning the activity of religious communities. He has met with church leaders and encouraged a growing activism by many religious groups. Some of this activity has conformed to patterns that Gorbachev intended, such as medical and charitable work and the effort to provide moral and ethical guidance as Communist

ideology evaporates. But, inevitably, religious leaders and believers have used their freedom to agitate for other causes, including the return of sequestered property and adjudication of long-standing disputes, such as those among Catholics, Uniates and Russian Orthodox in Ukraine. Far from always being an ally, religion may sometimes be a threat to Gorbachev's program.[17]

Of particular significance here is the multi-faceted character of religion. Islam provides a good example. Resurgent or fundamentalist Islam is often perceived as a serious threat to the USSR, to Russian rule over Central Asia, and sometimes to perestroika itself. But there are multiple strains within Islam, including conservative and reformist currents; and tensions have erupted in violence directed against other Muslims at least as often as against Slavs or communists. Like so many aspects of Soviet life, religion may be either an aid or a threat to reform, depending on how the diverse situations are handled. The adoption of a Law on Freedom of Conscience in September 1990 may yet help to regularize the relationship.[18]

2. Religious groups constitute only one example of the independent loci of activity developing in Soviet society. "Informal" organizations, too, have become a major feature of perestroika, leading some observers to state that a genuine civil/civic society is emerging. The definition of an informal group is vague, but the number of these organizations has been growing steadily. Their impact cannot be denied. Particularly in the major cities, "informals" have become a vital part of political life and a training ground for new political activists. There is data on the number of officially registered groups, but no full count of the unofficial informals. One of the largest categories of informal groups has been the vague category of "greens" in the ecology movement, and these organizations have been a particularly important recruiting and training ground for political activity.[19]

3. A few of the informal groups have been formed on the basis of gender, reflecting serious concerns about the status of women in Soviet society. Yet, despite the growth of womens studies, the sophistication needed to analyze a matrix of diverse cultures is only gradually being developed.[20] Most important, sensitivity to gender issues has to become much more widespread in the USSR itself, so that it becomes a mainstream concern. Although a general climate of reform and openness has encouraged discussion of womens issues, there is a danger that broader economic problems and other difficulties will be used as an excuse to postpone dealing with gender issues. Many Russian women have sought

to discuss male/female relationships, only to be told by men that they should save their energy for "real" problems.[21]

4. Soviet youth have been subjected to an enormous amount of abuse in parlor conversations about perestroika. Many observers believe that, unlike students in many other nations who have taken a leading role in political change, Soviet young people have been largely apathetic during perestroika. But the evidence thus far has been almost completely impressionistic. Western scholars studying youth culture have focused on rock groups and cultural content more often than on political activism. More public opinion and survey research will be needed to plumb the true state of young peoples' attitudes toward the changes affecting the USSR. Data indicate, for example, that a majority of young people now would prefer the private sector over the state sector in their future employment.[22] There have been notable examples of youth participation, particularly in the ecology movement and in movements for sovereignty in many republics. But we still lack systematic data on the extent and character of this activity.[23]

5. The revolution in Soviet military strategy has received an enormous amount of attention from scholars and policy analysts.[24] Regardless of how much credence one accords to the new pronouncements, or how durable they turn out to be, the tangible changes already carried out have revolutionized the military situation in Europe. Dozens of scholarly studies on such topics as Warsaw Pact military integration are now of mainly historical interest. "New thinking" in security policy and international affairs, which really incorporates concepts formulated in the Brezhnev era, has been concisely summarized by David Holloway:

> Among the main propositions of the new thinking are, first, the idea that universal or "all-human" (the term used in the Soviet press) values take precedence over class values in the modern world; second, that the world is becoming more interdependent; third, that in a nuclear war, or even a large-scale conventional war, victory is not possible, and that, therefore, security in the modern world has to be based increasingly on political rather than on military instruments of policy; and finally, that security in the modern world, and especially in the context of the Soviet-American relationship, must be mutual—it cannot be unilateral.[25]

6. Science and technology are most often dealt with in the context of the military. Yet the status of science and scientists deserves to be studied in its own right.[26] From its inception, the USSR proclaimed itself to be based on scientific principles, and to be able to organize the development of science to serve human needs. But its track record is mixed at best. The

Soviet Union has been able to create the world's largest scientific community, but the majority of that community's efforts have been directed at military needs. Equally damaging, the military sector, as well as much of Soviet industrial and even agricultural production, paid scant attention to long-term perspectives: neither overall economic returns nor collateral costs to health and environment were given due emphasis. The costs of such neglect will be enormous.

If many of the scholars in this volume are hesitant in their optimism over reform prospects, it is because of their concern about the durability of the domestic changes and their long-term implications. The Soviet Union and its erstwhile satellites aspire to join the Western economic system at a time when concerns about the renewability of resources and the consequences of their use are growing. Disputes over resource use and fair distribution are inevitable. Even if the U.S. has the resources for another Marshall Plan, should it use those resources in Europe or in the Middle East? Can it afford both? However, concerns about competing claims on resources are a far cry from worries over the gulag, military confrontation and nuclear war. Before becoming too depressed about the potential difficulties, we might take a moment to appreciate just how much did change in Gorbachev's first five years.

Yet the outcome remains in doubt. By the beginning of 1991, the prospects for evolution of the Soviet system looked far less promising. This does not change our account of what happened during Gorbachev's first five years, though it does influence our perspective. To bring the story up to date as of January 1991, we have added a short essay by Galina Starovoitova, a Soviet ethnosociologist and politician intimately involved in the events. The editor has provided an Epilogue incorporating recent scholarship and placing the events in context.

Notes

1. See the "Harbingers of Change" in the Selected Bibliography at the end of this volume.

2. Two of the more pessimistic commentators have been Peter Reddaway and Marshall Goldman.

3. For a sophisticated discussion of the meaning of "success" in the Soviet context see George W. Breslauer, "Thinking About the Soviet Future," in *Can Gorbachev's Reforms Succeed?*, edited by Breslauer (Berkeley: University of California, Berkeley-Stanford Program in Soviet Studies, 1990), pp. 1-34.

4. Moshe Lewin, *The Gorbachev Phenomenon* (Berkeley: University of California Press, 1988); S. Frederick Starr, "Soviet Union: A Civil Society," *Foreign Policy*, No. 70 (Spring 1988), pp. 26-41; Blair Ruble, "The Social Dimensions of Perestroika,"

Soviet Economy, Vol. 3 (April-June 1987), pp. 171-183; and Blair Ruble, "The Soviet Union's Quiet Revolution," in Breslauer, *Can Gorbachev's Reforms Succeed?*, pp. 77-94.

5. Z [Martin Malia], "To the Stalin Mausoleum," *Dædalus*, Vol. 119, No. 1 (winter 1990), pp. 295-344.

6. *Perekhod k rynku* (Moscow: Arkhangel'skoe, 1990); Ed A. Hewett, "The New Soviet Plan," *Foreign Affairs*, Vol. 69, No. 5 (winter 1990-1991), pp. 146-167.

7. Alec Nove, "An Economy in Transition," in Abraham Brumberg, ed., *Chronicle of a Revolution: A Western-Soviet Inquiry into Perestroika* (New York: Pantheon Books, 1990), pp 50-71.

8. Thane Gustafson uses the analogy of a "gnarled tree" to describe the deformations in basic economic structures. See Thane Gustafson, *Crisis Amid Plenty: The Politics of Soviet Energy Under Brezhnev and Gorbachev* (Princeton: Princeton University Press, 1990), p. 11. For more pessimistic assessments of Soviet economic prospects see Marshall Goldman, "Gorbachev the Economist," *Foreign Affairs*; and Anders Aslund, *Gorbachev's Struggle for Economic Reform: The Soviet Reform Process, 1985-1988* (New York: Cornell University Press, 1989).

9. Gertrude E. Schroeder, "Soviet Economic Reforms at an Impasse," in U.S. Congress. Joint Economic Committee, *Soviet Economic Prospects for the Seventies* (Washington, DC: U.S. Government Printing Office, 1973) pp. 11-28; Gertrude E. Schroeder, "Soviet Economy on a Treadmill of 'Reforms'," in U.S. Congress. Joint Economic Committee, *Soviet Economy in a Time of Change* (Washington, DC: U.S. Government Printing Office, 1979), pp. 312-340; Gertrude E. Schroeder, "Soviet Economic 'Reform' Decrees: More Steps on the Treadmill," in U.S. Congress. Joint Economic Committee, *Soviet Economy in the 1980s: Problems and Prospects*, Vol. 1 (Washington, DC: U.S. Government Printing Office, 1982), pp. 65-88.

10. For descriptions of formal structure of the political system, see Stephen White, *Gorbachev in Power* (Cambridge: Cambridge University Press, 1990), Chapter 2, and the excellent coverage of recent changes provided by Dawn Mann and others in the Radio Liberty *Report on the USSR*.

11. Also see Josephine Woll, "Glasnost' and Soviet Culture," *Problems of Communism*, Vol. XXXVIII, No. 6 (November-December 1989), pp. 40-50.

12. Vera Tolz, "Soviet Central Media Coverage of Events in the Baltics," Radio Liberty *Daily Report*, January 22, 1991 (received via Sovset').

13. Interview with V. Shkoda and V. Litov, *Sovetskaia Rossiia*, January 9, 1991, p. 5.

14. Also see Angela Stent, "The One Germany," *Foreign Policy*, No. 81 (winter 1990-1991), pp. 53-70.

15. See the sources in the Selected Bibliography at the end of this volume.

16. Jerry Hough, *Russia and the West: Gorbachev and the Politics of Reform* (New York: Simon and Schuster, 1988); and Hough, "Gorbachev's Politics," *Foreign Affairs*, Vol. 68, No. 5 (winter 1989-1990), pp. 26-41, particularly pp. 40-41.

17. Marjorie Mandelstam Balzer, "Nationalism in the Soviet Union: One Anthropological View," *Journal of Soviet Nationalities*, Vol. 1, No. 3 (1990), pp. 1-17, and S. P. Ramet, "Gorbachev's *Perestroika* in the Religious Sphere," in *Reli-*

gious Policy in the Soviet Union, edited by S. P. Ramet (New York: Cambridge University Press, forthcoming, 1991). Radio Liberty has provided consistent coverage in reports by Oxana Antic, Vera Tolz, and others.

18. The full text is in *Pravda*, October 9, 1990, p. 4.

19. Informal groups were growing in importance in Soviet society before Gorbachev came to power. In addition to the sources in the Selected Bibliography in this volume, see Victoria Bonnell, "Voluntary Associations in Gorbachev's Russia," in Breslauer, *Can Gorbachev's Reforms Succeed?*, pp. 63-76; Nicolai N. Petro, "Perestroika from Below: Voluntary Sociopolitical Associations in the RSFSR," in *Perestroika at the Crossroads*, edited by Alfred J. Rieber and Alvin Z. Rubinstein (Armonk, NY: M. E. Sharpe, 1991), pp. 102-133.

20. See the sources in the Selected Bibliography at the end of this volume.

21. Deborah Tannen, *You Just Don't Understand: Women and Men in Conversation* (New York: William Morrow and Company, 1990).

22. Bill Keller, "In Soviet Life, Thaw Becomes Chill," *The New York Times*, February 3, 1991, p. 12.

23. In addition to the sources in the Selected Bibliography at the end of this volume, see Iurii Shchekochikhin, "O 'liuberakh', i ne tol'ko o nikh," *Literaturnaia gazeta*, March 11, 1987, p. 1; T. B. Shchepanskaia, "Protsessy ritualizatsii v molodezhnoi subkul'ture," *Sovetskaia etnografiia*, No. 5 (September-October 1988), pp. 15-25; Richard Stites, *Soviet Popular Culture: Entertainment and Society in Russia Since 1900* (New York: Cambridge University Press, forthcoming, 1991), Chapter 7; and Richard Dobson, "Youth Problems in the Soviet Union," in *Soviet Social Problems*, edited by Anthony Jones, Walter D. Connor and David E. Powell (Boulder: Westview Press, 1991), pp. 227-251.

24. In addition to the books in the Selected Bibliography at the end of this volume, see David Holloway, "Gorbachev's New Thinking," *Foreign Affairs*, Vol. 68, No. 1 (winter 1988-1989), pp. 66-81; Dale Herspring, "The Soviet Military and Change," *Survival* (July-August 1989), pp. 321-338; F. Stephen Larrabee, "Gorbachev and the Soviet Military," *Foreign Affairs*, Vol. 66, No. 5 (summer 1988), pp. 1002-1026; William E. Odom, "Soviet Military Doctrine," *Foreign Affairs*, Vol. 67, No. 2, pp. 114-134; and Edward L. Warner, III, "New Thinking and Old Realities in Soviet Defense Policy," *Survival* (January-February 1989), pp. 13-33. Steven Foye has provided consistently excellent coverage in the Radio Liberty *Report on the USSR*.

25. David Holloway, "'New Thinking' Abroad and the Military's Stake in Reform at Home," in Breslauer, *Can Gorbachev's Reforms Succeed?*, p. 111.

26. See Loren Graham, ed., *Science and the Soviet Social Order* (Cambridge: Harvard University Press, 1990), and Harley D. Balzer, *Soviet Science on the Edge of Reform* (Boulder: Westview Press, 1989).

1

Stepping off the Treadmill of Failed Reforms?

Blair A. Ruble

The image of Russia trapped on a treadmill of failed reform has caught the imagination of the informed public in the Soviet Union as well as in the West. Distinguished historians write of a recurring cycle of incomplete reform throughout much of modern Russian history.[1] Western economists, frustrated by the unwillingness of Soviet political leaders to abandon their centrally administered economic behemoth, lament a more contemporary treadmill.[2] Taking either a fifteen-year overview or one of one hundred and fifty years, we find that conventional wisdom suggests a pattern in which an overly centralized Russian multinational state stagnates under a conservative leadership until some external event—usually defeat in war—prompts top-level authorities to attempt reform. Tsars and commissars have designed reforms intended to prod a torpid Russia into catching up to a world that is quickly passing it by. In light of either the steam revolution of centuries past or today's scientific and technical revolution, the centralized authoritarian state cannot keep pace with a changing world unless dramatic intervention comes from above.[3] Eventually, reformist storming exhausts itself, with reform initiatives remaining incomplete.

Cyclical explanations appear to be consonant with the events of recent years. Brezhnevian stagnation has been followed by Gorbachevian perestroika, which, in turn, appears to be running out of momentum after five years of upheaval and discord. Once again, it seems, Russian—and Soviet—centralized state authority may persevere, thereby preventing the emergence of a civil society.

Such reasoning accounts for the dramatic events spilling out of the Soviet Union into the daily press and onto television screens throughout the world. Nevertheless, at least three major cautionary notes should be sounded before such an explanation is accepted. First, the Brezhnev period was one not of stagnation but of profound social transformation. Second, the sustained social restructuring of the past quarter-century or so has fostered a revolution of the mind that recasts a wide array of social, economic, and political relationships. Third, between 1985 and 1990 Gorbachev and his advisers had begun to bring about a long-sought-after transfer of political power and authority from the center to the periphery, from the top of the political pyramid toward the bottom.

Brezhnev's Social Revolution

The Soviet Union has witnessed a prolonged process of social differentiation and fragmentation throughout the past several decades. This "spreading out" of traditional society may be seen in such extensive social changes as increasingly specialized employment patterns, reduced opportunities for social mobility across group boundaries, rising levels of education for all social groups, urbanization (not only rural-to-urban migration but also the formation of social strata that have been urbanized across one or more generations), complex ethnic relations and interactions among nationality groups, a shift in population growth to the south and the east, and the professionalization of the female labor force. Many of these processes originated in the immediate postwar period. They merged during the years in which Leonid Brezhnev served as the Communist Party's general secretary in a manner that emphasized the ever-more diverse nature of Soviet society.[4] Brezhnev's complacent style and rhetoric merely masked developments deep within Soviet society in much the same way that the era of "reaction" under Nicholas I obscured the formative period of the Great Reforms more than a century ago.[5]

Change in and of itself does not become politically significant until and unless the political system proves incapable of assimilating and coordinating emerging patterns of social interaction. Such inability was precisely what characterized Brezhnev's tenure as general secretary. By the late 1970s, the evolution of economic and political institutions had failed to keep pace with a process of social change that was creating entire new social groups: the working middle class, young urban professionals, specialized nationality élites, and the like. The lag led to severe social tensions and conflicts.

Individual space expanded as new room for personal action was reflected in the robust second economy of the period, the flowering second cultural life, and even a nascent second political system (as evidenced by dissent). When viewed as an outgrowth of the social revolution that took place while Brezhnev was in power, perestroika can be seen as an at-times frantic effort on the part of the Communist Party leadership to capture for the regime those energies released by deep-seated social differentiation that occurred before Gorbachev came to power. It might be helpful to explore briefly some of the changes that had been taking place within the Soviet working class, white-collar strata, and ethnic groups.

The New Working Middle Class

During the 1950s, the Soviet working class became remarkably homogeneous. Fresh from the countryside, or just one generation removed, Soviet workers remained undereducated and underskilled. Indeed, most workers had little more than a primary education, and those who did attain a higher level of educational achievement were often promoted into the ranks of the white-collar labor force.

By the 1980s, not only had the quantity and quality of education increased for the Soviet population as a whole but the level of educational achievement among workers had become more differentiated as well. On the one hand, many older workers who had only a primary education were still employed in the industrial work force. On the other, a new generation of workers had grown up during a period in which two-thirds of the general population and nearly three-quarters of the urban population had at least some secondary education. The spread in working-class education-al achievement expanded during the 1950s, 1960s, and 1970s, from an educational profile encompassing almost solely primary education to one reaching from incomplete primary school through some form of post-secondary training.[6] The percentage of Soviet blue-collar workers considered to be unskilled declined markedly during the same period, while the percentage of highly skilled industrial workers increased significantly.

By the 1980s, the levels of income, consumption, education, and prestige among workers had increased differentially. And when skill, sectoral, and geographic variables are taken into consideration, it becomes clear that some groups of workers received greater compensation than did white-collar employees.[7] The blue-collar/white-collar divide, once so pronounced in the Soviet social structure, became blurred by the emergence of a new working middle class.

In a system that bases its legitimacy on its ability to represent the interests of the working class, the potential significance of such broad social tendencies is considerable. During the 1950s, working-class interests could be thought of as relatively homogeneous, like the working class itself. Nikita Khrushchev's efforts to reduce wage differentials were seen as essentially "pro-worker" as well as "pro-peasant," inasmuch as blue-collar employees and collective farmers were concentrated almost exclusively in lower income brackets. (Once workers become spread out along a continuum of income levels, greater wage equality need not benefit all workers.) Soviet politicians of the 1980s, unlike their counterparts in the 1950s, had to select from among a range of labor policy options having a differentiated impact on the industrial working class. Choosing to link wages to productivity, as Gorbachev did early in his administration, has ensured that contemporary wage policies differentiate among industrial workers every bit as much as they separate blue-collar from white-collar workers.

Gorbachev must turn his back on the needs of less-skilled and -educated workers if he is to appeal to the working middle class for support. The resulting social tensions are potentially explosive, especially in an atmosphere of increased political liberalization, with social unrest and industrial disorder on the rise. The rash of wildcat strikes throughout the spring of 1989, as well as the better-publicized job actions taken by Siberian and Ukrainian coal miners and Leningrad rail workers in July of that year, demonstrated the volatility of a labor regime under which traditionally favored elements of the industrial labor force found themselves, for the first time, being left behind by other groups of workers. Miners and rail workers, once glorified as heroes, have languished in a cycle of deteriorating living standards.

Recent strike actions in the Soviet Union have amplified the problems confronting the Soviet trade unions and Communist Party agencies as a consequence of a four-decade trend toward greater heterogeneity within the Soviet working class. The problem facing the Soviet political leadership is not merely that Soviet workers—or any other social group—"want more." Rather, it is that the social organization of the Soviet working class has become sufficiently fragmented that choices must be made among social substrata that did not exist as recently as a generation ago.

White-Collar Professionals

Throughout the four decades between 1940 and 1980, the proportion of the Soviet work force employed in agriculture dropped steadily, from roughly one in two employees to one in five—a work force ratio between agricultural and nonagricultural sectors roughly equivalent to that found in Italy in 1971. Concomitantly, the Soviet Union's nonagricultural work force grew, with industrial and construction sectors dominating employment by the early 1960s.[8] Since 1965, however, the process of redistribution of the nonagricultural labor force among economic sectors has slackened. The Soviet Union has come to resemble other advanced industrial societies in its degree of urbanization (66 percent in 1987)[9] and, to only a slightly lesser degree, in its level of educational achievement. Consequently, the diversification that has been taking place in the Soviet white-collar world is every bit as complex as that which had occurred among industrial workers.

Dramatic changes in the structure of the Soviet economy have been accompanied by rapid expansion in the number of white-collar professionals based largely in leading metropolitan areas. Between 1960 and 1980, employment in trade, health, education, culture and the arts, science, finance, and state agencies more or less doubled.[10] In the area of science alone, the number of employees increased ninefold between 1950 and 1985, and the number of all advanced degree holders multiplied ten times during the same period.[11] Such growth took place at a time when the Soviet educational system discriminated against the children of working-class origin, thereby inhibiting upward mobility and encouraging élite regeneration.

The structure of Soviet society began to solidify around new groupings during the Brezhnev period. Society began to resemble a mature industrial social structure with relatively stable, multigenerational substrata. Social arrangements incorporating significant numbers of white-collar professionals and semiprofessionals, clusters that had not existed in a stable form in Soviet society for well over a half-century, were fashioned throughout the 1960s and 1970s. Given their élite status, white-collar professionals based in the country's leading urban centers offered important social and cultural role models for other social groups. And, many of these white-collar groups could be expected to respond in a differentiated manner to various elements of any package of political or economic reform put forward by the Communist Party leadership.

The emergence of a reasonably well-educated general population recast a multitude of social, political, military, and economic relationships. Indeed, higher levels of educational achievement are usually accompanied by skills that are readily transferable to a variety of institutional environments. In general, the more highly educated the person, the more independent he or she will be from traditional paternalistic institutional ties. And, authority based on long-standing personal and institutional relationships becomes more fluid and open-ended as employees become less dependent on employers. Societies experiencing the kind of broad social change reflected in increasing levels of education and urbanization frequently undergo dramatic reorientation in authority relations. Such change accompanied the emergence of a developed industrial economy in the Soviet Union during the 1960s and 1970s, as will become apparent in the discussion of political behavior that follows.[12]

Nationality Groups

Intellectual, professional, and cultural élites in societies undergoing rapid social change frequently turn to previous traditions to provide a sense of coherence and stability in an otherwise inconstant environment. And such searches for normative continuity tend to intensify the appeal of traditional forms of cultural expression, leading to efforts to demonstrate the exceptional and singular character of those groups. Over time, this striving for renewed group identity generates an agenda for political action.

Soviet élites among many of the country's 120-odd national and ethnic groups (including the Russians) have sought reassurance in traditional cultural forms. The search for cultural identity among several of the Soviet Union's various nationalities accelerated during the 1960s and 1970s, a time of seeming calm. Leading Soviet theorists, in dealing with ethnicity questions of the period, went so far as to postulate the gradual withering away of differences among Soviet nationalities.[13] In fact, the emergence of educated and culturally aware urban elites among the various nationalities of the Soviet Union created the necessary conditions for the public unrest that followed during the late 1980s.

Numerous factors contributed to the surface tranquility of ethnic relations during the Brezhnev period. One such factor was the vigor of the Soviet security apparatus. Another was the relatively high level of aggregate economic growth throughout much of the quarter-century following Stalin's death in 1953, which temporarily alleviated pressures generated by the social changes described in this chapter. Personnel and nationality policies throughout much of the 1960s and 1970s sought to integrate local élites into a national political hierarchy. These policies granted greater autonomy for republic and nationality-based regional party organizations within their own jurisdictions. The consequent expansion of operating space claimed by republic élites combined with sustained urbanization, increasing levels of educational attainment, and a quest for cultural continuity in such a way as to nurture younger cohorts of national political, economic, sociocultural, and intellectual leaders in many regions of the USSR (including predominantly Russian areas). These younger élites were becoming sufficiently articulate and well-placed within the

Communist Party's *nomenklatura* to manipulate that system. The stage was being set during the tranquility of the Brezhnev era for the ethnic conflict that would follow.

Despite outward stability, then, the Brezhnev period was one of fragmentation among the Soviet Union's nationalities. National relations were transformed in two ways. First, there emerged among various national groups an intense competition for jobs and resources. This instrumentalist ethnic orientation was reinforced by personnel and investment policies predicated on ethnic differentiation. Economic policies during the period sought a reduction in inequalities among various nationalities—a social justice orientation in investment policy that led some Russians to conclude that the Soviet system favored the interests of national minorities over their own. Second, the dislocation and disruption resulting from social change fostered a personal interest in ethnicity among many Soviet citizens. This concern has become a refuge against some of the more general dehumanizing effects of urbanization.

In summary, the 1960s and 1970s were a period of profound reevaluation of the relationships of many nationalities—including the Russians—to existing social, economic, and political institutions. This revolution in expectations was obscured by Brezhnev's manipulation of investment and political patronage to calm the ethnic waters.

A Perestroika of the Mind

Various interpretations of events in the Soviet Union over the past five years have emphasized widespread resistance to change. A number of Soviet and non-Soviet academic, political, and journalistic commentators have spoken of cultural factors that inhibit and ultimately may destroy Gorbachevian perestroika, such as quiescent and deferential attitudes toward authority as well as an innate distrust of entrepreneurship. Evidence of deep-seated resistance to change remains visible and powerful, but robust countervailing tendencies exist within Soviet society as well.

There can be little doubt that the Soviet economy is not performing well. Half-hearted attempts to stimulate growth of a private cooperative sector have failed to bring about noticeable changes in the quality of consumer life in the Soviet Union. At the same time, deep resentments have been building up across a wide spectrum of society over allegedly lavish and ill-gotten profits obtained by many cooperative managers. Muscovites regale visitors with tales of a "mafia" that has seized control of the city's fledgling cooperative sector.

Distrust is frequently well founded and must be taken seriously. The very conditions under which the cooperative sector operates in today's Soviet Union necessitate that enterprises essentially steal supplies from the state sector and resell products at higher prices—a practice many consumers rightly view with disdain and anger.

One might expect that the integration of the legal cooperative economy into the illegal "mafia" economy could turn the Soviet population against the cooperative sector. However, recent public opinion data suggest a more complex and fluid pattern in which both support and opposition to the cooperatives can be identified, even within the same individual respondent. The prominence of the cooperative sector and the criticisms of it have made views on the cooperative sector a test for broader attitudinal changes that may or may not have taken place within the Soviet population. The very intricacy of opinion suggests that a revolution of the mind is well under way in the Soviet Union.

Izvestiia reported in March 1990 that only 29 percent of a national survey of 101,000 respondents indicated any negative attitude toward cooperative enterprises.[14] Interestingly, the same survey found that just 15 percent of those questioned were unreserved supporters of cooperatives. Political and policy discussions are taking place along a continuum of opinion that reflects support for cooperatives and private enterprises, but not unrestricted endorsement. Preferences over placement along this continuum establish the contours of current policy debate.

Another recently released poll commissioned by two leading British media organizations—the *Manchester Guardian* and BBC Newsnight—indicates similar levels of support for cooperatives in Soviet industry.[15] The British-sponsored survey was conducted early in 1990 in six cities: Moscow, Leningrad, Gorkii, Irkutsk, Alma-Ata, and Tallinn. Its results reveal strong public support for cooperative enterprises. Nationally, the *Guardian*-Newsnight survey was roughly in line with the above-mentioned findings published in *Izvestiia*. But the British poll was perhaps of greater interest, for it revealed significant regional disparities in attitudes. Among the six cities surveyed, Tallinn was most hospitable to "the creation of individual industries run as cooperatives, free to make their own decisions about production, distribution, and pricing," with 73.1 percent of the respondents fully or partially approving such arrangements. Leningrad was least hospitable; yet even there, 57.9 percent of the respondents fully or partially approved such arrangements. Indeed, 52.9 percent of the respondents in Tallinn, 47.7 percent in Alma-Ata, 45.8 percent in Moscow, and 43.0 percent in Leningrad "fully approved" of cooperative arrangements, with support for "privately owned *industries*" only slightly less in each city surveyed.

Polls released at about the same time by the All-Union Center for the Study of Public Opinion on Socio-Economic Issues found that 61 percent of the respondents in a national survey thought that the authorization of private property would improve the Soviet Union's economic performance, in contrast to a mere 11 percent who disagreed.[16] Only 5 percent of the respondents opposed the transfer of land to the peasants; 15 percent advocated transfer of land on the basis of long-term leases; and 35 percent favored the creation of a land market, with authorization to buy and sell land. These findings are at odds with the widespread perception of popular hostility toward private property and entrepreneurship. They also provide insight into the growing desertion of the Soviet labor force from state enterprises in favor of the cooperative sector.

Cooperatives not only remain in business but are increasingly making their presence felt. Soviet data for 1989 and 1990 reveal the emergence of a dynamic private sector throughout the Soviet Union. According to the Russian Republic's State Committee on Statistics, more than 50,000 cooperatives were active in the Republic in 1989, employing in excess of 1 million people.[17] The preponderance of these cooperatives offered consumer services, with cooperative sales representing 15.6 percent of the Republic's total output in consumer services and 19.1 percent of all consumer goods production. Other data indicated that the number of cooperatives in the entire Soviet Union has been increasing by an average of 50 percent every three months, topping 171,000 by October 1989.[18] Four million people were employed in the cooperative sector at year's end, with 1989 sales totalling almost 26 billion rubles.

Much of the expansion of the cooperative sector has taken place in the service and scientific sectors. Cooperative enterprises have mushroomed in computer programming, office services, applied social science research, consultancy, and the like. White-collar entrepreneurs are hidden from public view as they work under contract with foreign companies, state agencies, and one another. Young professionals disenchanted with the constraints of official bureaucratic work environments are now taking risks, a pattern that stands in sharp contrast to the activities of security-craving Brezhnev-era Soviet professionals. Indeed, behavioral change points to a revolution of the mind that has accompanied the formation of a permanent urban professional class during the half-century following World War II.

The cooperative sector obviously does not dominate the Soviet economy. Nevertheless, cooperatives constituted the fastest-growing sector of the economy in terms of production, sales, and employment prior to the January 1991 monetary reform. The sustained and accelerating development of the cooperative sector is all the more impressive in light of the hostile regulatory environment in which cooperative entrepreneurs must operate.[19]

Manifestations of a perestroika of the mind are also apparent in Soviet political behavior. Soviet citizens have consistently challenged previous notions of the unthinkable in Soviet political life. Rowdy local caucuses nominated candidates for a new Congress of People's Deputies. Unpredictable elections to that Congress led to the defeat of a number of establishment Communist Party officials. Live nationwide television coverage of the Congress, the most open and contentious official gathering in three-quarters of a century, was followed by the convening of a new national legislative body, the Supreme Soviet, that immediately established its prerogative of review of all state agencies. A proto-opposition party, the Inter-Regional Group of Deputies, has also come into being, whereas the Communist Party's own monopoly of power has fallen by the wayside. By late 1990, a number of opposition parties were emerging throughout the USSR. And, finally, independent trade unions are being established, while liberal reformers have seized control of more than a half-dozen of the most important municipal governments.

All of these events have taken place in the Russian heartland. But activism on the non-Russian periphery is even more intense. At every stage in the process of perestroika, Soviet citizens have pursued demonstrations, strikes, protest actions, and electoral politics to push political leaders and institutions to new frontiers of liberalization and democratization. Meanwhile, government officials have been scrambling to create new institutions so as to channel and control these fast-moving events.

By mid-1990, four interrelated yet quite distinct struggles had emerged within the overall attempt to channel and manage change. First, the sustained effort of the previous years to shift the locus of political decisionmaking from the Communist Party *apparat* to state institutions had begun to be realized. Ambitious politicians such as Boris Eltsin, Gavriil Popov, Sergei Stankevich, and Anatolii Sobchak sought out new bases of power and authority in the freshly elected system of local, regional, and republican soviets. Mikhail Gorbachev, for his part, concentrated more of his own energies on his duties as president, leaving Communist Party affairs to others to manage.

Second, a new tension had become visible between the popularly elected soviets, which function as legislative agencies, and their executive committees, the *ispolkomy*. The full consequence of this contest has yet to unfold, as the dimensions of dispute remain largely hidden from public view. Two aspects of this contest are already quite apparent. The executive committees have retained control of most of the state's bureaucratic and financial resources at each administrative level. The Moscow City Executive Committee maintains and operates a fleet of automobiles, for example, while deputies to the Moscow City Soviet argue over the propriety of permitting each of their standing commissions to lay claim to the services of but a single car for all commission business.[20] Such seemingly minor debates have erupted in legislative councils across the Soviet Union as deputies seek to mobilize sufficient resources to force their nominally subordinate executive agencies to honor and implement newly approved laws and regulations.

These skirmishes obscure a more ominous trend—namely the tendency of the executive committees to become the repository of power for those officials driven out of Communist Party agencies for one reason or another. For example, the Iaroslavl Regional Communist Party Committee reduced its staff by half during the two months following the March 1990 regional and municipal elections. Most of these fired bureaucrats merely walked across Soviet Square to new offices in the city and regional executive committees.[21] The same *apparatchiki* reappeared with *ispolkom* visiting cards in their pockets rather than the more traditional party card.

Third, republics and regions are competing with one another as power flows downward and away from federal agencies. The inability of the USSR Congress of People's Deputies and the Supreme Soviet to legislate concise charters for various levels of government has created a legal vacuum in which representatives of nearly every public institution claim maximum authority to establish norms of behavior and levy taxes. From the point of view of municipal leaders throughout the Russian Republic, the Eltsin-inspired declaration of sovereignty on the part of the Russian Soviet Federated Socialist Republic (RSFSR) Congress of People's Deputies will have but marginal practical consequence if the prerogatives of power come to reside in republican ministries and agencies. Hundreds of Soviet politicians are scrambling to force the flow of resources, authority, and power away from the republics toward regions and municipalities. The precise contours of any settlement are not likely to be revealed for some time to come.

Fourth, the historic clash between town and country is shaping up as one of the most volatile and embittered conflicts of the early 1990s. The entrenched right-wing opposition so visible at the Twenty-Eighth Communist Party Congress rests on continued party hegemony in the countryside. The industrial *nomenklatura* may, in the end, be privatized during the transition from a centrally administered to a quasi-market economy as party and state bureaucrats seek out profit-making joint ventures and self-aggrandizing cooperatives. Collective and state farms have no opportunity for personal gain in the marketplace. Their niche within the Soviet political economy will simply vanish in the transition from a centrally planned command economy. Aware of their fate, the rural *nomenklatura* have launched a fight for survival, disrupting republican and national party conclaves and cutting off urban food supplies. More traditional skirmishes over capital and material assets have also erupted as both town and country pursue increasingly scarce resources within a declining economy.

Each of these conflicts is both a consequence of five years of Gorbachev-inspired perestroika and a determinant of perestroika's ultimate fate. Such struggles deserve sustained attention on the part of all who wish to understand the direction of change in the Soviet Union of the 1990s.

From the Center to the Periphery

Soviet society had been maturing and becoming ever-more diversified for more than a generation before Mikhail Gorbachev emerged as the Soviet Union's supreme political leader. These trends developed as a consequence of the structural changes that were taking place within the Soviet economic and social orders. The various social groupings forged by the press of Stalinism became increasingly fragmented throughout the years of Brezhnevian "stagnation." But this historic social transformation took place quietly. Few Western specialists on Soviet affairs seemed to be aware, for example, that a greater percentage of the Soviet population had moved from the countryside to the city during the Khrushchev and Brezhnev years than during the massive industrialization drive of Stalin's initial prewar five-year plans. As earlier noted, entire new social strata were formed, some for the first time in Russian history. This process of social differentiation released pent-up energies, expanded the personal space of Soviet citizens, and generally undercut the legitimacy of institutional structures that had remained essentially unchanged since the fully-developed Stalinism of the postwar period. The Soviet population increasingly came to resemble the industrialized world in terms of educational attainment, employment patterns, cultural taste, and, to a surprising degree, attitudes.[22]

Throughout most of their history, Russian and Soviet governments have lacked both the institutional arrangements and the leadership skills required to manage conflicts among diverse groups without resorting to repression.[23] The Soviet state's claims to legitimacy have long been based on an assumed harmony of interests among the "nonantagonistic" groups that constituted Soviet society. Faced with the growing differentiation that took place in Soviet society during the 1960s and 1970s, Soviet political leaders of the 1980s considered new economic and political arrangements intended to cope with the growing tensions between new and old within Soviet society.

The structural problems confronting Gorbachev and all Soviet political figures predate the Soviet period. The traditional Russian centralized state was both hyperinstitutionalized and underinstitutionalized: hyperinstitutionalized in the sense that hardly a sphere of human activity fell outside the purview of central state institutions; underinstitutionalized in the sense that few intermediary institutions either were created or wielded sufficient resources to mediate between state and society as well as among social groups. Russian and Soviet leaders consequently lacked adequate policy tools with which to govern—to manipulate policy and behavior—in an increasingly complex and interdependent world. At best, Russian and Soviet leaders have been able to motivate the population through loyalty, obedience, and, at times, the activities of an extensive security apparatus. But these hardly constitute the sort of refined policy instruments that have proven to be effective in managing intricate industrial and postindustrial societies. The flexibility required by modern states to respond quickly to a rapidly changing world has been undermined by hyperinstitutionalization in the center and underinstitutionalization on the periphery. Power must shift from the center to the periphery in order to redress this historical imbalance.

Prior to the steam-power and information revolutions of the nineteenth and twentieth centuries, autocrats sought to reform the Russian administrative system by modifying the structure of central authority. More far-reaching reforms were required by the mid-nineteenth century. The Great Reforms of the 1860s and the various reform efforts of the early twentieth century were built on changes implemented during seemingly repressive and quiescent periods in order to foster new political and economic institutions closer to society.[24] But the autocratic state never relinquished sufficient resources in the end to permit newly formed municipal administrations or the emerging land-holding peasantry to mature and prosper. The intermediary institutional layers required for flexible management of an increasingly complex society were still-born.

Stalin's drive for rapid industrialization and forced collectivization reversed whatever halting movement toward the creation of a mediating structure between the new Soviet state and society that might have occurred during the New Economic Policy (NEP) of the 1920s. The Soviet Union emerged from postwar Stalinism with a social structure on the brink of rapid transformation and an antiquated centralized state structure that could terrorize but was not able to manage social and economic development. International competition exposed the weakness of the Soviet state system by the time of Brezhnev's stewardship. The country desperately needed the sort of autonomous and independent intermediary institutions that provide stability and flexibility in the modern world: organized forums of interest articulation, autonomous trade unions, government institutions that are predicated on a plurality of interests, effective agencies of local administration, religious bodies, philanthropic organizations, self-governing professional societies, and so on.

Soviet leaders have moved with considerable determination to create just such a political system. Apparently, (or so it seemed before 1990) they realized that it may be necessary to relinquish some of the overt power of the hyperinstitutionalized state in order to overcome the shortcomings of the underinstitutionalized state. They set out to achieve these goals through the creation of a system of popularly elected soviets that could mediate conflicts among social groups precisely because they are institutions predicated on concepts of pluralistic competition. Power and authority were to be transferred from Communist Party agencies to those of this new state system and from the center to the periphery.

A Race Against Time

Efforts to establish an integrated system of popularly elected councils were announced at the Nineteenth Communist Party Conference in June 1988 and have been implemented with a remarkable degree of success. The process of creating state institutions has sparked the rise of semi-autonomous groupings within society; and new forms of economic organization are beginning to come into their own. Institutions and procedures to ameliorate and mediate the strains between the Russian and Soviet state on the one hand and society on the other—and among conflicting interests within society—were being put into effect by 1990. Indeed, Brezhnev's social revolution and Gorbachev's accompanying perestroika of the mind are being woven into the institutional fabric of Soviet political and economic life.

The long-standing problem of underinstitutionalization persists. Legislation granting municipal and regional governments greater revenue powers was promised for the summer of 1990. At the time of this writing, it has yet to be ratified and remains even further from implementation.

New local governments will languish without access to resources, as did their predecessors.

The long-standing tendency toward hyperinstitutionalization has not disappeared either. During the spring of 1990, Mikhail Gorbachev rammed through measures designed to establish a new Soviet presidency. This new supreme political office contains the seeds for future dictatorship, notwithstanding the benign comparisons with the French presidency offered by senior government officials. Gorbachev's reluctance to stand before the Soviet electorate in a general election must give pause to those who view the Soviet leader as a great democrat. The center has begun to fight for its survival through the deployment of security forces to the periphery. The outcome of this conflict remains in doubt as this volume goes to press.

Concomitant with the destruction of prolonged Soviet political and economic relationships has been the blending together of new organizational bonds among Soviet society and its political and economic institutions. The shock waves of institutions cracking under the pressure of perestroika have resounded across the Soviet Union. The emergence of new institutions has been a much quieter process—but one no less profound.

The stormy five years since Mikhail Gorbachev became general secretary of the Communist party of the Soviet Union have witnessed a contest between the new, which is only now coming into being, and the old, which is being torn asunder. Now clear, however, is the fact that the combination of striking new policy initiatives from above and dramatic social change from below has created an environment in which the Soviet Union just might finally be able to step off the treadmill of failed reforms.

Notes

1. See, for example, the essays contained in Robert O. Crummey, ed., *Reform in Russia and the USSR* (Champaign-Urbana: University of Illinois Press, 1989).

2. See, for example, Gertrude Schroeder, "Soviet Economic 'Reform' Decrees: More Steps on the Treadmill," in U.S. Congress. Joint Economic Committee, *Soviet Economy in the 1980s: Problems and Prospects*, Vol. 1 (Washington, DC: U.S. Government Printing Office, 1982), pp. 65-88.

3. Alfred J. Rieber, "The Reforming Tradition in Russian History," in *Perestroika at the Crossroads*, edited by Alfred J. Rieber and Alvin Z. Rubinstein (Armonk, NY: M. E. Sharpe, 1991), pp. 3-28.

4. This line of argument is put forward in Moshe Lewin, *The Gorbachev Phenomenon* (Berkeley: University of California Press, 1988); Gail Warshofsky Lapidus, "Society Under Strain," *Washington Quarterly*, Vol. 6, No. 2 (1983), pp.

29-47; and S. Frederick Starr, "Soviet Union: A Civil Society," *Foreign Policy*, No. 70 (spring 1988), pp. 26-41. It also appears in Blair Ruble, "The Social Dimensions of *Perestroika*," *Soviet Economy*, Vol. 3, No. 2 (April-June 1987), pp. 171-183; and Ruble, "The Soviet Union's Quiet Revolution," in *Can Gorbachev's Reforms Succeed?*, edited by George W. Breslauer (Berkeley: University of California, Berkeley-Stanford Program in Soviet Studies, 1990), pp. 77-94.

5. The origins of reform in the reign of Nicholas I have been chronicled most fully by W. Bruce Lincoln in *In the Vanguard of Reform: Russia's Enlightened Bureaucrats, 1825-1861* (DeKalb: Northern Illinois University Press, 1982), and most recently, Lincoln, *The Great Reforms: Autocracy, Bureaucracy, and the Politics of Change in Imperial Russia* (DeKalb: Northern Illinois University Press, 1990).

6. Over a decade ago, the late Arcadius Kahan published a seminal article on the economic and social changes that were reshaping the Soviet working class (Arcadius Kahan, "Some Problems of the Soviet Workers," in Arcadius Kahan and Blair A. Ruble, eds., *Industrial Labor in the USSR* [Elmsford, NY: Pergamon Press, 1979], pp. 283-312). Kahan foresaw much of the labor tension and worker unrest that is so visible throughout the Soviet Union today. A short while later, Alex Pravda published another important overview of the evolving profile of the Soviet working class in "Is There a Soviet Working Class?", *Problems of Communism*, Vol. 31, No. 6 (1982), pp. 1-24. These articles suggest some of the ways in which those analysts who examined Soviet political life during the Brezhnev era from the "bottom up" were closer to predicting the upheavals that followed Brezhnev's departure than were those who remained fixated on élite political struggles in the Kremlin.

7. This argument is developed more fully by Alex Pravda, "Is There a Soviet Working Class," as well as in Pravda, "Spontaneous Workers' Activities in the Soviet Union," in *Industrial Labor in the USSR*, edited by Arcadius Kahan and Blair Ruble, pp. 333-366.

8. *Narodnoe khoziaistvo SSSR za 70 let. Iubileinyi statisticheskii ezhegodnik* (Moscow: Finansy i statistika, 1987), p. 410; *Italy Today: Social Picture and Trends, 1985* (Rome: Centro degli studi investimenti sociali, 1986), p. 153.

9. *Narodnoe khoziaistvo*, p. 373.

10. *Narodnoe khoziaistvo*, p. 412.

11. *Narodnoe khoziaistvo*, p. 62.

12. For a suggestive discussion of the evolution of authority relations in the Soviet Union during recent years, see Thomas Remington, "A Socialist Pluralism of Opinions: *Glasnost'* and Policy-Making under Gorbachev," *The Russian Review*, Vol. 48, No. 3 (1989), pp. 271-304.

13. See, for example, Iu. Bromlei, "Etnicheskie protsessy v SSSR," *Kommunist*, No. 5 (March 1983), pp. 56-66.

14. E. Gonzal'ez, "Kooperativy: opiat' vyiasniaem otnosheniia," *Izvestiia*, March 2, 1990, p. 2.

15. Jonathan Steele, "Soviet Poll Backs Multi-Party System," *Manchester Guardian*, March 6, 1990, p. 9.

16. "Vesti dialog s liudmi," *Narodnyi deputat*, No. 2 (February 1990), pp. 23-27.

17. E. Ivanov, "Kooperativy Rossii," *Pravda*, January 9, 1990, p. 3.

18. M. Berger, "Rassvet na grani likvidatsii," *Izvestiia*, January 19, 1990, p. 5.

19. For further discussion of those conditions, see Anthony Jones and William Moskoff, "New Cooperatives in the USSR," *Problems of Communism*, Vol. 38, No. 6 (1989), pp. 27-39.

20. This issue was hotly debated by the Moscow Soviet on June 29, 1990.

21. This observation is based on a series of interviews with Iaroslavl' political leaders on June 18-27, 1990.

22. Such changes in attitude are particularly visible in Soviet popular culture over the course of the 1960s, 1970s, and 1980s. See, for example, S. Frederick Starr, *Red and Hot: The Fate of Jazz in the Soviet Union* (New York: Oxford University Press, 1983), as well as John Bushnell's recent analysis of Soviet graffiti, *Moscow Graffiti: Language and Subculture* (Boston: Unwin Hyman, 1990).

23. Various efforts to nurture such institutions are explored in Victoria E. Bonnell, "Voluntary Associations In Gorbachev's Reform Program," in Breslauer, *Can Gorbachev's Reforms Succeed?*, pp. 63-76.

24. See, for example, Bonnell, "Voluntary Associations," and Lincoln, *The Great Reforms*.

2

The Soviet Economy on a
Treadmill of Perestroika:
Gorbachev's First Five Years

Gertrude E. Schroeder

In his first five years of tenure, Mikhail Gorbachev has presided over an economy that has gone, in his words, from a state of "pre-crisis" to one of full crisis. His policies have brought the macro-economy from the comparative stability of central planning to a state of massive disequilibrium and the micro-economy from perennial but tolerable disarray to the brink of chaos. The mediocre economic performance of the "period of stagnation" (*zastoi*) has been followed by five years of low-level performance and incipient decline, a period now labeled "restructuring" (perestroika). On the economic reform front, Gorbachev has presided over two years of Brezhnev-style tinkering, followed by the introduction of self-styled "radical" reforms, and culminating in a degree of retrenchment. The economic difficulties contrast sharply with Gorbachev's notable successes in restructuring domestic political institutions and foreign relations.

The goals of economic perestroika have been clear from the start. Gorbachev wants to speed up the rate of economic growth and to raise living standards appreciably. Above all, however, he aims to achieve major breakthroughs in four areas: improvement of the efficiency with which the economy uses its resources, a rise in the quality of its products, an increase in the competitiveness of its manufactures in Western markets, and reduction of the large and growing technological gap with the West, which threatens the USSR's status as a superpower. In its first five years, economic perestroika failed to make much progress toward any of these goals; instead, it has left the country in the throes of three major crises—a disintegrating consumer market, a disrupted investment process, and a massive budget deficit.

Performance of the Economy

Perestroika has failed to produce the hoped-for upsurge in economic growth. In the years from 1985 to 1989, the gross national product (GNP) increased at an average annual rate of 1.9 percent, compared with 1.7 percent in the preceding five years (1980−1984). These are CIA estimates, used instead of Soviet official measures which have long been discredited in the West and now in the Soviet Union as well.[1] This small improvement in the growth of GNP reflects similarly small gains in the three major economic sectors−industry, agriculture, and services−which grew at only about half the planned growth rates. The average growth rates in industry throughout the two periods have been 1.9 percent and 2.2 percent, respectively. Corresponding percentages for agriculture are 1.4 and 1.6 percent; and for the services sector 2.3 and 2.6 percent. With the population increasing at just under 1 percent per year during the 1985−1989 period, the slight overall improvement registered in these figures was scarcely perceptible to the population. And as the growth rates of both total GNP and per capita GNP were appreciably higher in the US and Western Europe, the already-large development gap between the USSR and the West has clearly increased.

In the industrial sector, ambitious plans for growth of production and modernization of its structure were typically underfulfilled. Thus, growth rates in the "progressive" branches−machinery and chemicals−were lower during Gorbachev's watch than in the previous five years. Also notable was the much slower growth rate in the food processing branch. In 1989, industrial growth stagnated overall, notably in the machinery branch, owing to a cut in the production of weapons. Moreover, production declined in the chemicals branch, as did total energy output (for the first time since World War II). Indeed, total industrial production dropped significantly during the first 11 months of 1990.

In agriculture, too, the hoped-for acceleration in the growth of production failed to materialize, and year-to-year performance continued to be highly erratic. However, efforts and investment did produce markedly higher average levels of output of grain and livestock products. Grain production averaged 180 million metric tons in 1980−1984 and 204 million metric tons in 1985−1989, while meat production averaged 16 and 19 million metric tons in the respective periods. But demand for food rose much more rapidly, thus forcing the government to import large quantities of both products each year. As a consequence, increasingly scarce supplies of hard currency were severely drained.

Regarding the goal of accelerated improvement in the population's standard of living, events produced the opposite outcome. Real per capita consumption grew at an average annual rate of only 0.7 percent (1985–1989) compared with 1.2 percent during the previous five-year period. Again, rates of gains in living standards were much faster in the United States and Western Europe, thereby further widening the already large gap with the West in provision of goods and services to consumers. Moreover, because of price disequilibrium and the disarray in consumer markets in the USSR, the "welfare gap" with the West is much greater than that measured by quantities—and that gap has widened even further under Gorbachev. Per capita consumption actually declined in the USSR during Gorbachev's first two years, as a function of his antidrinking campaign, the curtailment of imports of consumer goods, and inadequate attention to growing consumer problems. Later quantitative improvement came largely as a result of the reversal of these policies.

The picture of the economy's performance is not wholly drab, however. For instance, labor productivity growth has accelerated markedly. In the economy as a whole, output per labor-hour increased from an average rate of growth of 0.8 percent annually in 1980–1984 to 1.7 percent annually in 1985–1989. Similar accelerations occurred in industry and agriculture, as state-owned firms and farms were motivated to shed workers under economic reforms that stressed self-financing, and as workers were lured to the private and cooperative sectors by higher incomes. (By contrast, capital productivity continued to decline, although the rate of decline slowed somewhat.) The economy's use of energy also improved a little. Whereas energy consumption per ruble of GNP had increased by 7.3 percent during 1980–1984, the ratio stabilized in the succeeding five years. Energy/GNP ratios in the USSR still remain high relative to the West, where they have been declining ever since the mid-1970s.

In other areas, however, perestroika has evidently accomplished little, if anything at all. Plan-fulfillment reports continue to bemoan the lack of progress in improving either the quality of products or the competitiveness of Soviet manufactures in Western markets. Numerous press reports cite large, and allegedly increasing, losses and levels of waste throughout the economy. Gorbachev himself sadly admits that no breakthrough has yet been achieved by perestroika.

Disintegration of the Consumer Market

Five years of perestroika have ended with the consumer market in massive disarray. Of course, this sector was already in disequilibrium in early 1985 as a consequence of bad pricing policies and excess money in circulation relative to the supply of goods. However, the situation has worsened dramatically since Gorbachev came to power, owing primarily to ill-conceived government policies and half-hearted reforms rather than to relatively mediocre economic performance per se. The first major blow to the consumer market was the antidrinking campaign launched in May 1985. It closed liquor stores, reduced hours of sale, raised prices, and cut back production of alcoholic beverages in state factories by 50 percent during 1985–1987.[2] In 1984, retail sales of alcoholic beverages amounted to about 51 billion rubles (approximately 16 percent of total retail sales); by 1987, sales of liquor had fallen to 35.7 billion rubles. This draconian measure thus deprived retail outlets of billions of rubles in potential sales of a product in high demand by consumers. Other negative consequences include the boom in production of home brew (*samogon*), a run on stores selling sugar (leading to its eventual rationing) and any product containing alcohol, longer queues at liquor stores, and an angry population. The campaign was abandoned in 1988, and alcohol sales rose by 39 percent in 1988–1989. But the damage had already been done.

A second major blow to the consumer market came from the government's decision to reduce imports of consumer goods in response to shortfalls in hard currency earnings resulting from the fall in the world market price of oil. The value of imported consumer goods allocated to retail trade dropped by nearly 8 billion rubles between 1985 and 1988.[3] These goods are both highly priced and highly prized by consumers; but their share of total deliveries to the trade network dropped from 15 percent to 11 percent during that period. The policy of reducing imports of consumer goods was reversed in 1989.

Despite stepped-up efforts to increase domestic production of consumer goods, plans were chronically underfulfilled, and the government was unable to make up for the tens of billions of rubles in lost sales from alcohol and imported goods. Another critical mistake was Gorbachev's failure to perceive early on that perestroika's success required a sharply increased priority for consumers in the allocation of investment; instead, investment policy continued to favor heavy industry. This decision, too, has now been reversed. Finally, major reforms in agriculture that might have rapidly boosted food supplies were not undertaken.

At the same time that the growth of supplies of consumer goods was being curtailed, various facets of Gorbachev's unfolding economic reform program accelerated the growth of the population's personal incomes, as did the government's decision to sharply increase wages and social benefits for groups that had lagged behind. The reforms included new laws designed to encourage private economic activity and the formation of producer cooperatives with considerable freedom to conduct their businesses as they saw fit. The number of persons engaged in this private sector rose to nearly 6 million by the end of 1989, when their average incomes were more than double those of workers in the state sector. In addition, wages increased sharply for the latter group as a result of general wage reforms and other provisions that gave firms and farms both the latitude and the incentive to raise the incomes of their workers. All of these forces accelerated the growth of personal money incomes. Whereas total money incomes increased at an average annual rate of 4.2 percent during 1980–1984, they rose by 6.5 percent annually during 1985–1989; the increase was 9 percent in 1988 and 13 percent in 1989. But supplies of consumer goods and services in real terms rose at average annual rates of only 2.1 percent and 1.7 percent in the two periods respectively, thus creating rapidly mounting inflationary pressures. The large imbalance between incomes and the availability of goods and services became even greater in 1990.

The consequences of this policy mix have been disastrous both for consumers and for the government. Longer lines formed in front of stores increasingly denuded of goods to sell, and black markets flourished. Distribution of goods through the workplace and other special channels proliferated. Rationing, entailing both the formal use of coupons and informal limitations or tie-in sales, became widespread–a phenomenon unique in peacetime anywhere. Finding few desirable goods to buy, people put their excess money in the state savings banks: Additions to deposits rose from fifteen billion rubles in 1984 to 41 billion in 1989. The statistical authorities reported that, in 1989, only 50 out of 1,200 standard consumer items were readily available in stores and that the population held 165 billion rubles in excess purchasing power–about 40 percent of the annual value of retail sales.[4] Despite the government's attempts to control inflation by holding prices down, open inflation increased from around 2 percent in 1984 to 6 percent in 1989, according to CIA estimates.[5] The degree of repressed inflation also rose sharply. Both open and repressed inflation continued to rise throughout 1990.

Difficulties in the consumer sphere have had a seriously adverse effect on labor discipline and work effort, quite the opposite of what is needed for the success of perestroika. In response, the government adopted a series of so-called "stabilization" measures that run counter to the spirit of the reforms. Throughout, the government has adhered to its long-time policy of holding stable the prices of basic foods and rents, while sanctioning public discussions about the need for retail price reform in order to create the true consumer markets that are the objective of the economic reform program. Such glasnost in regard to retail prices spawned rumors about impending price increases and possible monetary reform; it also led to runs on the stores, making the shortages even worse. Finally, the situation has been exacerbated by the behavior of individual cities and regions, which have used their newfound economic autonomy to ban exports to other areas, restricting the sale of available goods solely to local residents.

The Growing Mess in the Investment Process

Initially, Gorbachev seemed most worried about the Soviet Union's growing lag behind the West in the rate of what the Soviets refer to as "scientific-technical progress." One of Gorbachev's first moves was to convene a plenum on that subject. To accelerate the rate of technical progress, the final draft of the Twelfth Five-Year Plan (1986–1990) provided for an increase in the growth rate for investment, which was intended to be much faster than that of consumption. The plan also launched a grandiose program to modernize industrial capital stock and the mix of products by directing a sharply higher share of industrial investment to the machinery industries.[6] A growing share of investment was to go toward the reconstruction and reequipping of existing plants, rather than toward building new ones. Targets were set to double the retirement rates for outmoded facilities and to replace a third of the entire capital stock with modern facilities by 1990. With their massive (80 percent) increase in investment, the machinery industries were supposed to double the growth of their output, radically improve quality, and shift the mix toward new and progressive technologies. By 1990, 90 percent of all machinery was to meet world standards, compared with less than 20 percent in 1985. For the most part these ambitious goals have not been achieved.

The industrial modernization drive was pursued with sound and fury in the early years. The outcome was a classic case of trying to do too much too fast.[7] Now that investment resources were being heaped on them, the machinery industries were being pressured to do everything at once—to reequip their plants, sharply raise both the quantity and the quality of output, and change the product mix. As a consequence, much investment was wasted, and growth targets were missed by wide margins. Although the pace of retiring old capital speeded up a little, the rates are still only about half those of the United States and Japan and below those achieved in the USSR in the late 1960s. In short, the industrial modernization process seems to have proceeded at about the same slow pace under Gorbachev as it did in the past. But the attempt to accelerate modernization contributed not only to increased waste but also to growing disarray in the overall investment process.

Other factors contributing to this deterioration stemmed from decisions to reform the investment process by decentralizing the bulk of it to regions and to enterprises. A decree adopted in 1986 launched a major reorganization of the construction industry, thus essentially decentralizing much of it to the republics. Like the similar move made under Khrushchev, this approach unleashed the forces of "localism" and created significant confusion. More complications arose from the several later decrees that aimed to introduce more effective incentives to complete projects on time and in good condition. Moreover, under the general reform package adopted in mid-1987, individual enterprises were accorded much wider latitude to make their own investment decisions about projects financed from internally generated funds. By 1989, such funds financed nearly half of total state investment. A decision was made in 1988 to radically shift spending priorities once again, this time in favor of housing, the production of equipment to modernize consumer goods industries, and social infrastructure. Finally, the Chernobyl disaster and the Armenian earthquake, along with the defense conversion program launched in 1989 and the mothballing of many major building projects in response to mounting budget deficits, all contributed to the growing difficulties in the construction sector.

The mess in the investment sphere shows up dramatically in the following figures. During 1980–1984, investment growth averaged 3.4 percent annually, while project completions (commissionings) rose by 4.6 percent annually, thus reducing the backlog of unfinished construction work. But in the years 1985–1989, investment increased at an average annual rate of 4.6 percent, while project completions rose by an average of only 2.1 percent per year. As a result, the volume of unfinished construction shot up from the equivalent of 78 percent of investment in 1984 to 94 percent in 1989–the highest in Soviet postwar history and 27 percent above the state-set norm. By 1989, the time required to complete projects was double the norm, and many projects were rendered technologically obsolete long before their completion. In the same year, only half of the projects backed up with rationed materials were completed, thus adding to imbalances in the economy. The decentralization of investment decisionmaking and funding to firms and regions also led to a proliferation of project starts, as had previously occurred in the late 1960s, when limited decentralization was sanctioned. As in the consumer sector, the government adopted measures in 1989 and 1990 designed to obtain some control over the situation in the investment sphere, but many of these have run counter to the spirit of the economic reform program.

Monetary and Fiscal Crisis

At the end of his first five years of tenure, Gorbachev faced a monetary and fiscal crisis of "truly horrifying dimensions."[8] This situation, which poses a serious threat to the entire economic reform process, stems almost entirely from the cumulative effects of a series of specific policy initiatives and the apparent failure of the policymakers to perceive the gravity of the developing crisis until very late. By then, massive damage had already been done, and processes were set in motion that are proving nearly impossible to control. The monetary and fiscal crisis is characterized by three interrelated facets—an enormous budget deficit, a huge monetary overhang in the form of savings bank deposits and cash in the hands of the population, and large and rapidly mounting cash-equivalent balances in the enterprise sector.

Although by Western standards the Soviet budget has been in deficit for many years (contrary to perennially reported surpluses), the government has managed to finance its expenditures from ordinary taxes, by borrowing from the population through explicit state loans and by treating as budgetary income each year's addition to the population's deposits in state savings banks. Because these sources have been insufficient to cover rapidly growing expenditures, the government has resorted to simply printing money (through "borrowing" from the state bank) to make up the difference—and therein lies the essence of the current budgetary crises. During 1985–1989, total budget expenditures increased at an average annual rate of 5.8 percent, while ordinary tax revenues rose at only 1.4 percent annually. Whereas the budget deficit (as the Soviets define it) was negligible in 1984, it had shot up to 92 billion rubles (about 10 percent of GNP) by 1989. By comparison, the federal budget deficit that year in the United States was 3 percent of GNP.

Under Gorbachev, budget expenditures continued to increase rapidly. The industrial modernization program, rising subsidies on food and other consumer-related items, planned losses of enterprises, expansion of welfare programs, and defense outlays needed to be financed. The Chernobyl disaster and the Armenian earthquake added many billions of rubles to these expenditures. But in 1988, revenue from turnover taxes, which generally provide about one-fourth of total tax revenues, was only slightly above the 1984 level, primarily because billions of rubles were lost as a result of the cutback in sales of heavily taxed alcoholic beverages.

Failure to meet plans for domestic production of highly taxed clothing and consumer durables also contributed to the shortfall in turnover tax receipts. In 1989, however, turnover taxes rose sharply as a consequence of the upsurge in production of both alcoholic beverages and consumer durables. Budget receipts from profits taxes, the single most important source of tax revenue, were lower in 1989 than in 1986, owing mainly to the economic reform provision that permitted enterprises to keep a much larger share of their profits in order to finance their own investments.

The third major source of state revenue, income from foreign trade, also fell during the period, because of the drop in earnings from exports of oil and gas following the decrease in the world price for oil after 1985. But the revenue shortfall also resulted from the decision to cut back on imports of consumer goods, which are heavily taxed. Turnover taxes, profits taxes, and income from foreign trade constitute about three fourths of ordinary budget revenues; the remainder consists of income taxes, social insurance taxes, and a variety of levies that could not readily be changed. To make up the difference between revenues and expenditures, the government borrowed from the population by appropriating the annual additions to deposits in savings banks and by obtaining state bank credits in even larger amounts. The result of these cumulative budget deficits was a massive domestic debt of almost 400 billion rubles in 1989, the equivalent of about 45 percent of GNP.

The second facet of the financial crisis is the enormous ruble over-hang—money in the hands of the population that has resulted from much faster growth of incomes relative to the supply of goods and services. The bulk of excess purchasing power takes the form of savings bank deposits, which totaled 338 billion rubles at the end of 1989, the equivalent of 72 percent of the value of retail sales and paid services in that year. In 1984, total deposits were 202 billion rubles, the equivalent of 55 percent of sales of goods and services. The population also holds large amounts of cash, perhaps as much as 100 billion rubles. Thus, although Gorbachev inherited a bad situation, his policies have made it much worse. The presence of a massive ruble overhang fuels inflationary pressures, adversely affects work incentives, and seriously complicates government policy-making, particularly the decontrolling of retail prices.[9]

In the enterprise sector, too, the cumulative effects of the economic reforms have produced a large ruble overhang and unleashed inflationary forces. Robert Campbell estimates enterprise spendable bank balances as of January 1, 1989 at nearly 100 billion rubles—double the level recorded at the end of 1985.[10] Under the financial and credit reforms inaugurated in 1988, enterprises have been able to negotiate credit agreements with the banks at low rates of interest (2 to 4 percent), and the banks have evidently been quite accommodating. In addition, new cooperative and independent banks have sprung up and use of inter-enterprise credits is now permissible, thus adding to the supply of credit. Moreover, enterprises have been allowed to retain larger shares of their rapidly growing profits for purposes of investment and for bonus payments to workers. With such easy access to credit at low cost, enterprises have elected to use their profits to raise workers' wages, which have been increasing far more rapidly than productivity rates.

Economic Reforms—More or Less on the Treadmill

At the outset, Gorbachev clearly realized that the continuous reform attempts made by his predecessors had come to naught. But his first objectives were timid ones: to extend an experiment in broadening enterprise independence launched by Andropov, and to tinker with organizational forms and incentive arrangements on farms. At the Twenty-Seventh Communist Party Congress in February 1986, however, he spoke of the need for "radical" economic reform, including the need to address the formerly taboo matter of property ownership. The measures taken in 1986 in a veritable blitz of decrees were a mixture of traditional and somewhat bolder approaches.[11] Among the traditional approaches was the creation of new bureaus under the USSR Council of Ministers to coordinate the activities of groups of related ministries. In addition, the construction industry was reorganized once more; additional rights and responsibilities were delegated to union republics and local soviets; a sweeping overhaul of the wage and salary system required enterprises to finance the mandated rate increases from their own funds; and a new administrative system of quality control entailed the stationing of state inspectors in factories. Far less traditional, however, were the new laws broadening the scope for individual (private) economic activity, sanctioning the restoration of producer cooperatives in the consumer sector, and liberalizing the conduct of foreign trade—specifically, by permitting selected enterprises to bypass the state trading system and by authorizing joint ventures between Soviet and foreign firms. Implementation of these timid reforms, however, was accompanied by wide-ranging debates in the press, which touted even bolder proposals designed to cure the economy's ills through fundamental systemic reform.

In late June 1987, the piecemeal approach to economic reform taken during Gorbachev's first two years was replaced with a more comprehensive approach following CPSU Central Committee approval of a document entitled "Basic Provisions for Fundamentally Reorganizing Economic Management." These general guidelines were fleshed out in a new Law on State Enterprises (Associations) adopted by the Supreme Soviet and ten decrees of the USSR Council of Ministers spelling out various facets of the reform program.[12] This comprehensive program, labeled "radical" and "revolutionary" by Gorbachev, essentially amounts to a liberalized version of the 1965 and 1979 programs, but with a more specific and fairly rapid timetable for implementation.[13] The 1987 package, which focuses on broadening the independence of enterprises, modifies each of the familiar pillars of Stalinist centrally planned socialism without removing any of them. The new order of things was introduced in most of the industrial sector in 1988 and throughout the economy in 1989.

Under the new arrangements, the State Planning Committee (Gosplan) and the ministries, which have been reduced in number and size, have been enjoined to retreat from micro-management of enterprises and to focus on long-range strategic matters. As of 1989, all enterprises formulate their own plans, which are based on centrally determined "control figures," a portfolio of state orders (*goszakazy*) that are supplied with rationed raw materials, independently negotiated contracts with other firms for the sale of products and the purchase of materials for production not required to fill state orders, limits on centrally funded investment, and a set of normatives regulating such matters as wage increases and the use of enterprise profits. The share of state orders in total output was supposed to fall rapidly, along with a concomitant increase in the share of intermediate products and investment goods sold freely through wholesale trade. Enterprises must finance their activities from their own funds, under the threat of bankruptcy as the penalty for persistent losses. Enterprises are also required to set up elected Work Councils with broad decisionmaking authority, so as to give the work force a voice in management of firms.

Firms are accorded more leeway for negotiating product prices with suppliers and customers through contracts, and state-set prices for industrial and agricultural products were to be revised by January 1, 1991, the beginning of the Thirteenth Five-Year Plan. The matter of retail price reform has been left open for broad public discussion before action is taken. The reform package has also reorganized the banking system (without changing its nature) and spelled out new decisionmaking authority in economic matters to be accorded to regional bodies. Finally, two new laws adopted in 1988 have considerably liberalized the provisions governing the activities of cooperatives and the conduct of foreign trade and joint ventures. At the same time, the authorities sanctioned a variety of experiments involving the leasing of assets of firms and farms, the issuance of shares (bonds) by enterprises, and new organizational forms such as interbranch complexes and "concerns" independent of the ministries.

Implementation of these half-measures in conditions of growing financial disequilibrium generated few benefits and much aberrational behavior that only made matters worse.[14] As a result of loosened central controls, many firms raised wages and prices, reduced planned output, juggled product mixes in the interest of more profits, exported products that were in short supply domestically, and started numerous investment projects. The rapidly expanding cooperatives were able to take advantage of the situation by raising their prices and their own incomes even more, thereby generating a public outcry against such "abuses." Finally, regional bodies moved to protect their own populations against shortages of goods by restricting sales to outsiders.

In response to these growing difficulties, the government adopted several measures during 1989 that amounted to recentralization and retrenchment on reform. The various decrees imposed controls on enterprises' freedom to negotiate prices; greatly expanded the scope of mandatory state orders to include all consumer goods and services; sought to control the growth of wages by tying them to productivity and, when that failed, by imposing taxes on excessive increases; restricted the scope of activity for cooperatives and imposed controls on their prices and incomes; and banned the export of many consumer goods. Along with these recentralizing steps aimed mainly at stabilizing the consumer market, the government adopted a variety of measures intended to soak up purchasing power by authorizing the sale of state-owned housing, issuing new kinds of state obligations for sale to enterprises and the population, and raising rates of interest paid on time deposits.[15]

Meanwhile, the Supreme Soviet considered and adopted a bevy of reform-related laws on leasing, land, property, income taxes, and economic relations between the central and republic governments. A vigorous public debate culminated in an all-union economists' and planners' conference on economic reform held in Moscow in mid-November 1989. Without reaching a consensus, the conference participants discussed a new comprehensive reform program often referred to as the "Abalkin Blueprint," after its primary drafter Leonid Abalkin, chairman of the Commission on Economic Reform of the USSR Council of Ministers.[16] This document at the time represented a major step forward in the design of an economic reform program intended to move from central planning to a market economy.[17] It endorses the ultimate goal of creating a market economy, but one that retains a substantial state sector in industry and, presumably, in the social infrastructure as well. The draft prescribes "destatization" of property (*razgosudarstvlenie*), whereby legal sanction would be accorded to a variety of ownership forms and most state enterprises would be sold or leased to their worker collectives. It also prescribes a gradual transition to primarily market pricing, to be accomplished by means of a three-tier system like that used in Hungary: fixed prices, prices allowed to fluctuate within ranges, and free prices. The document lays out three transition scenarios—conservative, radical, and radical-moderate. Abalkin prefers the latter, which calls for a year of legislative preparation and economic stabilization (1990), followed by a phased introduction of various aspects of the new system (1991–1995), after which the new system is supposed to be in full force and operating as a normal market economy.

At the same time that the Abalkin program was being prepared, a government commission was drafting its own stabilization-reform program, the basic provisions of which were detailed in a speech by Prime Minister Nikolai Ryzhkov to the Congress of People's Deputies in mid-December 1989.[18] This document, which was endorsed by the Congress, details a wide range of specific measures to be taken during 1990–1992 aimed at containing the rapid growth of prices and incomes, reducing the budget deficit, and normalizing the consumer market. The government program also contains general goals for the Thirteenth Five-Year Plan for 1991–1995, among them a projected 4.6 percent average annual growth of national income. Although it endorses "radical" reform, the market, and diverse forms of property ownership, the program clearly opts for a continued large role for state ownership and control over the economy. New and much higher industrial wholesale prices and agricultural procurement prices were to be introduced on January 1, 1991. The matter of revising retail prices with some form of compensation was to be made the subject of a public discussion on particulars, with the goal of completing the process in 1992. Overall, the flavor of the government's program resembles that of the 1987 reform package rather than that of the Abalkin Blueprint.

That is where economic reform stood at the end of Gorbachev's first five years of tenure. But in accepting the office of president of the Soviet Union in March 1990, Gorbachev called for "radicalizing" the process of perestroika, "decisively accelerating economic reform," and "creating a full-blooded domestic market."[19] That speech touched off efforts to quickly draft still another reform document. In April 1990 the first-quarter plan-fulfillment report revealed further deterioration of the economy and no real progress on the stabilization front. Rumors that the government was considering "shock therapy" (as in Poland) to free prices and introduce markets quickly elicited denials from the government, as well as from Gorbachev. Both endorsed a gradual, "phased" approach to establishing the "regulated market economy" that was the proclaimed goal. This approach was incorporated in a revised government program that Premier Ryzhkov presented to the Supreme Soviet on May 24, 1990.[20] The major innovation in this revised program was an acceleration of the proposed timetable for retail price reform, which was to begin with a tripling of the prices of bread and similar products in July 1990. The population responded with a run on retail stores, and the Supreme Soviet directed the government to produce a new version by September.

In the meantime, with the economy continuing to deteriorate, a much more radical plan—what came to be called the "500 Day Plan"—was drafted at the behest of Boris Eltsin, Chairman of the RSFSR legislature. With Gorbachev's agreement, a working group led by economist Stanislav Shatalin was set up to try to combine the government's May program with the 500 Day Plan. The result—the so-called Shatalin Plan—was submitted to the USSR Supreme Soviet in September, along with a rewrite of that Plan ordered by Gorbachev, and still another version of the government's program.[21] Unable to decide among the three plans, the legislature requested that Gorbachev come up with a single program. The result was the so-called Presidential Plan, which was approved by the national legislature on October 19, 1990.[22] With the critical issue of the relationship between the central and republic governments still to be settled by some kind of a treaty, the national legislature then gave President Gorbachev the right to implement the new program by means of Presidential decrees. Also during 1990, the legislature and the government adopted several laws and decrees to further a market economy: laws on enterprises and on taxation of enterprises; and decrees on joint-stock companies, on small businesses, on monopolies, and on a State Property Fund to manage the disposition of state enterprises.

Compared to the reform package adopted in 1987, the Presidential plan is a radical document. The plan provides for a gradual, phased transition to a market economy, but with an explicit time-table. The plan aims first to stabilize the financial situation and consumer markets, and then gradually to free prices, create markets, and destatize or privatize most property. The task is to be carried out within a framework that recognizes "the state sovereignty and equality of the republics," as well as "the integrity of the Union as a whole." The goal of "economic recovery and changeover to a market economy" is expected to take as long as two years to achieve. Implementing the stabilization phase of the program, Gorbachev in late 1990 issued Presidential decrees freezing existing contractual relations among enterprises and republics through 1991, instituting large increases in state-set wholesale and agricultural procurement prices as of January 1, 1991, declaring invalid all inter-republic agreements that are in conflict with the Presidential decrees, and setting up a national economic stabilization fund, and introducing a rational gross sales (turnover) tax of 5 percent. But effective implementation of the Presidential Plan or any other plan for economic reform under present political conditions seems problematic.

Conclusions

The first five years of Gorbachev's stewardship over the Soviet economy have been a dismal failure. Most of the goals of his much-redrafted Twelfth Five-Year Plan (1986–1990) are far out of reach, and the economy's performance seems likely to be the worst in the postwar period in terms of growth rates. As Gorbachev frankly admits, many serious policy mistakes have been made; among the worst were the initial lack of attention to agriculture and to consumer needs, the antidrinking campaign, the reduction in imports of consumer goods, and the rapid implementation of inconsistent and contradictory economic reforms. Worst of all, perhaps, was the failure to perceive the consequences of a skyrocketing budget deficit until severe damage had been done. At the end of five years, Gorbachev finds himself with an unreformed economy in spectacular disarray and on the verge of a serious recession. No progress has been made toward his primary goal of reducing the economic and technological gaps with the West; rather, those gaps have widened. Soviet manufactures are no more salable in Western markets in 1990 than they were in 1984. The long-suffering populace is more miserable, and far more vocal. And, finally, major strikes and episodes of ethnic violence have erupted, further damaging the economy.

Yet Gorbachev's first five years have not been a total loss. Above all, Gorbachev himself has undergone a fantastic learning experience in economic perestroika. He finally seems to understand the full extent of the economy's ills and their roots in the institutions and policies of the now thoroughly discredited "administrative-command" system. He now knows that monetary and fiscal matters are of decisive importance in managing a reforming economy. He seems to have a much better understanding of both the costs and the benefits of marketizing and privatizing an economy, and has apparently shed much ideological baggage in the learning process. Moreover, he has presided over and consistently fostered a lively, wide-ranging public debate on economic matters not seen since the 1920s. As a result, the body politic is not only better informed, but also far more outspoken and politically active. And by opening up Soviet society to Western contacts, Gorbachev has produced an intelligentsia better equipped to design and manage a liberalizing economic reform.

In addition, Gorbachev's dramatic foreign policy initiatives are bearing fruit for the Soviet economy in the form of a significant reduction in the burden of defense. Not only were defense outlays reduced beginning in 1989, but major steps were taken to begin the difficult process of converting defense production facilities and resources, including human resources, to civilian uses. Although the results thus far are meager, Gorbachev has begun the long and arduous task of opening up the economy to the West and integrating the Soviet Union into the international trading system and its organizations. His freeing of Eastern Europe to go its own way will benefit Soviet foreign trade in the long run. Finally, the last two years have brought a significant and long overdue shift of production and investment resources in favor of consumer goods and services as well as modernization of the social infrastructure. The plans for 1991-1995 are strongly oriented in this direction as well.

What Gorbachev urgently needs to do now, if these positive developments are to yield tangible gains in consumer well-being, is to overcome the legacy of the failed economic policies of his first five years and to move forward vigorously to create an economic system that functions through markets and private property. To prevent the forces of nationalism and ethnic strife from undermining this process, he must also devise new and constructive approaches to center-periphery relations. If rapid progress toward the accomplishment of these difficult tasks cannot be made, the next five years will likely see a continuation of the treadmill of economic perestroika—that is, a lot of upheaval with little progress toward a healthy economy.

Notes

1. For a recent evaluation of the two sets of figures, along with some new ones made by Soviet economists, see CIA, Directorate of Intelligence, *Revisiting Soviet Economic Performance Under Glasnost: Implications for CIA Estimates*, SOV-88-10068 (September 1988). CIA estimates of Soviet economic performance are published in the Agency's annual *Handbook of Economic Statistics*.

2. For details see Vladimir G. Treml, "Gorbachev's Anti-Drinking Campaign: A 'Noble Experiment' or an Exercise in Futility?," in U.S. Congress. Joint Economic Committee, *Gorbachev's Economic Plans*, Vol. 2 (Washington: U.S. Government Printing Office, November 1987), pp. 297-311.

3. USSR State Committee for Statistics, *Torgovlia SSSR: Statisticheskii sbornik* (Moscow: Goskomstat, 1989), pp. 199-200.

4. *Pravda*, January 28, 1990; *Pravda*, February 8, 1990.

5. *The Soviet Economy Stumbles Badly in 1989*, a paper presented by the CIA and the Defense Intelligence Agency to the Technology and National Security Subcommittee of the Joint Economic Committee, U.S. Congress, DDB-1900-161-90, May 1990, p. 4.

6. For a description of the modernization programs see Robert E. Leggett, "Soviet Investment Policy: The Key to Gorbachev's Program for Revitalizing the Soviet Economy," in *Gorbachev's Economic Plans*, Vol. 1, pp. 236-256.

7. For details see Andrew J. Matosich and Bonnie K. Matosich, "Machinebuilding: Perestroika's Sputtering Engine," *Soviet Economy*, Vol. 4, No. 2 (1988), pp. 144-176.

8. For an excellent analysis of the financial crisis, see Gur Ofer's "Budget Deficit, Market Disequilibrium and Soviet Economic Reforms," *Soviet Economy*, Vol. 5, No. 2 (1989), pp. 107-161.

9. The enormous ruble overhang was one of the major reasons for the currency reform carried out in January 1991. All 50- and 100-ruble notes, reported to constitute approximately one-third of the cash in circulation, were declared void and selectively replaced.

10. Robert Campbell, "Perestroika and the Macro-Muddle," a paper presented at a symposium at Georgetown University, Washington, DC, March 8-9, 1990.

11. Measures adopted during Gorbachev's first two years are described in Gertrude E. Schroeder, "Gorbachev: Radically Implementing Brezhnev's Reforms," *Soviet Economy*, Vol. 2, No. 4 (1986), pp. 289-301.

12. The Law and decrees are published in *O korennoi perestroike upravleniia ekonomikoi: Sbornik dokumentov* (Moscow: Gospolitizdat, 1988).

13. The 1987 reform package is described and appraised in Gertrude E. Schroeder, "Anatomy of Gorbachev's Economic Reforms," *Soviet Economy*, Vol. 3, No. 3 (1987), pp. 219-241.

14. The consequences of the 1987-1988 reforms and the government's response are described in Gertrude E. Schroeder's "Soviet Economic Reform: From Resurgence to Retrenchment?", *The Russian Review*, Vol. 48 (July 1989), pp. 305-319.

15. Many of these measures are outlined in a recent decree of the USSR Council of Ministers. See the *Sobranie postanovlenii pravitel'stva SSSR*, No. 6, 1990 (Decree No. 33).

16. The general outlines of the Abalkin program are published in *Ekonomicheskaia gazeta*, No. 43 (October 1989), pp. 4-7.

17. See Ed A. Hewett, "'Perestroika Plus': The Abalkin Reforms," *PlanEcon Report*, Vol. 5, No. 48-49 (December 1, 1989).

18. *Izvestiia*, December 14, 1989.

19. *Pravda*, March 15, 1990.

20. *Pravda*, May 24, 1990.

21. *Perekhod k rynku* (Moscow, August 1990), Vol. 1, translated in JPRS-UEA-90-034, September 28, 1990.

22. *Izvestiia*, October 27, 1990. For a detailed analysis of both the Shatalin Plan and the Presidential Plan, see Ed A. Hewett, "The New Soviet Plan," *Foreign Affairs*, Vol. 69, No. 5 (winter 1990-1991), pp. 146-167.

3

Social Change in the USSR Under Gorbachev: Population, Health and Environmental Issues

Murray Feshbach

As in so many areas of Soviet life, until the advent of glasnost, little was said to indicate that anything was seriously wrong with the state of the Soviet people's health or of the environment they lived in. With the disclosure of formerly secret figures on such topics as life expectancy and infant mortality, and the explosion of public concern over pollution, it is clear that health and ecology are two of the most acute problems facing Mikhail Gorbachev.

During his first five years in power, Gorbachev replaced his minister of health twice and organized a new agency for environmental protection, whose first chief was dismissed and replaced by a non-Party member. Both the Ministry of Health and Goskompriroda (the new environmental agency) have experienced major difficulties in resolving the problems with which they are charged; but, in contrast to the pre-Gorbachev period, there is a qualitative difference in their approach. In addition, more money is becoming available for their enormous needs, and new approaches are being implemented. Nonetheless, Soviet health and environmental problems and their impact on the population are so serious and so widespread, that these problems will probably worsen before they improve. It will take at least a decade for positive changes to become visible.

Population Issues

Despite some elements of change since Brezhnev, one needs to look at the continuity of problems in health and environment. For example, proportional population shifts to the southern tier, where various medical and ecological problems are particularly pronounced, affect the Soviet Union overall. And distinct regional differentials in fertility, mortality, and morbidity have negative implications for the general health status of the Soviet population as the proportional share of the southern tier's population becomes even larger. Gorbachev will have to address the policy implications of these changes for resource demands, the military and the nationality problem.

The overall Soviet population continues to grow, but growth is slower among the Slavic population groups. The initial success of the 1981 pronatalist policy seems to have dissipated among the Russians, Ukrainians, and Belorussians. The results of the January 12, 1989 census show that Russians now constitute 50.78 percent of the total Soviet population (down from 54.6 percent in 1959, 53.4 percent in 1970, and 52.4 percent in 1979).[1] However, I believe that if the census had been taken in the spring of 1989, the number of Russians would have been even lower, and their corresponding share even closer to 50 percent. Numerous issues engendered by environmental degradation in Belorussia and the Ukraine suggest that the three Slavic nationalities—Russians, Ukrainians and Belorussians—can no longer be considered a single Slavic bloc. The key event behind this significant change was the publication on 20 March 1989 in *Pravda* of three maps and a full page of text revealing that local populations in various areas of the Ukraine and Belorussia, as well as in parts of the Russian Republic, had not been informed of the real and continuing hazards of the Chernobyl accident three years earlier.[2] They had been residing in an area with high levels of curies per square kilometer of cesium-137 radionucleides (with a half-life of 30.4 years) and believed, as they were told, that their areas had not been negatively affected by the Chernobyl accident and radiation release. Perhaps 1 million persons in the Ukraine alone are now estimated to be living in hazardous zones. Even if this circumstance does not "bother" the "Russian" Ukrainians (i.e., eastern Ukrainians), the other western (Polish) Ukrainians have become more radicalized than they might have been by appeals from Rukh (the Ukrainian popular front) alone.

Nor have the Belorussians been silent. They have made very strong comments in their local press, in *Moscow News*, and at the Supreme Soviet regarding the untruthfulness of the "center" and the deception by

Doctor L.A. Il'in of the Academy of Medical Sciences and by local medical and Party leaders. Perhaps these Slavs would have been less culturally "assimilated"—that is, less apt to call themselves Russians in the census—in April than in January, prior to publication of the *Pravda* article noted earlier. For this reason, I am less sanguine about adding the number of Ukrainians and Belorussians to the number of Russians to obtain a figure of some two-thirds of the Soviet population as Slavic, which in turn might permit Moscow to be less concerned about the growth of the population of Muslim origin.

The growth of the southern populations remains extraordinarily high. At the same time, there has been some reduction in their total fertility rates—that is, in the number of children born to women over childbearing age if current fertility patterns by age were to hold. Numerically, Tadzhiks increased by 45 percent during the intercensal decade of January 1979 to January 1989, and this Tadzhik and other Muslim population growth will lead to an increasingly young population in the southern tier. In contrast, the Russians increased by less than 6 percent over the same intercensal period, Ukrainians by slightly more than 4 percent and Belorussians by slightly more than 6 percent. Returning to the growth of the population of Muslim origin, we find that the number of Uzbeks grew to almost 17 million by 1989 from a total of 12,456,000 in 1979 (34 percent)—not quite as much as the Tadzhiks but still a rate more than five times that of the Russians. The Turkmens also increased by 34 percent and the Kirgiz by 32 percent.[3] This differential in growth rates has occurred in part because the fertility rates among the Slavs (whether additive or not) declined in recent years, and the corresponding figures for the populations of Muslim origin remain far above those for the Slavs. New pronatalist policies, issued in April 1990, seek to instill a new impetus among the population to reproduce; these policies are directed especially at the Slavs, since the Muslims do not need the encouragement of any legislation to produce large families.

Looking at the new age data from the 1989 census of population, we discover that differential rates of growth have affected the officially defined population of able-bodied ages (males 16 to 59 years of age and females 16 to 54 years of age, inclusive) and thus the regional labor supply. From January 1979 to January 1989, the total number of such persons in the country grew (on a net basis) by a total of 7 million. Of these, some 70 percent, or almost 5 million, resided in Central Asia and Kazakhstan. As of 1990, Central Asians and Kazakhs constitute more than 25 million of the 158.9 million able-bodied people throughout the country, or slightly less than 16 percent.

However, 70 to 75 percent of the industrial base (measured as gross industrial product) is located in the Russian Republic and the Ukraine, and the population of Muslim origin is not moving to these republics in any significant numbers. Perhaps the demobilized armed forces will be recruited for work at labor-short enterprises, thus deflecting for the moment any question of where to house the new increments to the civilian labor force. Aging of the population was demonstrated by the combined growth by 21 percent in the number of males 60 and over and of females 55 and over compared to a total population growth of only 9 percent. Limited regional data only very recently available reveal that this age group's share in the Slavic and Baltic republics is currently 19 to 21 percent of the total populations of each republic, compared to only 8 to 10 percent for the populations of the Central Asian republics, thus emphasizing once again the major structural differences in the populations of these republics. The increase in the population of Muslim origin would be much higher were it not for the extremely poor health conditions in these republics. Despite the appointment of Academician and Nobel Laureate Evgenii Chazov as minister of health at the beginning of 1987, there is an enormous amount of work ahead to solve the problems of health delivery, services, supplies, sanitation, infant mortality, facilities, lack of sewage and poor medical ethics, and so on, as Chazov himself made clear. (Chazov resigned on March 20, 1990, and Igor Denisov was appointed Minister shortly thereafter.) In the meantime, insufficiencies in these areas affect the number and health of the local populations, beginning with infant mortality and including the deaths of elderly people from respiratory and digestive illnesses caused by land, water, and air pollution.

Health Issues

Many years of bad planning and poor solutions to water problems in Central Asia (the dessication of the Aral Sea in particular) have resulted in an infant mortality rate in the Aral region as high as 150 deaths per 1,000 live born children in some localities[4] – about five to six times the rate for the District of Columbia, the highest rate in the United States at 25-30 deaths per 1,000 live born children. Moreover, two-thirds of the local populations have typhoid, hepatitis, and/or cancer of the digestive system, and all new mothers are forbidden to breast-feed their children owing to the chemical pesticides in their breast milk.[5] Obviously these diseases will also have long-term effects on the surviving children. The populations in other republics of Central Asia are similarly unhealthy.

Many young males have been correctly determined to be unfit for military service following revision of the conscription rules in September 1989;[6] prior to that point, for a number of years, the lame, the halt, and the blind were drafted. Although exceptions to application of this revision apparently still occur, they are probably minimal in comparison with earlier practices. Moreover, now that it has been revealed that draftees from the Transcaucasus and Central Asia constituted 37 percent of all draftees in 1988 (up from 28 percent in 1980), the question arises as to whether these recruits are healthy enough to survive the rigors of military service, and whether their Russian language capability is sufficient to allow them entrance into a milieu where Russian is the language of command, control, and communications.

Indeed, the 1989 census results have confirmed my previous conclusion that the 1979 Soviet census figures for Russian-language ability among Uzbeks were incorrect and inconceivable. Under glasnost, the fact that 90 percent or more of rural Uzbeks do not know Russian can now be revealed; even among urban youths, this figure is growing. The census results also tell us that the growth from 14.5 percent of all Uzbeks with Russian language fluency, according to the 1970 census, to the astonishing figure of 49.3 percent in 1979 could not be correct; this later figure has subsequently been "corrected" to 23.8 percent for the beginning of 1989. In other words, the 1979 figure was exaggerated by at least 100 percent. All the policy implications of that original figure—for example, that the Soviet general staff need not hesitate to include the population of Muslim origin in all their plans—now appear to require major revision. Moreover, expectations that the Azeris and Armenians could be posted together, or that the Baltic peoples would willingly serve outside their immediate region, also need major reconsideration.

One of the unanticipated consequences of glasnost in nationality-related military issues is the apparent refusal of many eligible young men to show up for the draft. Halfway through the May-June 1990 conscription period, the general staff noted the appearance nationwide of only 26 percent of draftees. Broken down by republic, the numbers are shockingly low and may well reflect negatively on the current capabilities of the armed forces if the authorities are not able to address the problem successfully. By the end of the draft period, figures indicated that only 27.5 percent of draftees reported for duty in Georgia, 33.6 percent in Lithuania, 54.2 percent in Latvia, 40.2 percent in Estonia, and 7.5 percent in Armenia. In the autumn draft period, only 10.0 percent of draftees reported for duty in Georgia, 12.5 percent in Lithuania, 25.3 percent in Latvia, 24.5 percent in Estonia, and 28.1 percent in Armenia.[7]

On a more positive note, the central leadership, having come to recognize the importance of the health of the population, has doubled state budgetary allocations to the health sector for the next five-year plan period (1991-1995). But this measure is far from sufficient to meet all the needs of the sector. It is now reported (again thanks to glasnost) that of all rural district hospitals in the country, 65 percent do not have hot water, 27 percent do not have sewage, and 17 percent do not have any water at all.[8] The consequences for the people's health are massive. In Uzbekistan, for example, this lack of sanitation contributes to a rate of hepatitis seven times higher than that in Estonia (per 100,000 population). In 1988, infectious and parasitic diseases as a cause of death among infants ranged between 4.4 per 10,000 live births in Estonia and 6.3 in Lithuania to 126.7 in Tadzhikistan (an increase in itself of over 10 percent from the previous year) and 142.7 in Turkmenistan, a difference of more than thirty-four times at the extreme. Apparently, Chazov's policy initiatives which entailed the assignment of 40 percent of new investment to maternal and child health care has not yet had an impact. Although the policy is only a year old (as of 1990), I doubt whether its effects will be felt in the southern tier anytime in the near future.

Perhaps the death of so many Central Asian children is the only reason for which the overall population growth rate was "only" seven and one-half times higher for Tadzhiks (45 percent) than that for Russians (6 percent). New evidence of an "injection epidemic" in one of the Central Asian republics (most likely Turkmenistan) indicates that children in their first year of life are given "200 to 400" shots, not the approximately 3 to 5 injections that American infants are given in the form of basic vaccinations along with liquid medications as necessary during illness.[9] This terrible medical practice is a reflection of the shortage of knowledge among medical personnel who give shots for everything, regardless of whether they are needed, whether the syringes or needles have been used previously (probably without sterilization, given the shortage of facilities), and whether the high rate of medication will affect the efficacy of such medicines when necessary in the future. Moreover, given the drastic shortage of single-use, disposable syringes and needles in the country, the potential for the spread of AIDS, to say nothing of hepatitis, is a clear and present danger for this population. The total Soviet demand for single-use medical syringes amounts to some 6 billion units per year; domestic production amounted to 8 million in 1988 and 192 million in 1989. With imports of 40 million and 500 million in 1988 and 1989, respectively, the total supply falls far short of the demand, thus increasing the potential for the spread of hepatitis, AIDS, and other diseases.

Environmental Issues

A new environmental agency, supplementing—but unfortunately, so far, not supplanting—the State Committee for Hydrometeorological Services (Goskomgidromet), came into being at the beginning of 1988. Finally recognized was the fact that green issues were serious, politically unavoidable, inherently linked to the health of the population, and have major consequences for the economy and the military. Finally formed almost two years after the Chernobyl accident (which itself took place one year after Gorbachev's accession to power and changed his agenda forever), the environmental agency (Goskompriroda) was initially headed by Fedor Morgun. An active participant in the debate to make this new agency a player of significance in the environmental arena, Morgun quickly came up against the power of Goskomgidromet and lost; he then resigned in 1989. It took eight refusals before Nikolai Vorontsov, a noted biologist but non-Party member (in the first ministerial position held by a non-Party member since the 1920s), agreed to face up to the problems in question. And his problems are enormous: As of June 1990, he still did not have a full budget for his agency; he still faced Goskomgidromet's monopoly over pollution monitoring; and he still did not have legislation giving him the power to enforce his agency's programs (which in turn had to be rewritten and redrafted from those prepared by Morgun a year earlier). The first annual review of the state of the environment of the USSR in 1988, published at the end of 1989, confirmed all of the problems previously known and more.

The Soviets measure air pollution by the extent to which maximum allowable concentrations (PDKs) of pollutants are exceeded. In 1989, Chazov and Morgun announced that 70 million people live in 103 cities where the PDK for air pollution is exceeded by 5 or more times; 50 million in cities where it is exceeded by 10 or more times; 43 million in cities where it is exceeded 15 or more times; and 22 million where it is exceeded by 50 or more times at some point during the year.[10]

Some cities have taken drastic measures. In the fall of 1988, thousands of families living in Khmelnitsky were provided with gas masks because of the air pollution being generated at the local meat plant.[11] In the village of Seitovka, near the Astrakhan gas condensate combine, sirens and loudspeakers have been installed in the event of a chemical accident, and residents there have been issued gas masks as well.[12] These and similar cases prompted the Russian Republic's minister of health, A. I. Potapov, to remark that "to live longer you must breathe less."[13]

Land pollution in the USSR is closely associated with two issues: the Chernobyl disaster and "nitrates" in food. As mentioned earlier, the extent of the radiation released at Chernobyl in April 1986 has only recently been made public. It now appears that, in addition to the 116,000 people evacuated from affected areas during the year following the accident, another 50,000 will have to leave as soon as possible.[14]

"Nitrates" have come to mean pesticide and chemical fertilizer residues in food products. According to ecologist Aleksei Yablokov, "the USSR currently permits use of 400 pesticides. Of these, approximately 120 are simply beyond the capacity of the regulating agencies to control. Only about 60 of the 400 in use are controlled on any significant scale."[15] Pesticide and fertilizer use is particularly intense not only in rural Central Asia, Azerbaidzhan and Moldavia but also in densely populated areas such as the Moscow, Leningrad, and Kiev oblasts, which Soviet scientist Boris Cherniakov characterizes as having endured "twenty-five years of intensive chemotherapy!"[16] Studies in the 1970s linked excessive pesticide use with an increased rate of miscarriages and birth defects, and the Ministry of Health found serious health problems among children and adults in six republics with heavy pesticide use.[17] DDT, though banned worldwide more than twenty years ago and by the Soviets since the early 1970s, continues to be used in the Soviet Union, to such a degree that in one area, the usage norm was exceeded by 2,500 times.[18] In Lithuania, a leading environmentalist has indicated that DDT is hidden under another name and used extensively throughout the country.

Water pollution has also affected all regions of the country. Morgun describes five major rivers (the Volga, Dnepr, Don, Kuban, and Dnestr) as practically exhausted, and the Ministry of Health has found that "one-quarter of the municipal water supplies they tested did not meet safety standards for concentrations of harmful chemicals and one-fifth did not meet bacteriological requirements."[19]

An enormous Soviet disaster ensued from the dessication of the Aral Sea. Once the fourth-largest body of inland water in the world, it has shrunk by 40 percent since 1960 because of irrational use of its feeder water for cotton irrigation. According to one prediction, it will disappear completely by 2010. Pollution of the sea itself has rendered water in the lower reaches of the Syrdar'ia and Amudar'ia rivers unsuitable for consumption. Salinization of the region has become so extensive that 20,000 people a year are fleeing one of the adjacent oblasts in Kazakhstan.[20] Since 1960, the salinity of the sea has increased from approximately 10 percent to 23 percent.[21]

Lake Baikal is another cause that has been taken up by environmentalists for more than twenty years, yet pollution of the unique Siberian lake continues. The amount of polluted drainage into the lake tripled in only three years, from 66 million cubic meters in 1986 to 192 million cubic meters in 1988.[22]

Even if Vorontsov were to succeed in securing a budget of 450 to 500 billion rubles for the years 1991–2005, it would not be sufficient to meet all Soviet environmental needs. Preliminary calculations indicate that the current cost of replacing worn water pipes alone amounts to about 800 billion rubles, approximately twice as much as the entire budget for the next fifteen years for all needs—air, land, forests, nature preserves, and education of the population, as well as all other water pollution clean-up needs.[23]

Ecological problems have political as well as health and economic implications. For instance, environmental concerns are a major factor behind Estonian demands to curtail the defense industry in that republic. Not only do defense enterprises attract Russians to Estonia (from 1979 to 1989, the number of Estonians in the country as a whole grew by only 8,000 persons whereas the number of Russians in Estonia grew by 66,000); but they also pollute. Moreover, like all of the other establishments of all-union ministries, defense enterprises ignore local authorities—a circumstance that does not bode well for Estonia's attempts to enforce its authority as a separate territory.

Other republics have their own environmental demands. The Supreme Soviets in Belorussia and the Ukraine have declared their republics ecological disaster areas; Siberian representatives have decried the spoilage of delicate tundra ecology by oil drilling; the Kazakhstan Supreme Soviet has adopted a resolution calling for the closure of the Semipalatinsk nuclear testing site; Uzbek and other Central Asian intellectuals have called for an end to the agricultural monopoly of cotton in the region; and the Armenian-Azeri conflict came to a head after Azerbaidzhan proposed the placement of a polluting chemical plant in the Armenian enclave of Nagorno-Karabakh.

Iurii Izrael's agency, Goskomgidromet—despite much criticism from Goskompriroda, the People's Control Committee and a wide variety of environmentalists, both official and unofficial—has been able to defend itself by calling on the support of the polluting ministries. These ministries are well aware that if the power to regulate the environment is transferred to Goskompriroda, that power will be used to fine them severely or to close their enterprises. In 1989, some 240 plants and shops were closed; many belonged to the biochemical industry. The Nairit combine in Erevan,

Armenia, is a prime example. The rates of leukemia and of respiratory and other illnesses are much higher among the people living in the plant's immediate district than among the residents of the city as a whole or for the outlying districts. But the medicines and basic chemicals produced by this combine are essential to the health of the population. Nonetheless, there seems to be relatively little understanding of the fact that scrubbers and filters for various sources of pollution actually need to be installed, and if installed, need to be maintained. Most are not. It appears that the economic impact of chemical plant closures in particular has prompted economic planners to convince Gorbachev to order that no more plants be shut down for reasons of environmental pollution. Nonetheless, many plants, enterprises and shops of enterprises were closed in the first half of 1990.

As for "cleaning up their act" without closing plants, the Soviets cannot point to a single plant specialized in production of scrubbers. In my discussions with people throughout the Soviet Union, many individuals did not comprehend my stress on ecology *and* economy, rather than on ecology *versus* economy. Although I cannot dismiss the costs of such installations in plants whose pollution leads to acid rain in the United States, I must add that the Soviet situation is still far worse than the poor ecological conditions in certain locations and industries in the United States. If the problem were not so severe, why did Gorbachev mention the environmental problems of his country and the world no fewer than nine times in his speech to the United Nations at the end of 1988 and a number of times in his accountability report to the Twenty-Eighth Party Congress in 1990? Indeed, the situation may well be even worse than we think.

Health and environmental problems will affect many aspects of future Soviet policy decisions. They will have an impact on resource allocations; they will affect the military and lead to a professional army within five years owing to the increasing importance of the south as a source of potential draftees; and they will be a major contributor to the further radicalization of many nationality groups, including the Russians, as the center continues to ignore the impact of poor health and environmental pollution. Unfortunately, given both the magnitude of the Soviets' problems in these areas and current levels of funding, health and environmental issues will remain acute into the twenty-first century.

Notes

1. Comparison of the results of the 1989 census, published as *Natsional'nyi sostav naseleniia: Chast' II* (Moscow: Goskomstat, 1989), with the 1979 results, *Itogi Vsesoiuznoi perepiski naseleniia 1979 goda* (Moscow: Goskomstat, 1989).

2. Iu. Izrael', "Chernobyl': Proshloe i prognoz na budushchee," *Pravda*, March 20, 1989, p. 4.

3. See Note 1.

4. See, for example, the three-part article by Galina Denisova, Elena Kourina, and Vladimir Zhuravlev, "More gibnushchikh nadezhd," *Meditsinskaia gazeta*, May 23, 25, and 27, 1990, which cited a figure as high as 187 for one village in the region.

5. E. Ponarina, "Aral ugrozhaet planete," *Sotsialisticheskaia industriia*, June 20, 1989, p. 2.

6. E. Agapova, "Kak zdorov'e, prizyvnik?", *Krasnaia zvezda*, November 16, 1989, p. 4.

7. N. Ter-Grigor'iants, "Itogi prizyva ne raduiut," *Krasnaia zvezda*, July 2, 1990, p. 4; and Moscow, TASS International Service (in Russian), 1740 GMT January 7, 1991.

8. See, for example, the interview with Chazov, "Sotni voitelei stoit odin vrachevatel' iskusnyi," *Ogonek*, No. 42 (1988), pp. 1-3.

9. V. Tatochenko, M. Kuberger, "Izbytochnaia terapiia," *Meditsinskaia gazeta*, March 22, 1989, p. 2.

10. S. Turanov, "It Is Still Not Too Late," *Sotsialisticheskaia industriia*, July 5, 1989, p. 3, translated in JPRS, *USSR Political Affairs*, JPRS-UPA-89-051, August 16, 1989, p. 1.

11. N. Barsegov, "Breathe Deeper," *Komsomol'skaia pravda*, November 15, 1988, p. 4, translated in JPRS, *USSR Political Affairs*, January 25, 1989, p. 61.

12. Moscow Home Service, April 10, 1989, translated in BBC, *Summary of World Broadcasts*, May 5, 1989, p. C4.

13. B. Pipia's interview with Potapov, "Ecological Journal: Cities in the 'Black Book'," *Pravda*, September 1, 1989, p. 8, translated in *Current Digest of the Soviet Press*, Vol. XLI, No. 3 (September 27, 1989), p. 27.

14. Izrael', "Chernobyl'."

15. A. V. Yablokov, "Razvitie ekologicheskikh issledovanii v SSSR," *Vestnik Akademii nauk SSSR*, No. 9 (September 1989), p. 41.

16. Boris Cherniakov, "Khimiia ili zhizn'. Kogda zamalchivanie prestupno," *Moskovskie novosti*, No. 25, June 18, 1989, p. 10.

17. A. V. Yablokov, "Pesticides, Ecology, and Agriculture," *Kommunist*, No. 15 (October 1988), 34-42, translated in *Current Digest of the Soviet Press*, Vol. XLI, No. 2 (1989), p. 20.

18. See interview with G. I. Sidorenko and other officials, "Vse men'she okruzhaiushchei prirody, vse bol'she okruzhaiushchei sredy," *Sotsialisticheskii trud*, No. 8 (August 1989), p. 38. How can there be a norm for something which is illegal?

19. *Sovetskaia Rossiia*, March 26, 1989, and I. Sivinskaia, "Threat to the Biosphere," *Sovetskaia kul'tura*, March 25, 1989, p. 2, translated in JPRS, *USSR Political Affairs*, JPRS-UPA-89-034, May 22, 1989, p. 94.

20. See, among others, Bill Keller, "Developers Turn Aral Sea Into a Catastrophe," *The New York Times*, December 20, 1988, pp. C1, C6; Moldakhmet Qanazov, "Barrier Upon Barrier," *Qazaqstan Ayyelderi* (in Kazakh), No. 8 (August 1988).

21. Rusi Nasar, "How the Soviets Murdered a Sea," *The Washington Post*, June 4, 1989, p. B3.

22. Goskomstat SSSR, *Press-vypusk*, No. 235, May 31, 1989.

23. Calculated using figures for Baku provided by Gina Despres, counsel to Senator Bill Bradley (D-New Jersey), in a letter dated March 2, 1988.

4

Perestroika as Process:
Lessons from the First Five Years

Harley D. Balzer

It is difficult to say who learned more in the first five years of pere-stroika—Mikhail Gorbachev or Western sovietologists. Gorbachev stated that "we did not know the country in which we live," and the sentiment has been echoed by his close advisers.[1] Many Western observers have been equally surprised: some by the content of the revelations, others by the simple fact that a Soviet government was finally willing to tell the truth—or something much closer to the truth than we had witnessed in more than sixty years—about the situation in the country.

In light of the gradually increasing and eventually radical departure from traditional Soviet patterns of behavior regarding information, perestroika has become an intensely personal experience for professional observers of the USSR. Each of us at some point has been forced to reconsider our fundamental assumptions about Soviet history, politics and political culture. One inevitable result is that many discussions of Gorbachev and perestroika devote as much energy to demonstrating why earlier analyses were correct (or incorrect) than to elucidating the nature of the new regime.

Given that our explanations of perestroika have as much to do with how Westerners seek to understand Soviet politics as with the politics themselves, this chapter will focus on two sets of lessons: the lessons I believe Western Sovietologists learned (or should have learned) during Gorbachev's first five years; and those Gorbachev learned. Despite the significant overlap, there are some advantages to keeping the two categories distinct. Since Gorbachev's learning curve is one of the things about which outside observers have learned, we shall begin with him.

In discussing Gorbachev's first five years, I have sought to retain a sense of the process of perestroika. (A chronology of important events and changes in leadership are provided in the "Chronology" and "Summary of Changes in Leadership" at the end of this volume.) The changes have been ongoing, dynamic, and not necessarily unidirectional, making the process at least as important as any outcomes thus far.

Gorbachev's Lessons

We should begin by noting the easily overlooked point that Gorbachev is the first Soviet leader since Lenin who has demonstrated a capacity not only to learn on the job, but to publicly discuss the lessons and adjust his policies accordingly.[2] That in itself is no mean achievement.

When he took office in March 1985, Gorbachev sounded a little bit like Leon Trotsky the day he moved into the Foreign Ministry in 1917, thinking all he had to do was publish the secret treaties and go have lunch. In both cases, the job turned out to be somewhat more complex.[3]

Gorbachev's initial program focused on economic reform. The buzz word was *uskorenie* (acceleration), an approach very much along the lines of Andropov's emphasis on discipline and sobriety.[4] He seems to have believed economic improvement could be achieved relatively painlessly through administrative reorganization and personnel turnover. Some ministries had their leading cadres shuffled, while others were transformed into giant "complexes" reminiscent of earlier eras when bigger meant better. Major examples were machine-building and the "Agro-industrial Complex," where massive combinations of enterprises were to be administered by new layers of bureaucracy cutting across existing departmental structures. Such "superministries" have been one of the recurring models of reform in the Stalinist system. But they have not improved economic performance.[5]

Politics during Gorbachev's first two years could be explained in terms familiar from previous Soviet leadership transitions: Any new general secretary seeks to put "his" people into key leadership positions, guaranteeing the "circular flow of power;" and reorganization of the economic administration has been a regular feature of Soviet life.[6] It was in many respects a traditional consolidation of power in the Soviet system.[7] But there were also indications that Gorbachev had more in mind than the Andropov agenda.[8]

By January 1987, Gorbachev had come to the conclusion that economic reform was going to require political reform, even if he wasn't quite sure what that entailed. In fact, he is still making it up as he goes along. The January 1987 Central Committee Plenum adopted an agenda of political reform aimed at creating favorable conditions for more extensive economic changes that were still in preparation. At this stage, political reform meant essentially reform of the Communist Party, as evidenced by Gorbachev's call for a special Party Conference to convene in the summer.[9]

The Party Conference amounted to only a partial victory for Gorbachev, leading him to consider broadening political participation beyond the Party. He appears to have hoped first for renewal of the Party itself, then for assistance from outside forces to push this renewal, and finally, by the end of 1989, for genuine (if limited) participation by both Party and non-Party personnel.

Simultaneous with the decision to seek political reforms, supporters of perestroika began to talk seriously about "new thinking" in a host of other areas, including foreign policy, ideology and ethnic relations. Initially insisting that economic change would be decisive (as is natural for materialist thinkers), reformers gradually came to comprehend that fixing the economy required not only economic and political reform but also social reform, psychological change, and even spiritual transformation. The active cooperation of religious groups, autonomous social organizations, and even new political associations has been encouraged. It is tempting to gloat when Marxists proclaim that psychological and spiritual regeneration of the people constitutes the basis for economic improvement. But we should not lose sight of just how remarkable a set of lessons have been assimilated in a surprisingly short period. We might also give some thought to the likely future backlash from such a rapid shift in doctrine. The backlash may be most violent in light of the results of new thinking in foreign policy, where the Gorbachev team formulated and acted in accord with a view of the world sharply at variance with what had been the Soviet norm.[10]

Despite the fact that Gorbachev learns, however, he has tended to learn more slowly than many of his well-wishers might have hoped. And many of his colleagues, even those who were elevated to top leadership positions with his help or at least his consent, have not necessarily learned the same lessons.[11]

What did Mikhail Gorbachev learn in his first five years? First, he learned the basic lesson of any politician: The people, and especially the voters, are ungrateful. Gorbachev seems to have thought that if the Soviet authorities took their boots off peoples' throats, the people would say "thank you." But this belief reflected a profound misunderstanding of human nature, leading him to misjudge what would happen both in Eastern Europe and in the Soviet Union.

I think that Gorbachev genuinely was shocked at how little gratitude his efforts elicited from populations experiencing their "second liberation" at Soviet hands. The collapse of Communist regimes in Eastern Europe and the reunification of Germany took place with a rapidity that stunned everyone, the Soviets included. Far from thanking the USSR for ending Communist rule, the new East European governments turned their attention to calculating the economic, ecological and human costs of Soviet domination. It quickly became clear that even showcase East German enterprises were in no condition to compete on the same field with capitalism.[12]

At home, Gorbachev still seems unable to fully comprehend that people are not grateful to the Communists for changing their ways. In his calculations, ceasing to do nasty things should be enough to cancel out seventy years of doing those nasty things. Perhaps some people will eventually come to think that way, but gratitude has been less prevalent than a desire for revenge. Much of the voting behavior in early Soviet elections amounted to a protest vote against the Communists. It is part of the price the Party has to pay for Stalinist excesses as well as for economic and ecological failures.

A second lesson that Gorbachev and his team assimilated was the need for changes in information policy—the domain of glasnost. Information policy has been characterized by a continual tension between efforts to manage information and the need for independent sources to ensure the acquisition of useful data.[13]

Having lived in the Soviet Union when the first halting steps of glasnost were taken, I can remember just how tentative and contradictory they were. I associate glasnost with the Chernobyl disaster. For months following a tragedy that was both an ecological catastrophe and also a public relations fiasco on a par with KAL 007, the regime sought to tell not the truth but a version of events that the rest of the world would find acceptable. The nightly TV news program "Vremia" groped for a new style and different formulations. It even created the USSR's first significant television news personality in Alexander Krutov.[14] Since 1986, controls over most forms of information have been relaxed, but the process has been neither unilinear nor based on a freedom-of-information philosophy. Here, too, the backlash potential is enormous, and by early 1991 a retreat appeared to be well underway.[15]

A third major lesson, and one Gorbachev may have learned even before he took power, is that the real problem facing Soviet reformers is not opposition; it is resistance and inertia. Just because this formula was one of the shibboleths of the early years of perestroika doesn't mean it isn't true. Resistance among the entrenched hordes of ministerial officials and Party *apparatchiki* has frustrated every Soviet leader, including Stalin.[16]

A great deal of attention during 1986–1990 was focused on the potential for a conservative coup in the Politburo, most often touting Egor Ligachev as an alternative leader.[17] Despite mounting evidence to the contrary, this scenario was still being envisioned as late as the eve of the Twenty-Eighth Party Congress in July 1990. Yet no one I know in the middle reaches of Soviet political life thought that Ligachev was a plausible candidate for General Secretary. There was not a right-wing faction in the Politburo that seriously threatened Gorbachev in this period.

Serious opposition to Gorbachev's personal leadership appears to have been a minority position. There were, and still are, many conservatives in the leadership. But once Grigory Romanov and Viktor Grishin were rejected as potential general secretaries, Gorbachev's power was ensured. How else can we explain his repeated ability to bring a restive Communist Party to heel, and even induce it voluntarily to abolish its monopoly on political power? The closest thing to a coup was the now famous Nina Andreeva affair, sparked by a letter to *Sovetskaia Rossiia* purportedly written by a Leningrad chemistry teacher. For more than a month, until *Pravda* responded, a chill was cast over the reformers. But once Gorbachev made his sympathies known, the opponents of reform were clearly defeated, with *Sovetskaia Rossiia* forced to publish the *Pravda* refutation. The conservatives were competing for influence over Gorbachev and the Party's policies, not for direct power.[18]

The threat of a coup was so low because both an alternative leader and a genuine alternative program were lacking. No one among the conservatives seemed able to articulate policies other than a return to one of the discredited models from the Stalinist past or a replay of the failed economic reforms of Khrushchev or Brezhnev. The people who were giving Ligachev economic advice had little to offer that differed from Gorbachev's program. They just didn't want to go as far or as fast.[19] The assertions by some conservatives that they were supporters of perestroika were not just a cover for sophisticated opposition tactics—no one could argue that the unreformed system was working.

It may be that the best analogy to perestroika is tax reform in the United States.[20] Just about everybody is in favor of tax reform. We all know it is necessary (or at least we thought so until 1986). We thought that tax reform meant that millionaires like Leona Helmsley would finally pay their fair share and just about everyone else would pay less. And most Americans hope that the "fat cats" will have their loopholes closed, but that no one will touch the mortgage interest deduction. The system should be made more fair, but somebody else should bear the brunt of the changes.

So it is with perestroika. The overwhelming majority of people in the USSR agree that the situation is impossible and that major changes are necessary. Almost everyone is a supporter of perestroika, at least on the surface. Yet everyone wants "it" done to someone else. The reaction is that the changes are absolutely essential, as long as they do not disturb my own work, situation, or "peaceful life." Official privileges must go, but not *my* privileges. Patronage networks are inherently evil, except when they involve *my* friends. And so on. The problem is most pronounced at the middle levels of the bureaucracy; and it is particularly severe in rural areas, where the managers of collective and state farms as well as the local party officials have little prospect of maintaining their lifestyles in a market environment. Managers and party officials in urban and industrial regions are more likely to have technical and managerial skills that enable them to function reasonably well in a non-command economy. But even they will have to work in very different ways, and not all relish the change.

Initially, many mistook perestroika for a new "party line," believing it would be enough to mouth the new slogans while continuing business as usual, or even working to undermine the reforms. Such resistance became more difficult as increasing numbers of people expressed their belief that change was necessary.

The effort to make local officials more responsive to demands from the center has been a constant theme in Soviet politics, leading to frequent campaigns for increased party discipline.[21] In 1989–1990, Gorbachev appears to have decided that this objective could be achieved only by ending the Party's monopoly and forcing it to compete for local power. Gorbachev seemed to be saying, "If I can't make them be responsible through the party, we'll make them responsible to the voters." The local party leaders who can't satisfy the voters don't deserve to be there.

Forcing *all* contenders to compete for political power emerged as one of the main lines of Gorbachev's strategy. Gorbachev sought to position himself between the Communist Party *apparat* and the new parliamentary system, seeking to use both while being the prisoner of neither. But the strength of the rejection of the Party was a shock. Not only inept local officials but most Communist officials were defeated, threatening to leave him with no institutional power base. His effort to convene the Twenty-Eighth Communist Party Congress and render it pliant was an attempt to hang on to what he regarded as the only "civilian" institution capable of providing some social glue.[22] The other two alternatives, the military and the KGB, are less satisfactory to almost everyone. The need for a powerful center at a time of crisis also underlies recent proposals for presidential rule and creation of executive plenipotentiaries.[23]

Gorbachev's learning curve was best on reforming traditional politics. This is the policy realm for which he has the best intuitive feel, and it is also the area in which, in the first five years at least, he was not faced with choices for which all the options involve a diminution of his capacity to influence events. Gorbachev also learned well, if reluctantly, in the realm of information. Glasnost has often been halting, but the benefits of a *relatively* freer environment seemed worth the inevitable increase in criticism and upset among the conservatives. His marks are lower in economics.[24] Gorbachev learned that fixing the economic mess requires reforming myriad other aspects of Soviet life. But he was not able to resolve the fundamental contradiction between generating the wealth promised by a free market and retaining the state control and social safety net of socialism. It is hardly surprising that Soviet citizens desire the material rewards, higher standard of living, and general "good life" associated with market economies, but also wish to keep the subsidized prices, guaranteed employment, free medical care and other benefits of socialism. The society is risk aversive, although in this respect it differs even from the "individualistic" United States only in degree.[25]

The realm in which Gorbachev was least prepared to learn, and in which he has had to learn the most, involves nationalities and ethnic issues. The Soviet Union is a multinational empire in an age when ethnic identity is gaining increased saliency on a global scale.[26] If there is any one lesson that Gorbachev probably wishes he had not had to learn, it is the nature and extent of the Soviet nationalities problem. This issue is discussed by Paul Goble in Chapter 5 of this volume, and has been treated extensively by other scholars.[27] I think that Goble is correct in his judgment that Gorbachev was not prepared to recognize the significance of the nationalities problem and has never really understood national feelings. Watching his attempt first to "jawbone" and then to bully the Lithuanian people into rescinding their declaration of sovereignty in early 1990 evoked the sense that, beyond his general preference for lecturing rather than listening, Gorbachev would not have comprehended the Lithuanians' message even if he had heard it.[28]

Yet even if he were much more aware and sensitive, Gorbachev could not make the nationalities problem go away. He might make fewer mistakes, but some problems are never solved. No solution exists to the

Soviet or any other nationalities problem. Certainly there is no single solution, and probably not even any combination of solutions that could permanently resolve the difficulties involved. Leaders can only try to *manage* the nationalities problem. Hence Gorbachev and the Soviet leadership must be evaluated not on the basis of how they "solve" the nationalities problem but on the basis of how they cope with it. They and their successors are likely to be coping with it for a long time.[29]

Outside observers who questioned the assumption that the Soviet Union would fall apart never argued that its cohesion was guaranteed. Any estimates of the likelihood of the breakup of the Soviet empire must take into account the possibility that sensitive issues will be mishandled. The most glaring example of botched policy during Gorbachev's first five years was the Tbilisi tragedy of April 1989, when troops attacked peaceful demonstrators. The desire for independence in Georgia has been increasing ever since. Similar increases in separatist sentiment have resulted from the central government's resort to violence in Baku, Vilnius, Riga and other places.[30]

The Tbilisi tragedy points to the most basic lesson still being assimilated by Gorbachev: Events, policies, and decisions have consequences that shape subsequent conditions and may limit options. In short, there is no way to avoid paying the bills.

We might also devote a moment to the question of what Mikhail Gorbachev has *not* learned. Almost anyone who watches his public appearances would agree that he has not learned how to express himself concisely. He retains a proclivity for long-windedness and a hectoring style in public appearances. In marked contrast to Boris Eltsin, who appears to have learned how to preside over a legislature, Gorbachev too often resembles a regional Party secretary ruling his feifdom.[31]

Gorbachev's loquaciousness is symptomatic of a far deeper problem: He does not understand what is involved in creating a political *system* — or else he understands it very well and has intentionally blocked the emergence of a new system. Rather than changes and adjustments to correct specific shortcomings, Gorbachev has preferred to create entire new institutions. It is an instrumental or even a consumer approach to political structures. New institutions are for him a means to a particular end, not an end in themselves. If the desired results do not appear quickly, another institutional configuration is devised. The Presidential Council, touted as a new "cabinet," never established a clear role. It was quickly replaced by a "Council of the Federation" consisting of the leaders of the fifteen republics. Leaving aside the question of how leaders who do not reside in Moscow can provide regular policy input, the Council appears to have only a vague mandate. Gorbachev's behavior gives the impression of desperate attempts to consolidate more power in the face of slipping authority.[32]

The same disdain for established rules of procedure can been seen when Gorbachev presides over meetings of legislative bodies. Basic rules of legislative and parliamentary business have not been established. Few people seem to know which bills can be approved by the Supreme Soviet and which require action by the Congress of Peoples Deputies.[33] The question of how to rotate the membership of the Supreme Soviet was put off for six months (until December 1990). Deputies are routinely asked to vote on bills they have not studied and to perform oversight functions without access to basic data on their subjects.

Some scholars have also noted what could be called the "disorganizing role" of Gorbachev himself.[34] He presides over sessions with aplomb, but exhibits little awareness of the need for standardized rules of procedure. Speakers are recognized according to his whims and moods, and motions are accepted or rejected on the basis of the leader's own political agenda. Most important, the microphones and television cameras are turned on and off at his bidding. Yet he has not always had full control, and he seems to do better with the microphones than with the media. In Fall 1989, when Gorbachev cut off the mike during an impassioned plea for democracy by Andrei Sakharov, the television and radio coverage continued; as a result, everyone in the USSR *except* the delegates in the hall was able to hear Sakharov's speech.[35]

Such behavior not only flies in the face of democratic procedure but also inhibits the development of a genuine parliamentary system. Many of these issues could be resolved when the new Constitution is approved, but only if everyone, Gorbachev included, agrees to set rules and abide by them. In the interim, the arbitrary character of political life may enhance Gorbachev's power, but in the long run it undermines institutional legitimacy.

Institutional legitimacy is crucial in the absence of ideological legitimacy. Communism had lost its appeal to a majority of people well before Gorbachev, but it still provided a rationale, an image of a future goal, and an common political vocabulary for regime supporters. Now there is no basis for the regime's legitimacy, nor for that of the empire, beyond Gorbachev's insistence on observing old documents with dubious claim to a higher legal standing.[36]

Lessons for Western Sovietology

The first lesson Sovietologists have learned—and in many ways the most important lesson—is that the prevailing models used to explain Soviet politics before 1985 were not much help in accounting for Gorbachev. The kindest interpretation is that these models offered some assistance in explaining how the Soviet political system functioned but provided few clues as to how it might ever change. Even the scholars who say that Gorbachev has failed—and, hence, that communism was unreformable—do not account for the appearance of a serious reformist Soviet leader. The few scholars who did forecast Gorbachev's revolution were treated as outside the mainstream by most Sovietologists.[37]

The most frequent argument in the West in 1986–1987 centered on whether Gorbachev was "for real." His policies did not seem to be a radical departure from accepted Soviet behavior, but his style and rhetoric definitely diverged from the norm. A few observers stressed the possibility that significant change was in the works, while others still pronounced it to be impossible. Many hedged their bets. In Washington, the "conventional wisdom" tended to lag two to three years behind events.[38]

Much of the discussion of Soviet politics in the post-World War II era has centered on the totalitarianism model, either as an explanation or as a target of attack.[39] The influence of the totalitarianism school is still manifest in analyses suggesting that the Soviet Union cannot change because the Soviet Union cannot change, and that if it does change it will no longer be the Soviet Union.[40] By making the Soviet regime something *sui generis* and outside history, such analyses are able to define it as something that could never be anything else.[41]

One reason we now lack conceptual models that might help us order the data we are receiving is that much of the Western interpretation of Soviet politics rested on some basic shared myths. The sum total of these myths is a distorted image of the Russian/Soviet political culture. In its worst forms, it is intensely Russophobic. How else can we explain optimistic assessments of the prospects for China and Eastern Europe, but prediction of dire disasters for Russia? There are parallels in the literature about other countries, most notably Spain. For Spain, too, the argument has been made that history, tradition, culture and national character all preclude democratic development.[42] The fundamental flaw in such arguments is that they ignore the connections between political culture and the social, economic, and intellectual life of the society. It is a static conception, assuming that the culture and, hence, the potential forms of political life are determined irrespective of social change.[43]

Shared Myths

The most widespread of the shared myths about Soviet politics and political culture involve the leader, the masses, and the character of the new regime.[44]

The Vozhd

The first and perhaps the most important myth is that of the *vozhd'* (leader) — the idea that the Soviet Union must have a Stalin in order to exist; or that an autocratic dictator ruling for twenty-five years is the typical experience for the Soviet political culture.[45]

Or to phrase the question slightly differently: Was Stalin the norm or an aberration? Judging from the individuals who led the USSR during the forty-five years that Stalin was *not* all-powerful, Stalin was not a typical Soviet leader. On the contrary, he was the exception — and a crucial exception at that, inasmuch as the Stalinist system and World War II were the fundamental defining experiences of Soviet life in this century. However, some commentators tend to ignore the struggle involved in creating the Stalinist system, arguing that Stalinism was the natural and logical consequence of the Leninist attempt to force Marxist revolution on an overwhelmingly agrarian society.[46] I do not believe that Stalinism was a natural product of Russian or communist political culture. Rather, the Stalinist system was imposed by force in a bloody civil conflict that Stalin himself equated with World War II.[47]

To say that the "seeds" of Stalinism were inherent in Leninism is not to say that Stalinism was either the inevitable result or the sole possible outcome. Even if it was the *most likely* outcome of Lenin's revolution, Stalinism was a product of specific social, economic, cultural, and technological as well as political circumstances. Stalinist totalitarianism could not exist in the era of Peter the Great because the technology for surveillance and communication had not yet been developed. And it may be that the regime that replaced Stalinist totalitarianism can not exist in the late 20th century because such a system is incompatible with modern technology.[48]

Recent scholarship focusing on the "social base" for Stalinism has demonstrated that there was a locus of support for the Stalinist system consisting of the recruits to the Bolshevik Party, workers and peasants — especially those promoted into education and responsible positions during the industrialization drive — and the army of officials who either believed in the new system or saw it as a patronage bonanza (or, more often, both).[49]

To state that there was a social base for Stalinism is not to imply that Stalin's policies were any less cruel or reprehensible. But it does raise two crucial historical issues. First, the entire era was not the product of a single demented ruler resuscitating vestiges from the time of Ivan Groznyi.[50] Second, and more important, if the social structure that supported Stalinism has changed, we might expect the potential for a return to Stalinism to be diminished.[51]

The Gray Masses

A second myth, in many respects the corollary of the myth of the leader, is that of the "gray masses."[52] Soviet Communist Party members, a large portion of the Soviet intelligentsia, and many Western scholars make the same mistake when evaluating the people of the USSR—in part, perhaps, because these three groups tend to talk largely to each other. In particular, many Western scholars tend to assimilate the views of their very interesting and respect-worthy friends in Moscow and Leningrad.[53]

The mistake is in believing that the population of the Soviet Union today is still the same dark mass depicted by Tolstoy or Chekhov. Some of my own friends in Moscow still think they are facing the situation that the character Vershinin outlined in Chekhov's *The Three Sisters*, where there are three cultured people living in the town today, and perhaps there will be six in the next generation. And "in two or three hundred years, life on earth will be unimaginably beautiful."[54] That description is no longer accurate. As Blair Ruble notes in Chapter 1 of this volume, and as he and others have demonstrated elsewhere, the Soviet Union has become a very highly educated and professionalized society.[55] Indeed, it is a much more politically literate and astute society than a lot of people are willing to give it credit for. Nearly every journalist, both Soviet and Western, who spent time in the Kuzbass or Donbass after the coal strikes in 1989 expressed astonishment at the miners' sophistication. Most striking, perhaps, were the miners who freely admitted their lack of political education, suggesting that they should develop direct contact with Poland's Solidarity to learn how to organize properly.[56]

The lesson that the people are not dupes was learned quite painfully by numerous Communist Party officials who failed to win election to the Congress of People's Deputies in March 1989, even when they were running unopposed. It was summed up very eloquently by Leningrad Party boss Iurii Solov'ev, who confessed to a reporter that "we never thought they would take the trouble to go into the booth and cross out a name."[57] Once people began to realize that the elections were not completely rigged and that their votes indeed had meaning, electoral involvement increased:

Soviet intellectuals frequently view the country as one in which they and their close friends are the sole intelligent, educated individuals. Unaware of the existence of tens of thousands, if not millions, of similar individuals, they seem to believe that their own ability to see through the veneer of official ideology and to learn about the outside world is some sort of cultural immaculate conception, never repeated elsewhere.[58] Yet survey data, education statistics and election results indicate the existence of a sizable educated middle class. Although the success of democratic institutions is far from guaranteed, we should not dismiss the possibility of their development *ipso facto*. The political culture does present difficulties in developing a democratic system, but they are neither genetic nor insurmountable.

In addition to their elitism regarding the people, members of the Soviet intelligentsia have tended to develop a very particular view of politics and politicians. Among the Academy of Sciences' candidates for the Congress of People's Deputies, those initially chosen were almost all directors of institutes. Many of the candidates from other organizations and in territorial districts were enterprise directors. Selection appears to have been based on the fact that the candidates were prominent individuals entitled to another "reward" for their services—a carry-over from the honorific character of the old Supreme Soviet.

Whereas office has been treated like yet another honorific title by Party types, the public has often elected former dissidents—that is, anyone who was brave enough to stand up to the Communists, such as Andrei Sakharov, Viacheslav Chornovil, or Roy Medvedev. To be a dissident, one had to be tough, single-minded, moral, and unwavering. One had to be utterly uncompromising. Such people, quite deservedly, are now public heroes. But the attributes that make heroes of dissidents are not necessarily the traits that enable a democratic political system to function. Parliamentary democracy depends on the capacity to compromise.[59] As Dante Fascell (among others) has put it, "sometimes you have to rise above your principles." Andrei Sakharov is a genuine hero. But he was not always tolerant of diverse opinions.[60] He did learn how to listen—a skill his successors need to cultivate.

There is a fundamental tension in democracy between electing the "best" or most deserving people and electing the people who will best articulate the wishes of the voters. The Soviet tradition has generally stressed the former, and many political positions have been considered honors that convey prestige but attach no obligation to do additional work. Now the concept of representing the electorate is beginning to intrude. This in itself suggests that the "gray masses" have become much more discerning.

The Benevolent Tsar

A third myth that has been demolished could be called the myth of "Tsar Misha the Good": the idea that Gorbachev began instituting change because, as was said of Iurii Andropov, he likes jazz and Scotch.[61] Gorbachev did not wake up one morning and decide that bourgeois liberalism and freedom of speech are preferable to what existed in the USSR. Perestroika (at least in its first five years) was not an attempt to build a Western-style democracy. And glasnost has never meant full freedom of the press (at least not to its initiators).[62]

In a very revealing moment during the session of the Congress of Peoples' Deputies in December 1989, Gorbachev allowed observers a glimpse of his basic political beliefs. During a rambling summary of the session he stated: "I am a communist. I shall remain a convinced one. For some people this may be a fantasy, something up in the air somewhere, but for me it is a goal. It is a long way off".[63]

Perestroika was introduced out of necessity, not because the people in charge wanted these kinds of change. The political leaders who initiated the reforms have not embraced Western parliamentary values. They introduced perestroika because for fifty years Soviet leaders tried just about everything else they could to make their system work, and they failed. The USSR could not remain a great power without major change. Indeed, the Soviet leaders understand that if they don't achieve moderate success with perestroika, the USSR will wind up as a ghetto in the global village.

However, there are some crucial corollaries to the "myth of the benevolent tsar." First, owing to the policy debates and academic discussions of the past thirty years, perestroika found a receptive audience.[64] The changes have been supported by many people who are more than willing to embrace Western values. Reform may have begun from above, as has so often been the case in Russian history, but as they were being carried out in a highly educated society, the reforms brought forth a host of supporters who have aspirations that may be very different from those of the reforms' initiators.

Gorbachev's strongest supporters have often been people who have wanted to move a lot farther and a lot faster than Gorbachev himself has been prepared to go. The phenomenon is most clearly visible in the press and in culture. In a similar manner, although Gorbachev may have little interest in or respect for new legislative institutions and little desire to create a viable political system, many of the politicians now working in these bodies are more concerned with building permanent institutions.[65]

A second corollary to the "socialist limits" of the good tsar is the simple rule "never say never." During Gorbachev's first five years in power, the journalistic landscape became littered with the carcasses of articles purporting to identify the new limits of acceptable expression.[66] The same maxim applies in politics, as exemplified by those who said the Communist Party would never surrender its political monopoly. We no longer know what Gorbachev or his successors are likely to permit. Anyone who tries to say, "This is the limit, the line that they cannot cross," is likely to find that the strictures are superseded very quickly. In politics, Gorbachev has been constantly capable of surprises.[67] The same caution applies to those who view the process as unidirectional or irreversible. It is complex, contradictory and, despite the importance of "new thinking," not based on Western values.

Politics and Participation

Perestroika and glasnost have created a field day for analysts of Soviet politics. In addition to unprecedented revelations about past events, we have seen scholars and journalists gain access to high-level participants in Soviet political life. The situation creates both unprecedented opportunities and new dangers.

We have learned a great deal about the Communist Party. Even before Gorbachev we knew that many of the "best and the brightest" in Soviet society were Party members.[68] If disillusionment with Party conservatism following the Twenty-eighth Party Congress resulted in a loss of membership, during the first four years of perestroika the trend was the other way, as many talented individuals sought Party positions to advance the reform effort.[69] It should not surprise us that 80 percent or more of those elected to new parliamentary bodies were Communists. It also shouldn't surprise us that the Party is riven by dissension and debate that have become both more acute and more public. By 1990 the rifts were put on full public display at the Twenty-Eighth Party Congress. Yet to say that 80 or 85 percent of the people anywhere are Communists does not say all that much about their political views. There have always been distinctions between activists and ordinary members; between *nomenklatura* and lesser officials; and between true believers and careerists.[70]

We now know unequivocally that Soviet politics involves genuine politics, with all of the messiness and all of the conflict and all of the political games that characterize politics anywhere. When politicians in the Soviet Union make statements we need to watch what they do, not what they say—the rule we would apply to politicians in any context. We must watch the spin, because some of them are becoming very good at spin control. Political speeches almost always are marked by local variations. George Bush doesn't deliver the same speech in Texas that he gives in Boston. Soviet leaders are similar. Gorbachev can't go to Central Asia without talking about water. When talking to people in the ecology movement, on the other hand, he is not going to mention river diversion.

We should have learned this lesson a long time ago. The existence of a single political party doesn't create an absence of politics; rather it drives all the politics inside that one party.[71] That has been true for a long time, and when scholars have looked for evidence, they haven't had much difficulty finding it.

In the Gorbachev era the Soviet Union has seen politics surface with a vengeance. Some mornings one might wake up, read the newspaper, and ask, "Who's in charge here?" Vadim Medvedev, when he was still the party secretary for ideology, stated publicly that Alexander Solzhenitsyn's *Gulag Archipelago* is a terrible anti-Soviet book that could not be published in the USSR. Within six months, it was published. Yet Medvedev remained in his post for another year.[72]

A second example of seriously mixed political signals was seen when General Dmitrii Yazov, the Minister of Defense, responded during his confirmation hearing in June 1989 to a question about students who had been drafted out of higher educational institutions by saying that it would be impossible to allow these students to return to school before they completed their full two-year term of military service. The policy of drafting students would cease, but nothing could be done about the individuals who had already been drafted. Within forty-eight hours, the Supreme Soviet voted to permit these students to return to their studies, Gorbachev signed the law, and 300,000 students returned to the classroom in September 1989. Who is the ultimate authority here? The answer is probably "no one". The political environment is becoming much messier and more complex.[73]

Similar rules of interpretation—watch what they do, not what they say—apply to the flap over Vladislav Starkov, the editor of *Argumenty i fakty*, in 1989. My interpretation of that episode is that Gorbachev handled it very astutely. After venting his spleen at a group of editors, he specifically threatened Starkov, who was capable of annoying him but was not in a position to do very much damage. Then Gorbachev turned around and used the occasion to dismiss Viktor Afanas'ev, the editor of *Pravda*, who was in a position to do a lot of damage. We need to pay more attention to the details of political maneuvering and infighting.[74]

We also need to pay more attention to the underside of politics. During the local election campaign in the spring of 1990 there was much coverage by journalists, both Soviet and Western, of dirty tricks. Indeed, the two themes that emerged most prominently in Western coverage of the elections were dirty tricks and voter apathy.[75] And yet, voter turnout was higher than in typical American off-year elections.

Dirty tricks are a fact of political life. But the interesting point about such shenanigans in Soviet elections is that they have frequently redounded against the perpetrators. Galina Starovoitova, a Moscow ethno-sociologist elected as a people's deputy from the Armenian capital of Erevan, describes how helicopters dropped leaflets in her district advising people to vote for an Armenian rather than the "false friend" Starovoitova. The provocation was so crude and obvious that most voters took the leaflets to be proof that Starovoitova had frightened the old authorities—and thus they had one more reason to vote for her. (Even the "gray masses" know that only the Communist Party and the KGB have access to helicopters).[76]

A similar tactic was used in one of the Belorussian electoral districts, where leaflets were distributed accusing a reformist candidate of having been a Nazi collaborator. Once again, the public reaction was to reject the provocation and support the "target." In June 1990, negative campaign tactics were used against the KGB whistle blower General Oleg Kalugin, who nevertheless won election in a region formerly under the control of RSFSR Communist Party leader Ivan Polozkov. Boris Eltsin cites several analogous examples in his autobiography.[77]

As the political system evolves, and as it becomes more "political" (or more like what we regard as politics), it is likely to take on various appearances in different regions of the country. That, too, should not surprise us. Those who have focused on the persistence of Communist Party dominance, clan politics and corruption in Central Asia might recall that the United States survived for nearly a century with a one-party system in one region of the country. Even if the equivalent of a "solid south" were to emerge in the Soviet Union, however, the overall character of the system would not be altered. Given the activism of democratically oriented popular fronts in Central Asia, such a bloc would likely last far less than a century.

We have also learned that the Soviet electorate, at least in 1988–1990, was to the "left" of Gorbachev, and that the much-vaunted Russian right, including the potential for anti-Semitism and fascism, was not much of a factor in the elections.[78] Of course the Russian right is hardly irrelevant. But many observers seem unable to accept the massive evidence indicating that the right, though noisy enough to get the attention of journalists and editors in both countries, has not been a mass political movement.

Throughout the 1990 local elections, the popular fronts and democratic movements in provincial cities repeatedly turned out thousands of people at their rallies. The right wing, by contrast, brought out only 50 or 100 most of the time.[79] The two largest Moscow demonstrations by the right-wing patriotic (and anti-Semitic) organization *Pamiat* numbered 500 and 1,500. The organization's most famous public appearance, when it disrupted speeches by Jewish writers, involved a dozen activists, and the leaders of the action were brought to trial.[80] Yet *Pamiat's* message and tactics continue to arouse fear.

In elections to the Congress of People's Deputies in the spring of 1989, *Pamiat* had some fifteen announced supporters on the ballot around the country. All lost their elections. Yet some observers, rather than focusing on the fact that all fifteen had lost, paid attention to a *Pamiat* spokesman who announced that there were secret supporters of the organization who had, in fact, been elected to the Congress, would work for their goals, and would reveal their identity "when the time comes."[81]

My personal favorite in the elections was the case of Iurii Bondarev, a Russian nationalist writer whose books sell millions of copies. He was a candidate for people's deputy in Volgagrad, a place that can hardly be accused of being a bastion of effete intelligentsia. His platform called for restoring the "traditional" name of the city—Stalingrad. He was decisively defeated.[82]

Results from the local and republic elections in 1990 indicate a similar pattern. Not only was there a massive protest vote against the Communists (it was necessary merely to state that someone was a party official to ensure that candidate would be defeated in almost any urban environment), but reactionaries performed poorly even in rural areas. The Communist Party did better in rural areas, and these two outcomes are related. Some Party conservatives are now making common cause with right wing and ultranationalist elements.[83] But each brings as many negative as positive trappings to the collaboration.

The popularity of right-wing periodicals has been cited as evidence of the appeal of reactionary and nationalist ideas.[84] But if one publicized case in Leningrad is any indication, even the number of newspaper and journal subscriptions may vastly overstate the popular appeal of the right-wing press. One retired junior-grade military officer in Leningrad was subscribing to 2,368 copies of the conservative weekly *Literaturnaia*

Rossiia. Another ten individuals subscribed to a total of nearly 2,000 copies, which means that these eleven people received more copies of this publication than the entire rest of the population of Leningrad and Leningrad Oblast. When asked how he could afford 1,500 rubles per month worth of subscriptions on his modest pension, the officer replied that "writers, artists and patriots" assisted him.[85] Presumably thc ploy, which doubled the periodical's subscriptions in the region, was designed to make the conservative press appear more popular and to help protect its share of rationed newsprint. (We might recall that, in the 19th Century, the tsars subsidized conservative and nationalist publishers like Mikhail Katkov and Prince Meshcherskii, whose readership and subscriptions were not sufficient to make their publications cconomically viable.)

Links among the Party, ultra-nationalists, and even anti-Semites have been reported in other places as well. In Kiev, a Radio Liberty correspondent attending a patriotic-religious gathering became part of a small crowd listening to a self-proclaimed worker from Moscow who held forth on Jewish responsibility for the nation's problems. When the crowd turned hostile, denouncing the speaker as a provocateur, the "worker" ran into a side street and was whisked away by a waiting limousine.[86]

This is not to say that the situation is impervious to change. But it ought to be kept in perspective. In evaluating commentary on the relative strength of political groups, Sovietologists might derive a lesson from the reign of Alexander II. In the 1860s and especially the 1870s, both the reformers and the conservatives thought that their own group was riven by dissent, faction and dispute, and that the opposition was a powerful united force.[87] People tend to stress their differences with those who are on their side, whereas they tend to perceive the opposition as a strong, cohesive group. But this perception frequently obscures divisions on all sides.[88]

The reign of Alexander II is probably the best place to look for analogies to the current state of affairs. The appropriate comparisons are *not* Ivan the Terrible or Peter the Great, and certainly not Stalin.[89]

One important lesson from the experience of reform under Alexander II is the need for a reformist leader to occupy the political middle ground. In almost any political system, leadership involves the effort to build a coalition. Much of the supposed vacillation attributed to Alexander II in the nineteenth century can be explained logically if we picture him as having tried to hold together a coalition that included both reformers and more conservative groups.[90] It is also noteworthy that some of the most important Great Reforms, including reform of the military and of local government, were promulgated *after* the supposed period of reaction had set in.[91]

The reign of Alexander II also helps us to remember that even though the country has become more open, the military has not become less important. After all, a significant portion Gorbachev's actions have been based on the premise that to be a great power in the twenty-first century, the Soviet Union has got to change.[92]

Beyond basic political lessons, we have learned some important lessons about the Soviet military system. Full discussion of these issues should be left to military specialists, but two may be noted briefly. First, the vaunted system of civil defense in the USSR turns out to have been largely an exercise in *pokazuka* (facade). Following the tragic earthquake in Armenia in December 1988, the system proved itself unable to organize even the most basic emergency services. Medical teams from outside the USSR were able to reach Armenia faster than Soviet groups, and the rail system functioned dismally. In 1990 the Soviet press extended glasnost to coverage of these grave shortcomings in civil defense and emergency services.[93]

A related lesson is that there is no peace dividend in either the U.S. or the USSR. As one Soviet official pointed out early in the process, in order to save $1.7 billion in the defense industry, the Soviet Union would have to spend $3.5 billion retooling, and converting the factories that are involved. Criticisms of the program of conversion have now proliferated.[94] In the United States, too, the costs, dislocations and problems involved in trying to scale back defense expenditures are likely to make it very difficult to reap any major benefits.[95] And in both societies, a budget deficit will eat up an enormous portion of any savings. In the Soviet case, however, there may be significant potential for a return if some of the massive military research and development effort can be reoriented. Positive results in this area would not be immediate, but over a five- to ten-year period the economy could benefit substantially.[96]

Conclusion

Predicting the political future of any nation is a task both precarious and thankless. It is also the province of op-ed pages, not of scholarship. Rather than suggesting that we know what will happen, Sovietologists should seek to identify the important currents in the society and frame the parameters of future developments so that we reduce the chances of being taken by surprise. We also have a responsibility to weigh carefully our assessments of possible developments so that, to the extent that our judgments have any influence on future events, that influence does not encourage irresponsible actions.

The most often asked questions during the first five years of perestroika were "Can Gorbachev succeed?" and "Is the process reversible?" I do not like either question, but their persistence requires taking them into account. Any answer to the first question depends upon the definition of success. Is the Soviet Union going to become an economic superpower like Japan within twenty or thirty years? Certainly not. Is it likely that there will still be something like the current Soviet Union in 2010? Possibly. Not definitely, but possibly, if they are intelligent in dealing with their problems. They will certainly not achieve success in the way that Gorbachev initially envisioned, by limited reforms under Communist tutelage.[97]

The second big question, concerning reversibility, is posed ahistorically most of the time. Many scholars note that every period of reform in Russian/Soviet history has been followed by a period of reaction.[98] They believe a similar fate must therefore inevitably await perestroika. In Chapter 1, Blair Ruble suggests the possibility that this cyclical pattern might finally be broken.[99] The emphasis here is on "might." To state a definitive answer would be the height of hubris. Of course perestroika could be halted, and indeed has constantly experienced rough fits and starts as well as significant regional variations. Any retreat from perestroika is likely to be equally ambiguous.

The important question is not whether perestroika is reversible, but rather how *likely* such a reversal is and what it would cost. It is now possible, for the first time in Russian/Soviet history, that the equation has changed. There are no guarantees; but there are some reasons for optimism.

The Soviet Union is not the same country that it was at the end of World War II. This is not to say that the process of change has been smooth, neat, or simple. The contradictions—dictated democracy, the "planned market," suspending freedom of the press to ensure "objectivity," and so on—would have delighted Lewis Carroll. But even Stalin was not always wrong: Contradictions are important, providing evidence of the tensions that always accompany change.

One of the greatest contradictions is that Gorbachev himself is both a leading force of and a major obstacle to evolution of the political system. By 1990 it became clear that the success of reform may be impossible if it remains inseparable from Gorbachev's personal success. The most positive outcome might be if Gorbachev turns out to be a crucial transitional figure. That is not what he intended initially, or even necessarily what he intends now, but it is no longer beyond the realm of possibility. Alternative political leaders are emerging—Anatolii Sobchak, Sergei Stankevich, Iurii Afanas'ev, Fedor Burlatskii, Gavriil Popov, Marju Lauristan, Mohammed Salekh, and Olzhas Suleimenov, and of course Boris Eltsin. It is obviously in Gorbachev's best interest to suggest that there is no alternative to his leadership, but it is no longer accurate.

Not only has Gorbachev been dragged unwillingly along the path of democratization, but there is a real question as to whether, for all his political skills, he understands it. His behavior often reflects his preference for older, "simpler" styles of political life. And in side comments he has frequently revealed his deep-seated sense that he alone should be defining what constitutes "democratic" processes. Words like "democracy" and "objective" have a different meaning in the Soviet political context.

The timing of political events may turn out to have a tragic dimension. Six years have passed with little accomplished in economic reform. Now reform is the responsibility of elected institutions, which are likely to afford those whose interests are being infringed new ways to protect their "turf." Political scientists know from long experience that democratic bodies are relatively good at expending resources but do less well when forced to make difficult choices about reducing funding. Calls for an "iron hand" have been made not only by right-wing extremists pining for the old days and by frightened individuals seeking a restoration of public order; they are also voiced by reformers who would prefer to achieve their projects through the edicts of an autocratic leader rather than see them watered down or defeated in a messy, painful, and time-consuming legislative process.[100]

The question of reversibility is thus raised again. Certainly perestroika and glasnost are reversible. Weimar Germany's descent into dictatorship is a good example of what can happen. But we should recall what was taking place in the global and German economies during that period to cause the collapse of democracy. A similar collapse is possible in the Soviet Union, but it is not necessarily the most likely alternative, and it is certainly not inevitable. The first five years of perestroika have taught us that there may be a number of potential outcomes, and not all are dire.

Notes

I am grateful to Marjorie Mandelstam Balzer, Blair Ruble and Valerie Sperling for comments on earlier versions of this chapter.

1. Mikhail Gorbachev, *Perestroika: New Thinking for Our Country and the World* (New York: Harper and Row, 1988), pp. 7-8; Gurii Marchuk, "Kakoi byt' nauke?", *Poisk*, No. 12 (July 1989), pp. 1-3; and references to comments by Aleksandr Yakovlev in Dusko Doder and Louise Branson, *Gorbachev: Heretic in the Kremlin* (New York: Viking, 1990), p. 69.

2. This is not to deny that other Soviet leaders learned lessons or adjusted their policies. But there is a qualitative difference in the way Gorbachev has integrated feedback into his reform program.

3. There is a debate regarding just how much Gorbachev understood the need for changes and the extent to which he moderated his policies while building support for more radical alternatives. See the Epilogue in this volume.

4. On Andropov's reform program see Ed A. Hewett, *Reforming the Soviet Economy: Equality versus Efficiency* (Washington: The Brookings Institution, 1988), Chapter 6, and Zhores A. Medvedev, *Andropov* (New York: W. W. Norton, 1983). For an excellent account of political developments see Stephen White, *Gorbachev in Power* (New York: Cambridge University Press, 1990), Chapter 1.

5. Both Gosagroprom and the MNTKs represented efforts to establish a new administrative body outside existing channels. While Gosagroprom was to be a superministry combining numerous existing enterprises, the MNTKs were are intended to separate out quality facilities from various administrative bodies. Gosagroprom proved too unwieldy; the MNTKs, in most cases, have lacked the power to elicit compliance with their activities. Harley D. Balzer, *Soviet Science on the Edge of Reform* (Boulder: Westview Press, 1989), pp. 175-178.

6. The classic statement of the "circular flow of power" is Robert V. Daniels, "Soviet Politics Since Khrushchev," in *The Soviet Union Under Brezhnev and Kosygin*, edited by John W. Strong (New York: Van Nostrand-Reinhold, 1971), pp. 20-23; on economic reforms see Gertrude E. Schroeder, "Soviet Economy on a Treadmill of 'Reforms'," in U.S. Congress. Joint Economic Committee, *Soviet Economy in a Time of Change* (Washington, DC: U.S. Government Printing Office, 1979), pp. 312-340.

7. Thane Gustafson and Dawn Mann, "Gorbachev's First Year: Building Power and Authority," *Problems of Communism*, Vol. XXXV, No. 3 (May-June 1986), and Jerry F. Hough, "Gorbachev Consolidating Power," *Problems of Communism*, Vol. XXXVI, No. 4 (July-August 1987), pp. 21-43.

8. Thane Gustafson and Dawn Mann, "Gorbachev's Next Gamble," *Problems of Communism*, Vol. XXXVI, No. 4 (July-August 1987), pp. 1-20; *Pravda*, April 26, 1985; *Pravda*, May 17, 1985.

9. Gorbachev speeches at CC Plenum on January 27 and 28, 1987. Economic reforms were adopted at the CC Plenum in June, to take effect January 1, 1988.

10. This is clearly seen in the military response to the Ministry of Foreign Affairs, *Sovetskaia Rossiia*, January 9, 1991, p. 5.

11. See the Summary of Leadership Changes at the back of this volume.

12. Joseph Rolthschild, *Return to Diversity: A Political History of East Central Europe Since World War II* (New York: Oxford University Press, 1989); Karen Dawisha, *Eastern Europe, Gorbachev, and Reform* (New York: Cambridge University Press, 2nd edition, 1990); and Charles Gati, *The Bloc That Failed: Soviet-East European Relations in Transition* (Bloomington: Indiana University Press, 1990).

13. Glasnost has been variously translated as "openness," "frankness," and "publicity." I prefer "frankness," but whatever the translation, the key element of the concept is a component of shared culture—the leadership assumes the population will use the opportunities to behave in a responsible manner, and will not violate cultural norms. Gorbachev's discussion in *Perestroika*—a book for Western consumption—is instructive: "Let the *Party* know everything." ". . . [T]hese bills are designed to ensure the *greatest possible* openness." "Criticism is, first and foremost, *responsibility*, and the sharper the criticism, the more responsible it should be." "To uphold the *fundamental values of socialism* is a tradition of our press" (pp. 61-66, my emphasis). Nikolai Chernyshevskii's comment that glasnost was a word devised *in place of* freedom of speech appears relevant here.

14. Ellen Mickiewicz, *Split Signals: Television and Politics in the Soviet Union* (New York: Oxford University Press, 1988) pp. 60-68.

15. For a good summary of the contradictions see A. Illesh and V. Rudnev, *Izvestiia*, October 9, 1990, p. 8.

16. Merle Fainsod, *Smolensk Under Soviet Rule* (Boston: Unwyn Hyman, reprint edition, 1989), particularly Chapters 7 and 10, and J. Arch Getty, *Origins of the Great Purges: The Soviet Communist Party Reconsidered*, 1933-1938 (New York: Cambridge University Press, 1985). The classic case is Nikita Khrushchev.

17. For example, the Radio Liberty *Daily Report*, No. 1, January 2, 1990, reporting on an article in *Sovetskaia molodezh'* from December 16, 1989.

18. On the Andreeva affair, see Doder and Bransom, pp. 304-313, and Seweryn Bialer, "The Changing Soviet Political System: The Nineteenth Party Congress and After," in *Politics, Society and Nationality Inside Gorbachev's Russia*, edited by Seweryn Bialer (Boulder: Westview Press, 1989), pp. 203-208. The comments about competition for influence *over* Gorbachev as opposed to efforts to replace him were made by Anatolii Salutskii during a conversation in Moscow in September 1989.

19. See Anatolii Salutskii's articles in *Nash sovremennik*, for example, "Umo-zreniia i real'nosti," No. 6 (1988), pp. 136-162; and "Artel'nye liudi," No. 12 (1988), pp. 137-165.

20. This comparison is not meant to suggest that the two phenomena are at all comparable in terms of magnitude, importance, or the stakes involved, only that the public/political reactions are similar.

21. See Fainsod, and Getty.

22. Alexander Rahr, "The CPSU After the Twenty-Eighth Party Congress," Radio Liberty *Report on the USSR*, Vol. 2, No. 45 (November 9, 1990), pp. 1-4.

23. The plenipotentiary proposal is vague. The classic account of this role is Jerry F. Hough, *The Soviet Prefects: Local Party Organs in Industrial Decision-Making* (Cambridge: Harvard University Press, 1969), pp. 3-6 and *passim*.

24. For critiques of Gorbachev's economic program see, in addition to the chapter in this volume by Schroeder and the sources in the Suggested Bibliography, Marshall Goldman, "Gorbachev the Economist," *Foreign Affairs*, Vol. 69, No. 2 (spring 1990), pp. 28-44.

25. The negotiations between the UAW and GM over a new contract in 1990 focused heavily on job security rather than wage issues. In an interesting cross-cultural research project, a Yale economist has found that American public attitudes on issues of economics and fairness are not very different from Soviet popular attitudes. "Soviets Understand Markets ... as Well as Americans Do," *The Wall Street Journal*, November 1, 1990, p. A22. Recent survey research suggests that in the USSR only eight percent of the people surveyed would like to have their own businesses. Rather than bemoaning this low number, it might be well to take note of recent surveys in California giving a figure of five percent for the number of Californians who would like to have their own business. For a review of recent Soviet public opinion surveys, see Stephen K. Wegren, "Market Reform and Public Opinion," Radio Liberty *Report on the USSR*, November 30, 1990, pp. 4-8.

26. Benedict Anderson, *Imagined Communities: Reflections on the Origin and Spread of Nationalism* (London and New York: Verso, 1983).

27. In addition to the Selected Bibliography at the end of this volume, see Ron Suny, "Nationalities and Nationalism," in *Chronicle of A Revolution*, edited by Abraham Brumberg (New York: Pantheon, 1990), pp. 108-128.

28. Lengthy segments of Gorbachev's public confrontations in Lithuania were shown on Soviet TV on January 11, 12 and 13, 1990.

29. The point about managing or coping rather than solving is made by Paul Goble and Gail Lapidus, "Gorbachev's Nationalities Problem," *Foreign Affairs*, Vol. 68, No. 4 (fall 1989), pp. 92-108.

30. Survey data in the Radio Liberty *Daily Report* of January 22 and February 11, 1991 (received via Sovset').

31. Based on observing both Gorbachev and Eltsin on Soviet television.

32. For a discussion of power and authority in the Soviet political context, see George W. Breslauer, *Khrushchev and Brezhnev as Leaders: Building Authority in Soviet Politics* (London: Allen and Unwin, 1982), particularly Chapter 1; and Gustafson and Mann, "Gorbachev's First Year."

33. Iurii Baturin, one of the individuals responsible for drafting the new Law on the Press and other key legislation, referred to the legislative jurisdiction issues as "a gray area."

34. Michael Urban, *More Power to the Soviets* (Aldershot: Edward Elgar, 1990).

35. Galina Starovoitova, lecture at Georgetown University, November 29, 1989.

36. Much of the literature on Soviet politics has stressed ideological legitimacy.

37. Archie Brown, "Gorbachev: New Man in the Kremlin," *Problems of Communism*, Vol. XXXIV, No. 3 (May-June 1985), pp. 1-23; Jerry F. Hough, "Waiting for Gorbachev," *Problems of Communism*. See Brown's account of how their suggestion was received at an international conference prior to Chernenko's death in "Gorbachev's Leadership: Another View," *Soviet Economy*, Vol. 6, No. 2 (1990), pp. 141-154, particularly Note 6, p. 143.

38. See Robert Huber's contribution to this volume, Chapter 9.

39. The classic statement of the totalitarianism model is Carl J. Friedrich and Zbigniew Brzezinski, *Totalitarian Dictatorship and Autocracy* (Cambridge: Harvard University Press, 1956), particularly Chapter 2. For a critique of the totalitarianism model see Stephen F. Cohen, *Rethinking the Soviet Experience: Politics & History Since 1917* (New York: Oxford University Press, 1985). Cohen stressed the Bukharinist tradition, which then appered to be the outer limit of what was possible.

40. Z [Martin Malia], "To the Stalin Mausoleum," *Dædalus*, Vol. 119, No. 1 (winter 1990), pp. 295-344; William E. Odom, "How Far Can Soviet Reform Go?", *Problems of Communism*, Vol. XXXVI, No. 6 (November-December 1987), pp. 18-34.

41. The other prevailing models of the Soviet political system, corporatism and neo-traditionalism, are equally weak in explaining socially-based change. Ken Jowett's discussion is a taxonomic *tour de force*, but he sees the potential for change in terms of protracted feudal-style conflict within the Party. He does not take account of the social-political interactions in what is esentially a middle class society. Ken Jowett, "Soviet Neotraditionalism: The Political Corruption of a Leninist Regime," *Soviet Studies*, Vol. XXXV, No. 3 (July 1983), pp. 275-297. Also see Andrew G. Walder, *Communist Neo-traditionalism: Work and Authority in Chinese Industry* (Berkeley: University of California Press, 1986). For a discussion of corporatism see Charles E. Ziegler, *Environmental Policy in the USSR* (Amherst: University of Massachusetts Press, 1987), Chapter 3.

42. For example, Howard J. Wiarda, "Toward a Framework for the Study of Political Change in the Iberic-Latin Tradition: The Corporative Model," *World Politics*, Vol. XXV, No. 2 (January 1973), pp. 206-235.

43. Not every pessimistic assessment of Soviet reform can be faulted for *a priori* judgements. Thane Gustafson expresses skepticism based on careful sifting of the evidence, rather than positing insuperable barriers. Thane Gustafson, "The Crisis of the Soviet System of Power and Mikhail Gorbachev's Political Strategy," in *Gorbachev's Russia and American Foreign Policy*, edited by Seweryn Bialer and Michael Mandelbaum (Boulder: Westview Press, 1988), pp. 187-230.

44. On Russian/Soviet political culture see Edward L. Keenan, "Moscovite Political Folkways," *The Russian Review*, Vol. 45 (1986), pp. 115-181; Robert C. Tucker, *The Soviet Political Mind: Studies in Stalinism and Post-Stalin Change* (New York: Praeger, 1963); Robert C. Tucker, *Political Culture and Leadership in Soviet Russia: From Lenin to Gorbachev* (New York: W. W. Norton, 1987); and Archie Brown, "Ideology and Political Culture," in Bialer, pp. 1-40.

45. For background, see Michael Cherniavsky, *Tsar and People: Studies in Russian Myths* (New York: Random House, 1969).

46. Z, and Mikhail Heller and Aleksandr M. Nekrich, *Utopia In Power: The History of the Soviet Union from 1917 to the Present*, translated by Phyllis B. Carlos (New York: Summit Books, 1986).

47. Stalin's comment to Churchill was made in 1942. See Winston S. Churchill, *The Hinge of Fate* (Boston: Houghton Mifflin, 1950), p. 498.

48. The argument for technology helping to influence the social and political system is made by S. Frederick Starr, "New Communication Technologies and Civil Society," in *Science and the Soviet Social Order*, edited by Loren R. Graham (Cambridge: Harvard University Press, 1990), pp. 19-50. Also see Seymour Goodman's chapter in the same volume, "Information Technologies and the Citizen: Toward A 'Soviet-Style Information Society'," pp. 51-67, and Leonard R. Sussman, *Power, the Press and the Technology of Freedom: The Coming Age of ISDN* (New York: Freedom House, 1989). For recent data on the topic see Michael Dobbs, "Workers of the World, Fax!", *Washington Post*, December 23, 1990, p. C3.

49. Moshe Lewin, *The Making of the Soviet System: Essays in the Social History of Interwar Russia* (New York: Pantheon Books, 1985); Sheila Fitzpatrick, *Education and Social Mobility in the Soviet Union, 1921-1934* (Cambridge: Cambridge University Press, 1979).

50. The most consistent invocation of the Ivan the Terrible comparison has been by Tucker, *The Soviet Political Mind*, Chapters 8 and 9, and Tucker "Czars and Commiczars," *The New Republic* (January 21, 1991), pp. 29-35. It is enormously popular among Soviet intellectuals, who also have a strong affinity for analogies to the "Time of Troubles" that followed Ivan's demise.

51. Z [Martin Malia] offers strong criticism of the argument based on the social base. See "To the Stalin Mausoleum," pp. 298-299. He is correct that Hough and Fitzpatrick greivously understated the number of purge victims—a mistake Lewin did not make—but he imputes to the "social science approach" a determinism that is not accurate. In fact, it is the reification of the "monolithic Party" that is deterministic: Cohen, Lewin, Starr, Ruble and even Hough speak about *potential* alternatives based on social structure, rather than inevitable outcomes.

52. I first heard this formulation from Marjorie Mandelstam Balzer. It appears in "Nationalism in the Soviet Union: One Anthropological View," *Journal of Soviet Nationalities*, Vol. 1, No. 3 (1990), pp. 1-17.

53. See, for example, Yuri Afanasyev, "The Coming Dictatorship?", *New York Review of Books*, Vol. XXXVIII, No. 3 (January 31, 1991), p. 38. Afanas'ev's characterization that "Many of our people seem reduced to a condition resembling that of cattle and, what is more frightening, they do not ask to live any other way" is disturbing. For a "democrat" to see his constituents as "cattle" and to be afraid of them is not a hopeful sign.

54. Anton Chekhov, "Three Sisters," in *Nine Plays of Chekhov*, (New York: Grosset and Dunlap, 1946), p. 107.

55. Moshe Lewin, *The Gorbachev Phenomenon* (Berkeley: University of California Press, 1988); S. Frederick Starr, "Soviet Union: A Civil Society," *Foreign Policy*, No. 70 (spring 1988), pp. 26-41; Blair Ruble, "The Social Dimensions of Perestroika," *Soviet Economy*, Vol. 3 (April-June 1987), pp. 171-183; Moshe Lewin, "Perestroika: A New Historical Stage," *Journal of International Affairs* (1989), pp. 299-315; and John Keane, ed., *Civil Society and the State* (London: Verso, 1988).

56. V. Kubas', "Rabochie komitety Kuzbassa," *Sotsiologicheskie issledovaniia*, No. 6 (1990), pp. 49-54.

57. Running unopposed, Solov'ev received 44.8 percent of the vote in his district. *Leningradskaia pravda*, March 29, 1989, p. 1.

58. For a good description of the hothouse atmosphere of Soviet urban intellectual life and the crucial and unique role of friendship, see Vladimir Shlapentokh, *Public And Private Life of the Soviet People: Changing Values in Post-Stalin Russia* (New York: Oxford University Press, 1989), pp. 170-177.

59. This discussion owes much to a lecture by Bogdan Denitch at the Washington AAASS Spring Symposium, May 10, 1990.

60. David K. Shipler, *Russia: Broken Idols, Solemn Dreams* (New York: Viking, 1984), pp. 370-372.

61. I first heard the characterization of "Tsar Misha the Good" from Paul Goble in a lecture at Georgetown Univesity.

62. In the wake of the December 1990 violence in Vilnius, Gorbachev suggested suspending the law on freedom of the press to ensure "greater objectivity" in media coverage.

63. Gorbachev speech at CPD, December 23, 1989, reported in FBIS-SOV-89-247, December 27, 1989, p. 81.

64. For discussion of the policy debates see the sources cited in the "Harbingers of Change" section of the Selected Bibliography at the end of this volume.

65. This is particularly true at the level of working groups on legislation.

66. Walter Laqueur, *The Long Road to Freedom: Russia and Glasnost* (New York: Collier Books, 1989), Chapter 11.

67. As Archie Brown puts it, there is "virtually no end to his pragmatism." "Gorbachev's Leadership: Another View," p. 148.

68. Jerry Hough has pointed out that Party membership in the USSR comes close to meeting many definitions of the society's "attentive public." Jerry F. Hough and Merle Fainsod, *How the Soviet Union is Governed* (Cambridge: Harvard University Press, 1979), p. 344.

69. I have spoken with dozens of individuals who joined the Party between 1985 and 1987 in response to Gorbachev's initiatives to broaden the Party's appeal to the intelligentsia. Some are now becoming important political figures, for example Sergei Stankevich. The high point of this movement was expressed in the edited collections *Inogo ne dano* (Moscow: Progress, 1988), and *Postizhenie* (Moscow: Progress, 1989). Since 1988, and particularly since resignations from the Party by a number of leading progressives following the Twenty-Eighth CPSU Congress in 1990, Party membership has been declining.

70. See the introspective piece by O. Bogomolov, "Ne mogu sniat' s sebia viny," *Ogonek*, No. 35 (August 1990), pp. 2-3.

71. Boris Nikolaevskii discussed this phenomenon in *Power and the Soviet Elite* (New York: Praeger, 1965). It is directly addressed by Kendall Bailes in *Technology and Society Under Lenin and Stalin* (Princeton: Princeton University Press, 1978), p. 140.

72. See Josephine Woll's discussion in Chapter 6 of this volume, pp. 114-115.

73. Some of the confusion results from Western observers not being used to seeing Soviet political disputes aired openly in the press.

74. There may be parallels in the battle over editorial policy at *Izvestiia*. See the Radio Liberty *Daily Report* for January 31 and February 1, 1991.

75. Linda Feldman, "Soviet Voters Apathetic on Eve of Key Local Vote," *Christian Science Monitor*, March 2, 1990, p. 1; Esther Fein, "Apathy Called Greatest Foe in Ukranian Election," *The New York Times*, March 1, 1990, p. A14; and Mark Nicholson, "Little agit and not much prop on the Moscow Campaign Train," *The Financial Times*, February 27, 1990, p. 3.

76. Galina Starovoitova, lecture at Georgetown University, November 29, 1989.

77. On Kalugin see David Remnick, "Critic of KGB Wins Election in Russia," *Washington Post*, September 4, 1990, p. A12, and Boris Eltsin, *Against the Grain* (New York: Summit Books, 1990), pp. 104, 131.

Since this chapter was completed, an older style of political dirty tricks has been used in the Baltic republics. See the excellent coverage in Radio Liberty *Report on the USSR*, and in the *Ekspress khronika*, as well as publications of groups monitoring events in specific republics.

78. The terms "left" and "right" have become so confused as to lose almost all meaning in the current Soviet political situation. The traditional left, meaning socialists, Social Democrats and Marxists, long ago ceased to be synonymous with the Soviet Communist party. Liberal democrats, usually described as centrist or just left of center, are the "progressives" in the current Soviet context. The terminological problems stem from the CP resisting change and liberalization. This makes the Communists the *de facto* "right," the conservatives, in the present configuration. It is probably preferable to speak of conservatives and progressives than left and right, but the directional terms are still widely used.

79. Good coverage was provided in the *Ekspress khronika*.

80. For a good analysis of Pamiat' see Nicolai N. Petro, "Perestroika from Below: Voluntary Sociopolitical Associations in the RSFSR," in *Perestroika at the Crossroads*, edited by Alfred J. Rieber and Alvin Z. Rubinstein (Armonk, NY: M. E. Sharpe, 1991), pp. 102-133.

81. See the coverage by Julia Wishnevsky in the Radio Liberty *Report on the USSR*.

82. Bondarev gave several speeches invoking the metaphor of Stalingrad, suggesting that the nation needs a similar victory to turn the tide against reform.

83. Radio Liberty *Daily Report*, November 27, 1991.

84. Yitzhak M. Brudny, "The Heralds of Opposition to *Perestroika*," *Soviet Economy*, Vol. 5, No. 2 (1989), pp. 162-200. Brudny's account is particularly strong in its coverage of the potential for a right-wing political alliance.

85. "Rekord patriota: 150 kilogrammov odnoi gazety na odnogo podpischika," *Izvestiia*, April 11, 1990, evening edition, p. 6.

86. Kathy Mihalisko, Radio Liberty *Daily Report*, No. 176, September 14, 1990.

87. P. A. Zaionchkovskii, *Rossiiskoe samoderzhavie v kontse XIX stoletiia* (Moscow: Mysl', 1970), Chapter 1, and Harley D. Balzer, "Educating Engineers: Economic Politics and Technical Training in Tsarist Russia," (Ph.D. dissertation, University of Pennsylvania, 1980), Chapter 2.

88. Z [Martin Malia] sees the sovietological profession dominated by a "liberal-to-radical mainstream" ("To the Stalin Mausoleum," p. 296). Stephen Cohen states that the totalitarianism model dominated the discipline for twenty years (*Rethinking the Soviet Experience*, p. 4). The tendency to fight most intensely with those one is closest to is hardly a trait unique to Russians or sovietologists: see William Safire, "Mutt and Jeff and Me," *The New York Times*, September 3, 1990, p. 21.

89. Bruce Lincoln, *The Great Reforms: Autocracy, Bureaucracy, and the Politics of Change in Imperial Russia* (DeKalb: Northern Illinois University Press, 1990); Ben Eklof and John Bushnell, eds., *Russia's Great Reforms* (Bloomington: Indiana University Press, forthcoming, 1991).

90. Alfred J. Rieber, "Alexander II: A Revisionist View," *Journal of Modern History*, Vol. 43, No. 1 (March 1971), pp. 42-58.

91. P. A. Zaionchkovskii, *Voennye reformy 1860-1870 godov v Rossii* (Moscow: 1952).

92. Gorbachev, pp. 4-9.

93. For example, the interview with Civil Defense Chief of Staff General V. Kozhabakhteev, *Krasnaia zvezda*, January 21, 1990, p. 2.

94. For example, V. Urban, "Nuzhen li zakon o konversii?", *Krasnaia zvezda*, October 27, 1990, p. 1; V. Romaniuk, "Konversiia u nikh i u nas: Zametki s mezhdunarodnoi konferentsii OON v Moskve," *Izvestiia*, August 18, 1990, p. 2; and Aleksei Iziumov, "Konversiia? Konversiia! Konversiia . . .," *Literaturnaia Gazeta*, July 12, 1989, p. 11.

95. Arthur J. Alexander, "Defense Industry Conversion in China, the Soviet Union, and the United States," unpublished manuscript, May, 1990.

96. Balzer, *Soviet Science*, p. 201, and John Tedstrom, "Conversion and the Problem of Industrial Science," Radio Liberty *Report on the USSR*, August 25, 1989, pp. 19-20.

97. See the discussion in Breslauer, *Can Gorbachev's Reforms Succeed?*, particularly pp. 4-5.

98. Tucker, "Czars and Commiczars"; Alexander Yanov, "In the Grip of the Adversarial Paradigm: The Case of Nikita Sergeevich Khrushchev in Retrospect," in *Reform in Russia and the USSR: Past and Prospects*, edited by Robert O. Crummey (Urbana: University of Illinois Press, 1989), p. 157.

99. Also see Alfred J. Rieber, "The Reforming Tradition in Russian History," in Reiber, pp. 3-28.

5

Imperial Endgame: Nationality Problems and the Soviet Future

Paul Goble

History has rendered its verdict on empires. On ancient ones, a long time ago; on colonial ones, quite recently; and on others, just now.
                                                    —Aleksander Yakovlev (April 23, 1990)

The Soviet Union has never been an empire like any other; its approaching end seems certain to be different as well. But the recent rush of events has obscured this uniqueness, leading many to jump from a belated recognition that the USSR is after all an empire to the conclusion that it must necessarily "decolonize" according to some standard model. That leap has had three unfortunate consequences. First, it has contributed to a Soviet domino theory according to which the departure of any one region will eventually entail the departure of all. Second, it has promoted an all-or-nothing view about the meaning of independence for any region. And, third, it has led to a reification of Soviet-imposed borders, to the belief that all successor states will have the same shapes as the republics do now.

Together, these assumptions severely limit the ability of participants and observers alike to think about the Soviet future. To escape their influence, we need to consider three groups of questions: First, how does the Soviet Union compare to other empires? Second, how and why has it been shaken to its foundations in the last five years? And, third, what kinds of imperial devolution are in fact possible for the Soviet Union? Only in this way can we finally ask what role there is for outsiders who want to maximize human freedom while avoiding serious international destabilization. These are the questions I want to begin to answer here.

An Empire Unlike Any Other

Until very recently, Soviet officials have stoutly resisted any effort to label the USSR an empire. They have done so for two reasons. First, the word *empire* has become a term of political abuse rather than a category of analysis, a virtual denunciation of the state to which it is applied and a demand that it be deconstructed. And, second, many writers who do apply the term to the USSR apply it in an overly simple way, implicitly assuming that the Soviet empire is like the British and French empires and that it should suffer the same fate.

Although the Soviet disclaimer of imperial identity is understandable, it is not entirely defensible because the concept of empire sheds important light on key aspects of Soviet reality. But to gain insights into that reality, we must have a more general understanding of empires, of the enormous range of regimes that fall into that category, and of the ways in which the Soviet empire is both similar to others and unique in itself.

Historically, there have been many kinds of empires—that is, regimes in which one political center rules over a variety of peoples and states. Obviously a complete survey of all such regimes is beyond the scope of any single chapter, but a sense of their diversity can be captured by considering some of the continuua along which they can be grouped. Some—such as Austro-Hungary, have been contiguous; others, such as Denmark's rule over Greenland, have been non-contiguous. Some have been based on ethnic claims of superiority—as in England; or on the recovery of a single people's lands—as in Germany. But still others have had no ethnic basis at all, such as the Holy Roman Empire. Some have been openly exploitative, such as Spanish rule in South America; others have been ideocratic, such as Chinese control in Tibet. Some have been highly coercive, such as the Soviet Union under Stalin; others have been permissive, such as British indirect rule. Some have been ethno-transforming and assimilationist, such as English absorption of various groups within England; others have been ethno-intensifying, ethno-exacerbating or have even created national feelings where none existed before. Some have ended peacefully, others in violence; and still others have ceased to be empires as a result of social and ethnic change.

The list could be extended almost at will; and because each empire is invariably a combination of various characteristics, each is largely unique. The Soviet Union is no exception. But the application of the term *empire* to the Soviet Union in nonetheless instructive because it highlights certain kinds of power relationships there and explains parts of the political landscape in a way that no other term could. In this chapter, then, I shall consider briefly the characteristics of the pre-1917 Russian empire, the unexpected impact of the revolution and civil war, and finally the Stalinist synthesis that defined virtually all of Soviet political life prior to Gorbachev and set the stage for the turmoil that his policies have unexpectedly unleashed.

The pre-1917 Russian empire is a good place to begin because both Soviet authors and Western students of that country accept the idea that this political regime was an empire. Its chief characteristics—which continue to affect Soviet reality—are easily summarized. First, the empire was built before the nation at its center was fully consolidated, thus leaving open the question of the boundaries of identity for the metropolitan country and its periphery. Second, economic marginality and foreign threat led to an absorption of society by the state—that is, to the politicization of all relationships. Third, expansion was justified in terms of a radical messianism that sanctioned unexpected cruelty but opened the way for integration of those who accepted its terms. Fourth, the empire was organized not along ethnic or political lines but, rather, for purposes of administrative convenience. And fifth, the central authorities pursued a highly differentiated approach to different ethnic communities under the imperial domain depending on political calculation and ethnic distance from the dominant community. Thus, some nationalities were seriously repressed, while others enjoyed special protection and still others were excluded from the direct attention of the center.

Such an autocratic arrangement worked under conditions of underdevelopment and premodern social relationships. But the rise of capitalism and the expansion of communication and education undermined the traditional relationships and, by the end of the nineteenth century had made the old order untenable. Several large Western nationalities such as the Poles, the Finns, and the Ukrainians were actively seeking independence; others were demanding one or another form of autonomy or, at the very least, recognition from a regime that steadfastly refused to identify people on the basis of nationality alone—religion and language, yes; but not nationality in most cases.

World War I and then the February 1917 revolution accelerated these changes, leading to demands both for recognition of the nationality principle by all groups, including the Russians, and for independence by an increasing number of ethnic communities. In the ensuing chaos, many successfully achieved independence for a brief period, all were able to achieve recognition of the nationality principle for state arrangements, and some were able to win genuine independence. Had this process proceeded without interruption, the Russian empire would have developed as the

Austro-Hungarian one did; and most would have achieved some form of democratic or guided democratic regimes. But as everyone knows, that did not happen.

In ethnic terms, the October 1917 revolution was a profoundly reactionary movement. In the name of socialist internationalism, and with the aid of a powerful army fed simultaneously by ideology and xenophobic anger at foreign intervention, Moscow reconquered the empire, and reordered it at the same time. This reordering took the form of and was reflected in three developments: the creation of a new form of official nationality that required individuals to identify themselves in ethnic terms—something that many people had never done before and that had the effect of intensifying this form of identity; the establishment of pseudo-statehood for the largest nationalities, which were thus given the institutionality of independence without its realization; and the increase of the Russian nationality from 43 percent of the population immediately before 1917 to more than 60 percent in 1921 as a result of the departure of Poland, Finland, the Baltic states, and two provinces in Turkey.

Pseudo-statehood and Russian numeric preponderance were central to the elaboration of the repressive Stalinist system, which lasted with only relatively minor modifications until recently. On the one hand, the non-Russians received institutions that could only encourage them and threaten the Russian core with devolution or even dissolution; on the other hand, the Russians, who had also undergone the nationalizing experience, felt that they should be the beneficiaries of these changes. Stalin offered the Russians a Faustian bargain: They could hold the empire but only at the price of denying some of their own aspirations, since to flaunt those openly would render maintenance of their control impossible. The Russians also had to be willing to subject themselves to greater repression than otherwise would have been necessary. In short, the Russians were offered the choice of being free or being powerful; not surprisingly, they chose the latter at the behest of Stalin and thus became the sociological basis of the Stalinist state.[1]

Shaking the Foundations

In 1985, the Stalinist system remained more or less in place, although there was some sense that it could not endure much longer. Still, most Soviet leaders were confident that the system would somehow endure and that in any case it was not threatened with collapse. In 1990, only five years later, Mikhail Gorbachev has conceded that the nationalities crisis threatens both his reforms and the integrity of the Soviet Union. Some junior officials are even more explicit. For instance, Vyacheslav Mikhailov, the CPSU Central Committee official responsible for overseeing ethnic developments, has conceded that the Soviet Union "will not survive in its present form" and that it definitely will be "smaller than it is today." He has also suggested that the "critical period" for the country would be the last months of 1990.[2] How did things come to such a pass so quickly?

The tempting and most often heard answer—to paraphrase Tom Lehrer—is that one man deserves the credit and one man deserves the blame: Mikhail S. Gorbachev. Unfortunately, however, this tempting answer is almost certainly inaccurate. Rather, the fact that all fifteen union republics have declared independence or sovereignty, that ethnic violence engulfs whole areas of the country, and that groups never heard of outside ethnographic departments are taking political stands reflects the convergence of three powerful forces, of which Gorbachev and his policies are only one: first, the massive social change sponsored by the Soviet state; second, the double generational change that brought the Gorbachev group to power; and third, Gorbachev's own approach, as manifested both in the unintended ethnic impact of his general policies and in the ways in which his specific nationality policies have backfired.

The most powerful force, and the one that conditions all the others, is the massive social change that the Soviet state has sponsored throughout the USSR. Its policy of mass mobilization not only transformed the country's economy but also brought more ethnic groups into contact with one another. In 1917, relatively few Soviet citizens lived in ethnically mixed regions; now more than one Soviet citizen in five lives in an area dominated by people of another ethnic group. That experience of strangeness is perhaps the most ethnically sensitizing of all. Moscow's policy of promoting equalization among the nationalities had the effect of eliminating one of the most potent arguments for Russian dominance. Non-Russians who might have been willing to accept a Russian role when they lacked the necessary cadres were no longer quiescent once they acquired their own intelligentsias. Moreover, the rise of non-Russian intelligentsias created a political class that by the 1980s could not be absorbed by the slowing Soviet economy, thus leading to a situation familiar to many Third World countries. And the system's promotion of growth—which has often been more rapid on the periphery than at the center—launched a revolution of rising expectations that both the system's own inefficiencies and its inability to move from secondary to tertiary and quaternary economic arrangements would not allow it to meet. As a result, frustration levels rose; and these frustrations were invested with ethnic meaning.[3]

The second factor in this triad is even more often neglected than the first. The remarkable longevity of the Brezhnev generation and its succession by a group of men nearly twenty years younger reflect both the peculiar demographics of the Soviet Union and the likely change that any such succession would entail in values and outlook. The men of 1938, of whom Brezhnev and his generation were the chief representatives, held power for so long not only because of the repressive nature of the system but also because the generation that should have succeeded them in the 1960s did not exist. The Brezhnev generation was born circa 1910; the Gorbachev generation, circa 1930. The generation in between—those born around 1920—was almost obliterated by World War II; as its representatives have claimed, it was not in a position to support Khrushchev, and it could not challenge the Brezhnevites.[4]

The shift from the Brezhnev generation to the Gorbachev generation was therefore a double-generation transfer. The senior group simply wanted to hold onto power; the junior and vastly more educated and knowledgeable generation wanted to make the power worth having. The former knew little but its own country; the latter had a comparative framework, and what it knew was distressing. As a result, the Gorbachev generation is willing to take risks that the Brezhnevites were not, in an effort to get its country moving again. The shift was just as large and even more dramatic than that between Eisenhower and Kennedy in the United States in 1960; and this generational base helps to explain both why Gorbachev has emerged and why he has so much support compared to his conservative opponents. Clearly Gorbachev could not have acted alone and certainly could not have succeeded alone; and the emergence of this new generation suggests that we should not spend so much time asking whether Gorbachev will succeed, but, rather, should discover whether this generation will.

Nonetheless, Gorbachev's role should not be underestimated. In this connection, I want to focus on three matters: what he brought to the job in ethnic terms; how his general policy thrusts had unintended consequences given the country's ethnic mosaic; and, finally, how his specific nationality policies have backfired in ways that he neither expected or desired.

To a remarkable extent, Gorbachev is a Soviet man, perhaps the last Soviet man. He spent most of his career in an ethnically homogeneous environment and, with rare exceptions, has surrounded himself with people like himself. In contrast with his predecessors, he had little experience with ethnicity, little interest in it, and even less patience with ethnic aspirations. Gorbachev is the first Soviet leader since Lenin to have come to power without ever having worked in a non-Russian region of the country; and he is the only Soviet ruler who had never written an article or given a speech on nationality issues before his elevation. In sum, he does not think in ethnic terms, and—as his experience with the RSFSR Supreme Soviet in the spring of 1990 showed—cannot credibly present himself even as a Russian. On the contrary, he is a modern rationalist who identifies with the Soviet system. Unfortunately for him, rationality and Sovietism are not sufficient in a country of more than one hundred ethnic groups.

In keeping with his earlier inattention to ethnicity, Gorbachev neither focused on it during the first years of his reign nor developed policies designed to cope with the country's ethnic mix. Instead, he launched a series of broad policy thrusts, each of which made rational sense and would have worked if the country had been monoethnic, but all of which had serious repercussions in a multiethnic society. Here I would like to consider five of these policy thrusts.

Reduction in Coercion and the Rise of Glasnost

By reducing coercion, Gorbachev hoped to free up public activism. That he has certainly done. But he has also transformed the role of intermediate political leaders (i.e., the heads of union republics) from representatives of the center to mobilizers of the people and representatives of their wishes. Prior to Gorbachev, republic party leaders were Moscow's men on the scene, ready to do Moscow's bidding and to use force to impose central policy. Now, in the absence of coercion, they must represent the population, thereby giving national content to the pseudo-institutions that Stalin created and setting the stage for imperial devolution. Moreover, in allowing greater press freedom, Gorbachev failed to recognize that the Soviet media are divided along ethno-territorial and ethno-linguistic rather than functional lines. As a result, any expansion in press coverage will reflect a nationality bias and promote nationality sensitivities—because there is no issue that does not look different to different parts of the population.

The Cult of Rationality

Gorbachev is a committed rationalist. Unfortunately for him, that stance has ethnic consequences. His attacks on Marxism-Leninism and on Soviet history have deprived the Soviet state of its ideological legitimacy—proletarian internationalism, after all, was the only real justification for the state to retain its current size. And his elimination of affirmative action for non-Russians and of reserved slots for Russians angered both groups, disappointing those who had expected to retain if not improve on their current ethnic situation. Judging people on meritocratic criteria may improve efficiency, but the careful balance implied by the Stalinist synthesis outlined earlier is unfortunately called into question in the process.

Economic Collapse

Gorbachev has overseen perhaps the worst Soviet economic recession since World War II, and his continued tinkering with the economy has created new classes of winners and losers. Each of these developments has had ethnic consequences as well—in the first case, by leading virtually every group to invest economic difficulties with ethnic meaning; and in the second, by prompting the newly disadvantaged first to see a conspiracy behind the shift to market forces and then to resist them as such.

"New Thinking" in Foreign Policy

Gorbachev's new approach to foreign policy has had serious consequences for the cohesiveness of the country. As one Novosti correspondent put it, "no one can say how long the 'welded forever' Soviet Union would have lasted" had it not been for the "psychology of a beleaguered nation with a common destiny" that was promoted by the cold war.[5] Once that discipline was lost, more and more non-Russians began taking a new look at their country, and Russians increasingly did so as well. It is not only the United States that would suffer by being deprived of an enemy, as Georgiy Arbatov had threatened. Moreover, Gorbachev's decision not to prevent the collapse of Communist power in Eastern Europe—the outer empire—raised the question of whether he would be willing to defend the inner empire as well. Baltic moves in early 1990 cannot be understood outside the context of what happened six months earlier in Eastern Europe.

Holding Elections

Perhaps the most ethnically significant (if ethnically unappreciated) of Gorbachev's policies was his decision to allow republic governments to be elected when he himself had never faced a competitive public election. Indeed, by holding elections in the three Slavic republics on March 4, 1990, Gorbachev allowed the creation of legitimate governments in the heartland at a time when he had not been similarly legitimated himself. That decision not only weakened his authority; it also meant that these new republic leaders had to seek out nationalist themes in order to legitimate themselves. Boris Eltsin is no accident; he is the unintended consequence of Gorbachev's own policies.

If Gorbachev did not want to focus on ethnic issues initially, he soon found that he had no choice, given the nationalist upsurge throughout the country. His initial reaction, however, underscored the extent to which he failed to understand the situation: In early 1988, one of his aides insisted that ethnic unrest would boost perestroika, a line repeated by some in the West.[6] But Gorbachev gradually came to understand that he had to focus on the issue and to adopt policies to cope with nationalist aspirations. According to one Soviet writer, this change began in 1987 and was fully in evidence in 1988 and 1989.[7] Unfortunately for Gorbachev, his earlier inattention was fully in evidence here as well. Let us consider five cases:

Punishing the Wrong People. Gorbachev's approach to the Caucasus and the Baltics showed that he was far more willing to move harshly against those who had avoided violence than against those who used it — hence his far harsher policy against Armenia and Georgia than against Azerbaizhan. That sent precisely the wrong signal to the many who wanted to use the system, thus suggesting that extrasystemic approaches might be more effective.

Supporting the Russian Language. Gorbachev's decision to call for Russian to become the Soviet state language was a response to republic moves to give non-Russian languages official status. Unfortunately, his decision prompted virtually all republics to respond, thereby promoting in the republics Russian flight and Russian anger that in themselves have been destabilizing.

The Blockade of Lithuania. Gorbachev's blockade of Lithuania following Vilnius's declaration of independence on March 11, 1990, had the effect of radicalizing not only the Balts but also many others. Ukrainian nationalists asserted that the blockade proved independence was the only option for them—hardly the conclusion that Gorbachev wanted anyone to reach.[8] The blockade also prompted the Russians to move toward a rapprochement with the Balts that undercut Gorbachev's future options.

The Law on Secession. In crafting a law on secession, Gorbachev hoped to slow the process of devolution. Instead, he created a situation in which virtually everyone decided to ignore his wishes, thus undercutting the value of the law and guaranteeing that all would scramble to leave in their own ways. In addition, the process further undermined whatever confidence anyone had in either Gorbachev or Moscow as honest brokers in such a process.

A Call for a New Union Treaty. Perhaps the greatest mistake of all from Gorbachev's point of view was his call for a new union treaty. That decision, taken very late, had three serious consequences, none of which he wanted. First, it implied that the union was now in a state of *dies non*, that it no longer existed, and that virtually any arrangement was now possible. Second, it encouraged non-Russians to put their maximum demands on the table as part of the negotiations, demands that rapidly took on a life of their own and encouraged further radicalization. And, third, it drove Gorbachev into the arms of the Russians because, in Boris Eltsin's words, "Moscow without the RSFSR was a general without troops."[9] Thus the decision to call for a new union was virtually an obituary not only for the old union but for any future one as well.

A Typology of Affected National Groups

To make some sense of this confusing mosaic we have to divide the nationalities according to the way they are perceived in Moscow. Roughly, there are five categories. The first consists of the fourteen non-Russian Union Republics, whose population amounts to 40-45 percent of the total. These, in turn, can be broken down into four basic groups, defined by what they want. The first are the Balts, who actively want independence and are working toward it. The second are the three Republics of the Soviet West—Moldova, Ukraine, and Belorussia. Now that a revolution has occurred in Romania, some Moldovans want to become Romanians. (When Ceaucescu was in power, not even Romanians wanted to be Romanians.)

Ukraine is divided into three parts. As I have noted elsewhere, the citizens of the extreme west, who constitute one-sixth of the population, probably want to achieve complete independence. But the much larger eastern portion of the Republic has given us such well-known Ukrainian nationalists as Nikolai Ryzhkov and Nikita Khrushchev. I do not think that Ukraine is going to be making the kinds of demands for total separation that we've seen in the Baltics.

I would argue that the great unheralded national movement is the one in Belorussia. There is enormous anger over the authorities' lies about the consequences of Chernobyl, and about the failure of the local authorities to permit the emergence of a People's Front. The headquarters of the Belorussian people's front had to be established in Riga, Latvia. The organization managed to turn out 100,000 people for a demonstration that included the slogan: "Ingrelia, let us Romanize our leaders," by which they meant to follow the Romanian example in deposing Ceaucescu. The demonstrators took control of Minsk television and radio for nearly four hours to broadcast their story. The Belorussian situation is potentially explosive. The movement is not structured: The level of institutionalization is considerably below the level of mobilization in Belorussia.

Next are the peoples of the republics of the Caucasus, all of whom hate Moscow almost as much as they hate one another. Everybody thinks that these three Republics—Georgia, Armenia, and Azerbaizhan—are all pushing for independence. Certainly all of them want a new deal with Moscow. But I would argue that none of them wants independence in the short term. Independence would shrink Georgia by 50 percent in size and 60 percent in population; and it would be reduced to a state that would not be viable at all because of the minorities around it and within its borders, all of whom don't like the Georgians. The Armenians might have a vision of what could happen to them wedged between Azerbaizhan and Turkey, and they continue to be worried about that. Both Moscow and Teheran have a vested interest in not letting Azerbaizhan become the focal point for the 12 to 15 million ethnic Azerbaizhanis in Iran.

The point is not that these people are going to stop pressing their demands, but, rather, that they're not likely to be granted independence, and that it might not be their best option.

To those in the West who, following the demonstration by the women of Stavropol krai, said that Azerbaizhan had the potential to become a domestic Afghanistan, I would respond that it took fewer than 5,000 troops, when Moscow finally got around to sending them, to restore some semblance of order in that republic. The Soviets didn't do nearly so well with 100,000 troops in Afghanistan.

Finally, there is Central Asia, where widespread communal violence continues, with Muslims killing Muslims. The violence is likely to worsen with Russians leaving Tadzhikstan at the rate of about 5,000 a month and departing the other Central Asian republics at only a slightly lower rate.

The next category of nationalities is the one that gives Moscow the most grief, because Moscow doesn't have any good answers for its constituents—the various "punished peoples." These include the Germans, the Crimean Tatars, and the Meskhetians who were deported by Stalin and who certainly can't go home again. The Germans can't go back to the Middle Volga, the Crimean Tatars can't go back to Crimea and the Meskhetians can't go back to Georgia, because the people who now live in these places don't want them back. Precisely because they are relatively small in number and because they lack political institutions, the kind of activities they engage in will be extra-systemic and tend toward violence, especially in the case of the Meskhetians but, to a lesser extent, the

Crimean Tartars as well. The Germans are going to join the reunited Germany as quickly as they possibly can.

The third big group of nationalities comprise the 60 million Soviet citizens who live outside their home ethnic territories. This group represents Gorbachev's second biggest problem. One consequence of the devolution of authority and power in the Soviet Union from Moscow to the republics was a change in the basis of nationality oppression in the USSR. If hitherto the Russians were oppressing non-Russians, the non-Russians are now oppressing minorities. And they are not suppressing only the Russians. For a good example of what human rights is not about, look at what the Lithuanians have been doing to the Polish minority in Lithuania.

Now that these groups are at risk, Moscow's general failure to come to their aid means that people are moving back to their "home" republics. There are now between 750,000 and one million refugees in the Soviet Union — not just from Armenia and Azerbaizhan, but from many other areas as well. These population movements constitute an enormous problem. And to the extent that the republics become more ethnically homogenous, which is what refugee movements tend to promote, Moscow will find it increasingly difficult to manage the situation.

The fourth group of nationalities, and one that I follow with great interest (though not with the skill and sophistication of Marjorie Balzer), is composed of the micro-nationalities of the Far North in Siberia. In April 1990 they convened their first All-Union Conference to create institutions intended to pressure the government. While these 38 or 39 groups, who number fewer than a quarter of a million in toto, would not seem to constitute a large problem, they are strategically located. They enjoy enormous support from some key Russian leaders, who see them as local tenants for the only pure part of Russia that is left. And they are in a position right now to cause some very serious policy difficulties.

One need not subscribe to the fictionalized accounts Edward Topol presents in *Red Snow* to consider the difficulties that Moscow is going to face if the Sami of the Kola Peninsula decide to disrupt the movement of electric power by blowing up even a single transmission line. There are demands among these people, who have suffered perhaps as much as anyone, for getting the facilities that have spawned Soviet ecological disasters closed down quickly.

Finally, there are the Russians. The Russians are very angry. From their point of view they have not done very well. They see themselves as having carried an enormous burden. Now that they have experienced a real election, they have a real Supreme Soviet and a president — a new president with power equivalent to a U.S. governor who controls everything west of the Mississippi River. Their potential for causing trouble for the center is very great. Increasingly, the Russians are against everything, not for something. This tendency was reinforced by the way in which the elections were conducted.

One of the biggest challenges for the Russians may be to hold the Russian Republic together. Increasingly, there are demands for the formation of an Independent Siberian Union Republic, or even an Independent Siberia. The leader of that movement is someone who, as the newspaper *Novosibirsk* put it, was arrested eight years ago for calling for a Siberian Union Republic. Now, he has been elected to the legislature for calling for the same thing.

Different Devolutions

Historically, both Soviet writers and Western students of Soviet society have discussed the nationality problems of the USSR as a question, implying that there is a single answer to the issue that will allow it to be solved.[10] More recently, the possibility that there may be multiple answers has come to be appreciated. But at least there is still a tendency to assume that there are answers.

Elsewhere, I have argued that nationality developments are tending in three main directions: toward independence, toward federalism, and toward cofederalism.[11] I have also argued that Moscow has five main tools to manage and contain the process: coercion, devolution, the elaboration of a new ideology, economic revival, and charismatic appeals by the leadership, Moreover, I have suggested that only coercion and devolution are immediately available, and that independence and cofederalism are the most likely outcomes. Such conclusions highlight the extent to which I, too, have been a prisoner of the old conceptions.

Here I would like to suggest that the future is likely to be far more complicated than has been adumbrated by Gorbachev. The Soviet empire is likely to devolve into a series of cross-cutting alliances for a variety of specific purposes. Some republics will achieve political independence but will be locked in military and economic alliances, others will have less political freedom but greater economic autonomy,and so on. Gorbachev is correct in saying that the future will not be like the past, but even he has not gone far enough. The end of the Soviet empire will mean the elaboration of a new state system—one in which the USSR may resemble the Warsaw Pact and Comecon, and in which creative new arrangements are likely. Any effort to impose a single common outcome will fail.

Notes

1. Paul Goble, "Russische Nationalismus in der Sowjetsystem," in *Die Russen*, edited by Andreas Kappeler (Koln: Markus, 1990), pp. 3-10.

2. *The Los Angeles Times*, June 24, 1990.

3. Paul Goble, "Gorbachev and the Soviet Nationality Problem," in *Soviet Society Under Gorbachev*, edited by Maurice Friedberg and Howard Isham (New York: M. E. Sharpe), pp. 76-100.

4. N. Egorychev in *Ogonek*, No. 2 (1989).

5. Vladimir Simonov, "Soviet Federalism: The Shape of Things to Come," *Novosti*, July 2, 1990.

6. Valentin Falin to Reuter, March 14, 1988; and Jerry F. Hough, "The Non-Russians as the Stabilizing Element in the Soviet System," Notes from the Harriman Institute Seminar No. I, (November 11, 1988), p. 2.

7. Sergei Cheshko, "Filosofiia i mistika natsional'nogo voprosa," *Obshchestvennye nauki*, No. 3 (1990), p. 113.

8. Paul Goble, "Gorbachev's Baltic Policy Backfires," Radio Liberty *Report on the USSR*, April 1990.

9. Paul Goble, "Gorbachev's New Federalism Won't Work," Radio Liberty *Report on the USSR*, July 1990.

10. Paul Goble, "The End of the National Question," in *Ideological Decay in the Soviet Union*, edited by Sylvia Woodby et al. (Boulder: Westview Press, forthcoming, 1991).

11. Paul Goble, "The Fate of the Nationalities," in *Russia in the Year 2000*, edited by Walter Lacqueur (New York: St. Martin's, 1990), pp. 121-134.

6

Glasnost: A Cultural Kaleidoscope

Josephine Woll

In the early days of Gorbachev's rule, his twin policies of perestroika and glasnost were frequently contrasted with each other. Every manifestation of glasnost, whether the publication of poetry by the previously banned Nikolai Gumilev or the rehabilitation of Nikolai Bukharin, was applauded. But the applause was accompanied by a wariness, understandable in light of Soviet history, that unless perestroika established institutional guarantees to safeguard the cultural horizons expanded by glasnost, the astonishing revelations of glasnost would be ephemeral. Glasnost was even dismissed as superficial and amounting to little more than changes in personnel.

In fact, the significance and impact of glasnost cannot be overestimated. It has not merely introduced to the public particular individuals, living and dead, and given access to particular items of information and art; it has also transformed public consciousness by creating a different set of expectations and a new kind and level of public discourse on every issue, artistic and political.

In the arts, Soviet culture for virtually its entire history has been poisoned by lies, both explicit and implied. In the worst years artists had to be active propagandists for official ideology; even in the best times they could rarely ignore the official line, let alone openly contradict it. Those who did risked professional isolation and sometimes legal sanctions. Over the past five years, the lies have been exposed. For more than sixty years the state controlled the creation and distribution of cultural products—literature, art, film, music—as well as the gathering and dissemination of information. Now culture has largely been freed from that control.

Certain limitations notwithstanding, glasnost has meant a major expansion of artistic opportunities available to creative artists and their audiences. The cultural fruits of glasnost are tangible and ubiquitous. Books have been and continue to be published, movies appear on theater and television screens at home and abroad, and paintings hang in museums and exhibit halls that even a few years ago would never have reached the readers and viewers for whom they were intended.

For Russians, as for other ethnic and national groups, glasnost has meant a recovery of their cultural legacy from the distant and the more recent past. Three categories of work constitute that legacy: art (in every medium) created for the drawer (i.e., not for distribution), primarily during the Stalin years; art, usually literature, that circulated unofficially within the Soviet Union in manuscript or typescript through unofficial channels (*samizdat*), or that was sent abroad for publication (*tamizdat*); art produced by every wave of emigration. Although the Soviet intelligentsia, particularly its Moscow- and Leningrad-based members, was able to read *Doctor Zhivago* and *Invitation to a Beheading* twenty-five years ago, the vast majority of Soviet readers had no such opportunity. For them glasnost has meant access to Pasternak and Nabokov, to Aleksandr Solzhenitsyn's *The Gulag Archipelago* and Vladimir Voinovich's *The Life and Extraordinary Adventures of Private Ivan Chonkin*. A plethora of such works has been published in large-circulation magazines since late 1986. In the non-verbal arts, access was severely restricted for everyone, including members of the intelligentsia, simply because the equipment and/or space necessary to see films, paintings, plays, and sculptures were the exclusive domain of the state. Now two concurrent trends have changed that situation: State space has become hospitable to work that was once off-limits, and private or cooperative forums have been established that compete with the state.

Access has meant more than simple availability. The recovery of the Russian cultural heritage has as a corollary its integration into Soviet culture. In the past, even those critics who read proscribed authors could neither write about them nor discuss their role in and contribution to Russian/Soviet culture. Because of such taboos, appraisals of Russian culture were inevitably distorted and falsified. In 1990, five years after the onset of glasnost, one almost forgets how certain individuals were made into nonpersons, their names dropped from the lexicon of cultural analysis. Discussions of post-1960 cinema, for example, ignored Andrei Tarkovskii after he emigrated, despite the importance of his films. Surveys of post-1960 fiction ignored Vasilii Aksenov after his departure—despite his immense popularity throughout the 1960s and 1970s.

With the serialization of émigré Mark Aldanov's historical novels (a favorite among Soviet readers), the philosophical thought of Nikolai Berdiaev appearing on the pages of *Novyi mir,* and the flying lovers of Marc Chagall reproduced in *Ogonek* and hanging on gallery walls, glasnost has validated a complex concept of one Russian culture, connected over—or despite—geographical and political boundaries. It is a concept that was impermissible for nearly sixty years, ever since the door was slammed and bolted in 1929.

Theater and Cinema

The dissemination of cultural artifacts is one issue; their production is another. Theater and film unions were among Gorbachev's first and most energetic supporters. One reason was purely pragmatic: Even in Moscow, theaters stood half-empty; and in other cities people on stage sometimes outnumbered those in the audience. Both union bureaucrats and artists hoped that audiences might be enticed back with the kind of repertoire that they assumed would ensue when censorship was lifted and their industries were reorganized.

In fact, despite a general reorganization of theaters in the direction of far greater artistic and financial responsibility, theater seats are often still empty; public interest is relatively low. The only plays that have consistently aroused audience enthusiasm in the last few seasons are dramatic versions of recently published fiction (Anatolii Rybakov's *Children of the Arbat,* Mikhail Bulgakov's *Heart of a Dog,* Vladimir Voinovich's *Fur Hat,* Vasilii Aksenov's *Surplused Barrelware*) and memoirs (Evgeniia Ginzburg's *Journey Into the Whirlwind*). Controversial plays such as Mikhail Shatrov's "Further . . . Further . . . Further," in which Stalin is accused of ordering the murders of Kirov and Trotsky,[1] are also popular, but the political significance of such plays is moot: Famous historical figures often appear in order to testify to the author's progressive ideas.

Critics continually lament the state of the theatrical repertoire. "A time which has been politicized to monstrous dimensions, as ours has, is dangerous for art," wrote one critic. "The audience is obsessed not so much by the plot as by associations."[2] Iulii Kim, commending a production of Camus' "Caligula" to readers of *Moscow News,* prefaced his praise with the rueful comment that "our historic times have politicized [theatergoers] to such a degree that they prefer an evening in front of the TV set to a night at the theater."[3]

Recent cinema has also been charged with sacrificing art to politics. New Soviet films convey "a feeling of alarm, disturbance and unsteadiness" that, critic Boris Berman implies, accurately reflects today's society. Yet the relevance and topicality of these films do not compensate for their "cinematographic impotence . . . . These films," he writes, "are fit to be broadcast over the radio."[4]

Certainly there is an enormous public hunger for accurate facts and statistical data. The audience for investigative journalism on television (i.e., for programs like Leningrad's "Six Hundred Seconds") is huge; millions of readers subscribe to *Argumenty i fakty*, a weekly newssheet full of "hard" information. There is an equal hunger for popular culture, often of a crude variety distasteful to Russian intellectuals. Given the history of falsification on the one hand and of drabness and puritanism on the other, both are perfectly understandable. Commercialization, what one critic called "shock, rock and car chases at full volume,"[5] is not the least acceptable price of freedom.

To a Western observer, Soviet cinema looks much healthier than it did several years ago. There has been an explosion of documentary films, often broadcast on all-Union television with its vast audience. Whether dealing with legacies from the Stalinist past or with contemporary social and ecological problems, documentaries like *Solovetskii Power* (which interviews former inmates of the Gulag) and *This Is No Way to Live* (about the degraded level of life in the Soviet Union) are startlingly powerful. Weaker documentaries, too, offer insights into Soviet reality. Feature films naturally vary in sophistication and originality, though a surprising proportion are quite good. They reflect a range of genres from the grim hyperrealism of Pichul's *Little Vera* through Iurii Mamin's laughter-through-tears satire *The Fountain* to Karen Shakhnazarov's remarkable surreal nightmare, *City Zero*.

For film studios and theaters, the financially self-supporting system envisioned a few years ago, like other dreams of *khozraschet* (cost accounting), has been undercut by the reality of the *nomenklatura*'s entrenched interests, the lack of hard currency, and the realization (hardly confined to Soviet filmmakers) that art and bureaucracy don't mix. Studios are virtually autonomous, with total control over selecting scripts for production, budgeting, casting, and hiring. Scenarists and directors can now bring their projects directly to a studio (or another association), and request funding; if funding is granted, they can then proceed without looking over their shoulder or requiring approval from either studio officials or censors.

They can even go outside the studio system entirely. The film cooperative Podarok, essentially the team that made *Little Vera,* was able to capitalize on the international success of that film to finance a new film, *Black Nights on the Black Sea.* Avoiding both the Soviet studios and Goskino (the State Film Committee), Podarok arranged foreign distribution through an Italian firm and received a 500,000-ruble loan from the Bank for Social Innovations.[6]

Despite bureaucratic roadblocks, film distribution has been substantially decentralized and is becoming more sensitive to market forces. The Film Distribution Board of Goskino used to bear total responsibility for setting prices and deciding the number and destination of film prints. Now a national film market (the first of which convened in late 1988), is supposed to meet quarterly. Prices are set on the basis of attendance forecasts, and buyers, using funds provided by their local soviets (councils), decide how to spend their money—and hope their decisions prove profitable. Mosfilm, the largest of the studios, now has the right to distribute its entire library of 2,500 films, plus any future films, directly, without using the official government export agency (Sovexport).

Because distribution is now governed by market considerations, noncommercial cinema finds itself in an increasingly untenable situation. To prevent the total domination of commercial criteria, the Filmmakers' Union recommended earmarking a portion of the annual government budget to culture, to guarantee some protection for experimental work or art otherwise unlikely to bring in a profit.[7] A sliding tax scale encourages the production of certain kinds of high quality, low profit films: Children's movies, for instance will be taxed at a low rate, horror films at a high rate, and opera/ballet films will be tax-free. A number of joint ventures are under way, including a Mosfilm/Warner Bros. extravaganza about the battle of Stalingrad; meanwhile a Soviet-German corporation is planning to distribute German and Soviet films in both countries and to supply the Soviets with sorely needed equipment and film stock.

One of the first projects undertaken by the revamped Cinematographers' Union was to examine films that had been "repressed" during the Brezhnev years. There were about one hundred of these films. Nearly all have been released. Some (such as Aleksci German's *Roadcheck,* and Gleb Panfilov's *Theme*) date from the late 1970s; a few are much older. Aleksandr Askoldov's *Commissar,* with its portrait of a Red Army commissar torn between her duty and the baby she eventually leaves with a poor Jewish family, was made in 1968 and released two decades later. Scripts once deemed "unfilmable" have also reached the screen. Evgenii Grigorev's 1968 screenplay for *Our Armored Train,* for instance, was finally shot at the Belorussian Film Studio by director Mikhail Ptashuk: The film depicts both the durability of Stalinist fanaticism in a group of "formers" — a former guard commander at a labor camp, a former head of the camp, a former personnel manager—and the moral self-examination of one former security *apparatchik*.

Not everything gets through without a fight, however. Aleksandr Kibkalo's documentary *Day of Revelation*, for instance, has footage of militia and civilians ripping placards out of the hands of demonstrators at Pushkin Square. According to Kibkalo, the film was blocked by Goskino for six months, during which time the press, with the exception of *Moscow News*, was also silent: "It turns out that there's some kind of list at Glavlit [the censorship office] of works that shouldn't be referred to in print. The censor admitted that we were at the top of the list." Nevertheless, the film did come out. "At the Congress of People's Deputies," Kibkalo observed, "sharper things were said than in our film. Goskino called me in and suggested a compromise: They would okay the film's release, and I would add a disclaimer—that the opinion of the authors was not necessarily the last word, and that we hoped to stimulate discussion. I added such a phrase."[8] A compromise, true, but hardly a blow to Kibkalo's artistic integrity.

Literature and the Press

Literature, with its relative speed and ease of production, was the first artistic medium to manifest the effects of glasnost. In autumn 1986 readers found the hitherto-taboo poetry of Nikolai Gumilev (who was shot in August 1921 for alleged counterrevolutionary activity) on the pages of the weekly magazine *Ogonek*. And it is literature that has benefitted most immediately from the steady expansion of opportunity and the gradual erosion of prohibitions. The Law on the Press, effective August 1, 1990, officially abolishes prior censorship; yet even before its adoption, Glavlit had lost most of its teeth. Many editors, once the first-line censors, now fully exercise their new power to make decisions with almost no regard for political or ideological criteria, though often with an eye toward increasing circulation.[9]

The Press Law forbids state censorship of media and gives Soviet citizens the right to establish their own publications. Registration requirements are simple: applicants (any state body, group of people's deputies, public organization, political party, or individual) must indicate the language and number of copies of the prospective periodical, and the source of financing. Central or local government agencies must render a decision within one month, and grounds for refusal or cancellation of registration are severely restricted: periodicals may not advocate war, the violent overthrow of the state, racial or ethnic intolerance, or pornography (the last undefined). Glavlit, according to the law, is supposed to function solely to check foreign publications and audio and video material sent in to the Soviet Union. However, months after the Press Law took effect, *Izvestiia* complained that Glavlit was still hard at work compiling a new list of taboo subjects.

One immediate effect of the law was the legalization of formerly unofficial journals. In the first two months after the law took effect, more than 400 periodicals were registered, including publications of thirteen newly created political parties. The law stipulates that each publication has the right to decide who its "founders" are, and those founders have broad rights including the right to fire an editor whose editorial policy displeases them. Many journals have used that provision to free themselves from control of such "sponsoring" organizations as the Communist Party and the Writers' Union, though the latter is not prepared to let go of its periodicals without a fight, since a great deal of money is involved.

Problems abound, as emerging institutions of democracy contend with conservative party and government officials who retain a lot of power. The Press Law does not deal with the ownership of printing facilities, 90 percent of which belong to the Communist Party, nor with access to and distribution of paper, which is also still in Party hands. So the newly independent periodicals face myriad practical obstacles, including price rises in printing services that necessitated raising subscription and newsstand prices (in turn causing a sizeable drop in subscribers). Moreover, Soiuzpechat, the state agency that controls subscriptions and retail sales of periodicals, has been refusing to accept subscriptions to independent papers and to sell them in state-run kiosks, so that publishers have had to mail or distribute their papers themselves.

After more than five years of glasnost, two salient characteristics dominate the literary scene. First, the range of work available is extraordinarily wide, and second, although some of that work is of enduring value, much is aesthetically insignificant but responsive to immediate and short-term needs. (In this connection, see Helena Goscilo's analysis of major trends in current literature in Chapter 7 of this volume.) Literary discussion has become increasingly polarized; the cultural middle ground has concomitantly diminished. Both trends are connected with perestroika's economic and political vicissitudes.

It is sad, and ironic, that of all the artistic industries, the structures involving literature have been so resistant to change. Books get published much as they did five years ago; the copyright agency, VAAP, although no longer all-powerful, operates under old laws. Unwieldy five-year plans still dominate in the world of Goskompechat, the State Publishing Committee, despite its inability to compete with new market-oriented and relatively flexible publishing houses. More reader-responsive than it once was, Goskompechat still schedules one stultifying volume by one of its editorial board members (if not two or three) for every edition of the much more popular Varlam Shalamov stories promised, notwithstanding a continuing paper shortage so severe that 105 books planned for publication in 1989 had to be put off until 1990 for lack of paper.[10]

Despite restrictive laws, cooperatives are gaining a foothold in the publishing market. Yet Goskompechat retains the power to confiscate print-runs—as it did in autumn 1989, for instance, when it seized a cooperative-published volume of Freud (for violating "obscenity" regulations) and promptly vaulted the copies into the hard-currency bookstores.[11] Not all pertinent laws hamper the cooperatives, however: Unlike state publishing houses, they are not obliged to publish unprofitable literature such as textbooks, scientific books, and children's literature.[12]

As for the Writers' Union, only now is it finally being forced by economic pressures to consider its structure, function and future as an organization. Because so many of its former publications have become independent, the Writers' Union faces a dramatic loss of income. At a two-day meeting in November 1990, members vociferously debated restructuring the Union as a voluntary association of equal republican unions, if not doing away with it altogether.[13]

The *apparat* of the Writers' Union—especially of the Russian Republic (RSFSR) branch, which constitutes almost half the total membership of the Union—is the most conservative of all the creative unions.[14] (One writer, Leonid Zhukhovitskii, ruefully noted that the founders of "Memorial," the admirable organization formed to identify, publicize and memorialize the victims of Soviet history, included the Filmmakers' Union but not the Writers' Union.)[15] Its executive office is bloated with "released secretaries,"—namely, bureaucrats "released" from such distractions as writing to devote themselves to organizational matters. With much to lose and nothing to gain from either perestroika or glasnost, they are therefore hostile to both.[16]

After the Eighth Congress of the Writers' Union (in July 1986), where proponents of perestroika briefly took the reins and in the aftermath of which many liberal journal editors were appointed, the Writers' Union has been steadily dominated by conservatives. Since 1987, the floor at RSFSR Writers' Union plenums has regularly been given to and held by writers who imprecate liberals, "cosmopolitan enemies of Russia," and a favorite target, "Russophobes."[17] One of the most eloquent adversaries of the conservatives, the critic Igor Vinogradov, describes them as

> Young Guardist brothers, who . . . under Brezhnev grew so diehard and crawled into every possible high post, decorating themselves with medals and titles, filling the editorial plans with their own works and waxing fat on their million-copy printings and endless bonuses—who turned into a real mafia: aggressive and scot-free. Is it any wonder that today when this paradise of theirs threatens to recede into the past, they are so feverishly mustering their subunits? Is it [a] surprise that the command system, readying its forces for its final skirmish with developing democracy and well aware that the traditional official ideology has lost almost all credibility with people, is willing to use that ideological venom supplied by the ideological oprichnina raised on it and crying the loudest on Russia's behalf?[18]

The "ideological venom" spewed freely at the Sixth Plenum of the RSFSR Writers' Union Secretariat, held in November 1989.[19] Much of the Plenum was devoted to denouncing the *betes-noirs* of the conservatives: The writer Andrei Siniavskii, whose iconoclastic volume on Pushkin (*Strolls with Pushkin*) is perceived to be a blasphemous assault on Russian culture, and editor Anatolii Anan'ev, who had the audacity to publish excerpts from it in his journal, *Oktiabr'*. Anan'ev is also guilty of publishing Vasilii Grossman's *Forever Flowing*, an impassioned, thinly fictionalized tract on the spoliations of Stalinism and Leninism that is considered a defamation of the Russian people. Anti-Semitism was both explicit (in the remarks of Anatolii Builov and Tatiana Glushkova) and implied, in the distinction drawn between "Russian" and "Russian-language" writers. The few members who tried to protest were shouted down.

The liberals have thus far been unable to wrest from the conservatives even a measure of control over the Writers' Union. But they are hardly quiescent. Liberal writers formed a committee called "April," precisely in order to change the way the Union functions and to gain more independence for its members. "April" has been trying to break the Union's monopoly on publication so as to enable writers who are not necessarily in the best graces of the Union secretariat to get their work into print. Its meetings have been the focus of verbal attack and, on at least one occasion, physical disruption by members or sympathizers of the right-wing Russian nationalist group *Pamiat'*. In October 1990, the ring-leader,

Konstantin Smirnov-Ostashvili, was sentenced to two years in jail for "fanning interethnic enmity."[20]

Cultural Civil War

The battleground of what has been called a "cultural civil war" has shifted to the media, especially to the journals, many of which are headed by pro-reform editors. Conservatives control three main monthly magazines, *Nash sovremennik*, *Molodaia gvardiia*, and *Moskva*, as well as the newspapers *Sovetskaia Rossiia* and *Literaturnaia Rossiia*, and the in-house paper of the Moscow chapter of the Writers' Union, *Moskovskii literator*. Liberals run the flagship publications of perestroika and glasnost—the weeklies *Ogonek*, *Moscow News*, and *Argumenty i fakty*, the monthlies *Znamia*, *Oktiabr'* and *Druzhba narodov*, and the newspaper *Sovetskaia kul'tura*.

Two periodicals, *Literaturnaia gazeta* and *Novyi mir*, attempt to provide a forum for all voices within the spectrum. *Literaturnaia gazeta* runs a regular column called "Weekly Dialogue," in which leading liberal critics butt heads with their conservative opponents. The newspaper, which covers political and economic as well as cultural news, has become more controversial under the stewardship of Fedor Burlatskii, an early and aggressive supporter of glasnost. *Novyi mir* has long published both the "left" and the "right." Between October 1989 and January 1990, for instance, articles by émigré literary critics Peter Vail and Aleksandr Genis, poetry by Evgenii Popov and Evgenii Rein, prose by Iurii Dombrovskii, and a round-table discussion on the post-avant-garde, appeared side by side with material by the émigré religious philosophers Sergei Bulgakov and Nikolai Berdiaev, economic analysis by the Christian "nativist" [*pochvennik*] Vasilii Seliunin, and prose by Viktor Astaf'ev.

Novyi mir's editor, Sergei Zalygin, was one of the first glasnost-era champions of Solzhenitsyn. In 1988, when an alliance of official spokesmen along with a minority of pro-Leninist liberals argued against publication of some of Solzhenitsyn's work (most liberals strenuously urged publication), Zalygin promised his readers *The Gulag Archipelago*. But the October 1988 issue was delayed because its back cover advertised Solzhenitsyn's work for 1989, and when the magazine finally appeared, its future contents page made no such commitments. After several discussions with Gorbachev, however, Zalygin made good on his promises. In July 1989, he published Solzhenitsyn's "Nobel Lecture," and subsequent issues carried *The First Circle* and major sections of *Gulag*.[21] In September 1990, *Komsomol'skaia pravda* (with 22 million subscribers) published a long article by Solzhenitsyn in which he advocated the dissolution of the Soviet Union, the return of private property, and the creation of locally elected councils. Not surprisingly, it provoked vigorous discussion.[22]

Vestiges of pre-glasnost high-handedness can affect even so august a journal as *Novyi mir*. With a circulation of more than 2.5 million, *Novyi mir* earns the state a great deal of money; yet the March, April and May 1990 issues have appeared months late. The official excuse—a lack of paper—may have been true. Nevertheless, Zalygin, together with his editorial board, published a letter in *Literaturnaia gazeta* charging the authorities with punishing the magazine by withholding paper—in part, according to the prose editor Vadim Borisov, for publishing Solzhenitsyn.[23] If indeed the decision was political, or quasi-political, Solzhenitsyn was probably not the main culprit. The facts and views aired in *Gulag* are less immediately irritating to the Party than articles by the émigré historian Mikhail Voslensky (on the privileges of the Party élite), by historian Viktor Danilov (on mismanagement of the economic crisis), and by Aleksandr Tsipko, an "official" philosopher who argues for a return of Christian values and principles as the sole remedy for the Stalinist legacy.[24]

Thus one battle persists—between officialdom, especially its Stalinist *cum* Brezhnevite relics, and the men and women actively engaged in producing and disseminating art. As of the beginning of 1991, the official instruments of control were weakening, steadily if sometimes unevenly; and if the Soviet Union continues to move in the direction of a law-based state, those instruments are almost certain to continue to lose their significance.

The second battle can fairly be called pluralism. Its conservative voices can be heard loudly disparaging virtually all manifestations of modernism, avant-gardism, and pop culture in Soviet life, from abstract painting to pornography. Its liberal voices are more broadly inclusive in their toleration of and tolerance for diversity, though they may dislike post-modernism, beauty contests, and sexually explicit scenes on stage or screen as much as their adversaries do. This battle is sometimes civilized and sometimes vicious, sometimes sophisticated and sometimes primitive, sometimes loftily theoretical and sometimes unpleasantly personal. But as it goes on, those who profit from it most are Soviet citizens. As readers, as viewers, as listeners, they have been participants in the dynamic cultural and intellectual process that glasnost signifies.

Notes

1. See David Joravsky, "Glasnost Theater," *New York Review of Books* (November 10, 1988).

2. Anatolii Smelianskii, "Everything'll Be as it Was When Grandma Was Alive," *Moscow News*, No. 43 (1989), p. 13.

3. Iulii Kim, "Roman Emperor at the Mossoviet Theater," *Moscow News*, No. 27 (1990), p. 14.

4. "Is There Light at the End of the Tunnel?", *Moscow News*, No. 42 (1989), p. 11.

5. Georgii Kapralov, "The White Heat of Passions and the Road to the Temple," *Pravda*, July 30, 1989.

6. Anna Lawton, "Happy Glasnost," *The World and I* (December 1989), p. 43. See also her article on *This Is No Way to Live*, "The USSR's Hottest Movie Ticket," *The World and I* (December 1990), pp. 200-205.

7. Andrei Smirnov, "Hurray! Crisis Is There," *Moscow News*, No. 20 (1990), p. 16. Smirnov mentions that three films rejected by film and video distributors won prizes at a nation-wide festival of "unbought" films.

8. Sergei Romanovskii, "People on the Square," *Sobesednik*, No. 39 (September 1989).

9. For an account of the censors' recent role at *Ogonek*, see Abraham Brumberg, "The Turning Point?", *New York Review of Books* (June 28, 1990).

10. Yet the vicissitudes of the Soviet system continue to manifest themselves. The press of the Moscow Polygraphic Institute somehow managed to acquire enough paper for a five volume edition of Anna Akhmatova. Evgenii Kuz'min, "With a Feeling of Deep Satisfaction," *Literaturnaia gazeta*, February 14, 1990, p. 4.

11. Tatyana Tolstaya, "On Publishing and Publishers," *Moscow News*, No. 37 (1989), p. 11.

12. See Iurii Aleksandrov's interview with Goskompechat' official V. Rakhmanov, "Cooperatives and Books," *Literaturnaia gazeta*, August 9, 1989, p. 7. See also V. Eremenko, "The Market Threatens Books," *Knizhnoe obozrenie*, October 12, 1990, p. 2.

13. See Julia Wishnevsky, "Press Law Makes Trouble for Writers' Unions," Radio Liberty *Report on the USSR*, November 2, 1990.

14. John and Carrol Garrard, in *Inside the Soviet Writers' Union* (New York: Free Press, 1990), offer a thorough analysis of how and why that came to be true.

15. "About Conservatism, Informal Groups, and the Oldest Profession," *Sovetskaia molodezh'*, September 23, 1989, p. 5.

16. See Natalia Il'ina, "Welcome, Young and Unknown Tribe . . .," *Ogonek*, No. 2 (1988), pp. 23-26, for a lethal exposé of the range and magnitude of their perquisites.

17. Igor' Shafarevich's book, "Russophobia," which appeared in *Nash sovremennik*, No. 6 (1990), as well as in a separate edition, has shaped much of the discussion. See Liah Greenfeld, "The Closing of the Russian Mind," *The New Republic* (February 5, 1990), and Josephine Woll, "Russians and 'Russophobes':

Anti-Semitism on the Russian Literary Scene," *Soviet Jewish Affairs*, Vol. 19, No. 3 (1989).

18. Igor Vinogradov, "What Did Not Happen?", *Moscow News*, No. 5 (1990), p. 14.

19. Extracts appeared in *Ogonek*, No. 48 (1989) and *Literaturnaia Rossiia*, December 1, 1989. For English excerpts see *The Current Digest of the Soviet Press*, Vol. XLI, No. 52 (1989) and Vol. XLII, No. 1 (1990), and "'Literary' Ugliness in Russia," *Dissent* (Spring 1990), pp. 198-200.

20. Francis X. Clines, "Soviets Jail Man for Anti-Semitic Threats," *The New York Times*, October 13, 1990, p. 3.

21. See John B. Dunlop, "Solzhenitsyn Begins to Emerge from the Political Void," and Douglas Smith, "Reappraisal of Solzhenitsyn in the USSR," both in Radio Liberty *Report on the USSR*, September 8, 1990.

22. See, for example, Igor Vinogradov, "Through Wide Open, But Not Rapturous Eyes . . .," *Moscow News*, No. 41 (1990), p. 14. Michael Scammell examines the substance of Solzhenitsyn's proposals in "To the Finland Station?", *The New Republic* (November 19, 1990), pp. 18-23, while in the same issue, Conor O'Clery describes Soviet reactions (pp. 22-23).

23. As reported by David Remnick, "Soviet Editors Charge Censorship," *The Washington Post*, May 25, 1990.

24. On Tsipko, see Dimitry Pospielovsky, "Russian Nationalism: An Update," Radio Liberty *Report on the USSR*, February 9, 1990, pp. 14-15.

7

Alternative Prose and Glasnost Literature

Helena Goscilo

Tous les genres sont bons hors le genre ennuyeux. (All genres are fine except for the boring genre.)
—Voltaire

History [is] a distillation of rumor.
—Thomas Carlyle

The historian, essentially, wants more documents than he can really use; the dramatist only wants more liberties than he can really take.
—Henry James

Identifying the Beast: A Taxonomical Tease

In the context of the complex, contradictory developments that have prevailed in the Soviet Union over the past five years, what are the major trends in current Soviet literature? How may one characterize the fiction published under the aegis of glasnost? The first problem is one of definition, for the elastic and imprecise rubric "glasnost literature" encompasses at least five dissimilar and largely incompatible categories: (1) the "archeological" fund—literature belonging to earlier eras but banned until now primarily on "ideological" grounds (e.g., Evgenii Zamiatin's *We* and Mikhail Bulgakov's *Heart of a Dog*); (2) more recent works whose successful or attempted publication resulted in the author's public vilification, imprisonment, or expulsion (e.g., Vladimir Voinovich's *The Life and Extraordinary Adventures of Private Ivan Chonkin* and the writings of Alexander Solzhenitsyn and Andrei Siniavskii), as well as works of approximately the same period that circulated only unofficially in the Soviet Union but were published in the West unaccompanied by scandal (e.g., Venedikt Erofeev's *Moscow to the End of the Line* and Andrei Bitov's *Pushkin House*); (3) manuscripts "kept in the drawer"—written in the 1960s, 1970s, and early 1980s, but rejected by editors or not even submitted for possible publication by authors who simply bided their time (e.g., Anatolii Rybakov's *Children of the Arbat* and Vladimir Dudintsev's *White Robes*); (4) current fiction by writers who thrived throughout the stagnation (*zastoi*) of the Brezhnev years, but who now *perestroilis'*; i.e., have leapt on to the careening bandwagon of thinly-veiled journalism (e.g., Liudmila Uvarova); and (5) works by authors whose debut or belated discovery happens to have either coincided with glasnost or proved useful to its advocates but whose vision of the world evolved prior to glasnost, even if the publication of their works did not (e.g., Tat'iana Tolstaia and Viktor Erofeev).

The majority of Soviet readers frankly favor the first three categories, to which the thick journals (the chief purveyors of literature in the USSR) likewise give priority. The titillation of biting into formerly forbidden fruit (about the only fruit available in Soviet supermarkets) undoubtedly accounts in part for this taste, though few would recognize or admit the mechanism at work here. Grigorii Baklanov, the editor of *Znamia*—a standard-bearer in the tireless procession of reclaimed materials—asserts that pre-perestroika fiction by the likes of Boris Pil'niak (1894-1937), Varlam Shalamov (1907-1982), Vasilii Grossman (1905-1964), and Vladimir Tendriakov (1923-1984) overshadows new submissions: "There are still no contemporary books equal to the importance of the current period of change."[1] A cursory glance at recent issues of Russian periodicals confirms that such an estimate is not peculiar to Baklanov alone. Alla Latynina, a centrist literary critic akin to Sergei Zalygin whose moderate liberalism mediates between extreme positions, and a frequent contributor to *Novyi mir*, *Literaturnaia gazeta*, and *Moscow News*, has echoed that sentiment: "Literature of the past has become today's literature."[2] Others concur.

To what extent, however, does this privileging of a recovered legacy edge out potentially gifted newcomers? One must invest inordinate trust in the taste and judgment of editors like Baklanov not to challenge both his sweeping claim and his editorial decisions. Is that trust warranted? What standards does Baklanov apply to candidates for publication? Clearly, ideological rather than aesthetic ones. However impressive in their high-minded censure of ethical misconduct, virtually all of the glasnost "blockbusters" (Rybakov's *Children of the Arbat*, Grossman's *Life and Fate* and *Forever Flowing*, Dudintsev's *White Robes*, Daniil Granin's *The Bison*, and Chingiz Aitmatov's more recent *The Executioner's Block*) have come from clumsy and often artless, if well-meaning, pens. Wooden dialogue, characters that fail to come alive, interminable harangues, shaky transitions, and faltering command of viewpoint substantially compromise their status as artistic creations. Yet their phenomenal success is evidence that what Soviet editors (and, apparently, the public) esteem above all else nowadays is topical exposé, publicistic statements that, *mutatis mutandis*, still operate stylistically within the dispiriting framework of social realism or "poor man's realism." In that respect, Siniavskii's shrewd remark that Soviet literature has entered the Solzhenitsyn era is a genuine aperçu, substantiated, moreover, by Viacheslav Kondrat'ev's admission that in the Soviet Union "today Solzhenitsyn is perhaps the only writer who has been accepted by everyone."[3] Belated semijournalistic unmasking of the past or invectives against the present, masquerading as literature, now verge on a new orthodoxy—a new social, if not socialist, realism—and, as befits Soviet orthodoxy, find voice in a prose that bears the stamp of the period and its exigencies rather than that of the artist. Though praiseworthy in their moral fervor and their probity from the standpoint of refurbished liberal ideology, these texts lack individuality and could be signed "glasnost representative No. 1," "No. 2," and so on, instead of carrying their authors' names.

Yet very few Soviet or, for that matter, Western critics have expressed qualms about the effect of journalism on the fiction most closely identified with glasnost. Isolated exceptions include (implicitly, at least) the writer Venedikt Erofeev,[4] the Slavist Nora Buks,[5] and especially the prolific Soviet literary critic Natal'ia Ivanova, whose principled commitment to openness has not blunted her aesthetic sensitivity. As early as 1986,[6] she drew attention to how noticeably the artistic level of fiction has suffered from massive infusions of journalistic features—precisely those features that writers like Ales' Adamovich recommend as the sole means of elaborating the "superprose" (*sverkhproza*) that can answer the needs, and be commensurate with the realities, of Soviet society today. Ideology and social relevance, the hallmarks of socialist realism, remain the imperatives of Soviet literature, albeit now reoriented in accordance with the devaluation of former truths and truisms and the concomitant valorization of erstwhile heterodoxy.

"Privychka svyshe nam dana" (Habit is given us from above—Pushkin)

In that sense and others, some of the touted changes in new literature and its publication are more apparent than real. Perhaps censorship more than any other facet of the "literary process" discloses how, at this stage in history, musty old wine can still get decanted into vaunted new bottles. To assume that the current acceptability of previously taboo works (the mere possession of which earlier carried the risk of incarceration) means the abolition of all censorship is to ignore, for instance, what happened with Sergei Kaledin's story "Construction Battalion." Military censors withdrew the text, already set in type in *Novyi mir*, because of its demoralizing portrait of military life, albeit during Brezhnev's premiership.[7] (The Brezhnev years remain a sensitive area, because many of today's foremost proponents of change occupied high positions under Brezhnev; the problem of their involvement in the infamous violations and injustices perpetrated by the state during the period of stagnation has yet to be tackled with any consistency.) The reduced intrusion of the state censorship agency Glavlit, which now confines its jurisdiction to security matters, has signaled not the disappearance but the transfer of proscriptive power to other areas. According to the film director Alexander Proshkin, the USSR Academy of Sciences interfered in his documentary on the life of Nikolai Vavilov (the geneticist persecuted by Stalin's favorite, Trofim Lysenko), because Proshkin did not intend to portray Vavilov's brother Sergei, president of the Academy during Lysenko's ascendancy, as a positive character.[8] Censorship in Central Television, too, has elicited sharp criticism in the media (where the new winds of glasnost blow strongly), and the film director El'dar Riazanov, responsible for Central Television's programs on culture, resigned from his post in 1988 after censors cut an episode from one of his films dealing with the tragedies of the poets Nikolai Gumilev (executed), Osip Mandel'shtam (perished in a prison camp), Sergei Esenin, Vladimir Maiakovskii, Marina Tsvetaeva (suicides), Anna Akhmatova, and Boris Pasternak (both expelled from the Writers' Union and persecuted by the authorities).[9]

As the critic Michael Massing discovered during recent interviews with press personnel, although Party leaders still monitor all newspapers, the censorship function long monopolized by the state is gradually being transferred into the hands of individual editors.[10] In addition to the authors themselves, who have internalized decades-old prohibitions, individuals at all levels of the publishing process now censor works. Prudery regarding sex, violence, various unglamorous bodily functions, profanities and obscenities still causes texts to be bowdlerized, though now on a more random basis, depending on the tastes of those who exercise their editorial privileges. These come into play most noticeably in the thick journals, which reach an appreciably broader audience than the collections published in book form, typically in insufficient runs to satisfy the demands of Russian readers.

The fate of Venedikt Erofeev's *Moscow to the End of the Line*—written in 1969, circulated in manuscript form in 1970 in the Soviet Union, and published eleven years later in Paris in its entirety—demonstrates how Soviet puritanism leads to startling idiosyncrasies in the system. When the weekly *Nedelia* printed a chapter from the novella in September 1988, it expunged a humorous passage that satirically linked Russians with homosexuality and the Arab-Israeli conflict.[11] Similarly, in comparing the version of Liudmila Petrushevskaia's story "Our Crowd" that appeared in *Novyi mir* in January 1988 with the fuller text as printed in her collection *Eternal Love*, one finds a remarkable sea change in the service of propriety. Presumably offensive words like *perdet'* (to fart), *der'mo* (shit), and *sblevat'* (to throw up) (p. 111) have been replaced by the more sedate *puskat' gazy* (pass gas), *eto delo* (this stuff), and *vydat' meniu* (bring up the menu) (p. 111) respectively.[12] Moreover, entire sentences dealing with sexually related phenomena that official Soviet morality condemns as immoral or perverse are absent in the *Novyi mir* text (though reinstated in the anthology). For example: *Andrei ushel v okean, a prishel ottuda — privez iz Iaponii malen'kii plastikovyi muzhskoi chlen. Pochemu zhe takoi malen'kii, a potomu, chto ne khvatilo dollarov. A ia skazala, chto eto Andrei privez dlia docheri* (Andrei went abroad, and on his return brought a small plastic masculine organ from Japan. Why so small? Because he didn't have enough dollars for a larger one. And I said that Andrei had brought it for his daughter (p. 198); or *U Tani byl syn, izvestnyi tem, chto v mladenchestve polzal po materi i sosal to odnu grud', to druguiu, i tak oni i razvlekalis'* (Tania had a son famous for having as a baby crawled all over his mother and sucked first one breast and then the other, and that's how they entertained themselves) (p. 200). References to a ruptured maidenhead and to someone's looking very Jewish likewise have been expunged from the journal variant of the story. Public response to even the more genteel version, and to Viktor Erofeev's readings from his fiction, indicates that a society reared on palliatives and "supervised," expurgated texts may not yet be ready to cope with unsanitized prose. According to Petrushevskaia's own comments[13] and the letters that bombarded *Novyi mir*, "Our Crowd" offended many and earned her enemies among the very intelligentsia who purportedly are the strongest supporters of glasnost. Analogous complaints have sounded against the violence, preoccupation with physiological matters, and profusion of verbal impieties that constitute the authorial signature of Viktor Erofeev. Yet for the Western reader familiar with Jarry's Theatre of Cruelty and with the biological orientation of Jean-Paul Sartre and the Existentialists, both Erofeev's nihilism and the aggressively modernist narration and offhand references to various sexual acts found in Alexander Ivanchenko's *Safety Measures I*[14] have scant shock value. In fact, the authors' self-conscious effort at polemical outrage could strike the educated Westerner as quaint or, even worse, anachronistic posturing.

What might distress both Soviet and Western readers who expect scrupulous scholarship and responsibility from publishers of texts that have gained acceptance only under glasnost is that works advertised as making their debut in the original language often make no mention of previous publication abroad, as in the case of Bulgakov.[15] Soviet rediscovery of what has been common knowledge or standard reading in the West sometimes suffers from sloppy handling—a consequence of journalism, which by definition prizes speed over thoroughness and, all too often, over accuracy. Incidents of this kind indicate that the present marriage of literature to journalism, *pace* Adamovich, augurs nothing intrinsically auspicious for the emergence of significant new fiction. In fact, one could argue quite the contrary.

The Shock of the New?

However unpropitious the current circumstances, original talents (in compliance with the unfathomable dynamics of artistic creativity) have materialized in the last few years (recall our fifth category of glasnost literature). Some, like Vladimir Makanin, have gained prominence rather late in their careers, while others have attracted a following with the publication of their first work (e.g., Mikhail Kuraev with *Captain Dikshtein* [1987]).[16] Whereas the rise of certain authors (such as Tolstaia, who began writing in 1983) has been meteoric, others (such as Petrushevskaia, who tried to break into print in the 1960s)[17] have struggled a decade or more to attain recognition or, as in the case of Alexander Ivanchenko, access to print. In its technically novel treatment of any and all aspects of life, the "new" prose has revived the modernist tradition long stifled by prescriptive Stalinist aesthetics and thus may more appropriately be characterized as "renewed" or "renovative." A grain of truth may be buried under the mountain of abuse heaped by Dmitrii Urnov on this "alternative" or, as he pseudo-ingenuously labels it, "bad" prose:[18] Part of its appeal for Soviet readers (trained to read literature as encoded political statement) may indeed reside in the involuntary frisson produced by texts glamorized through prohibition (though that cannot explain the popularity of Tolstaia, who encountered no serious obstacles in getting published). More likely, however, the liberal intelligentsia welcomes "alternative prose" not because of its piquancy but as a promising liberation from hoary formulas—a chance for writers to pursue flights of individual imagination instead of adhering to collective stereotypes.

Radical differences in authorship, subject, and manner notwithstanding, the novellas and short stories (if not the novels) by the period's most gifted prosaists share a number of refreshing tendencies: a more subtle or original perspective on familiar phenomena; a focus on the inner world of human experience, with the external defamiliarized or relegated to the periphery; attentiveness to the stylistic, rather than ideological, aspects of prose; a scrambling of temporal and spatial categories; a propensity for irony and fantasy; a postmodernist explosion of intertextuality; enriched vocabulary; and a generally freer approach to language. The heterogeneous, unaffiliated group associated with this trend—Tolstaia, both Erofeevs, Kuraev, Valerii Popov and Evgenii Popov, Viacheslav P'etsukh, Ivanchenko, Valeriia Narbikova, the Viktor Konetskii of "Cat-Strangler Silver" (1987),[19] and Andrei Bitov, especially in "Pushkin's Photograph (1799-2099)" (1987)[20]—has greater affinities with Vladimir Nabokov, Sasha Sokolov, and the writers of the 1920s than with its immediate Soviet predecessors. Most seem to have imbibed, at creative (re)birth, Siniavskii's prophetic intuition that the future of Russian literature lies not in a drab art of Purpose, but in an absurd, fantastic, phantasmagoric art of hypotheses (*What Is Socialist Realism?* [written in 1956]).

Kuraev's *Captain Dikshtein* splendidly illustrates how artistic complexity can vouchsafe a more nuanced treatment of a subject that seems doomed to simplification in the hands of overt polemicists. *Captain Dikshtein* comprises a lengthy "historical" account of the Kronstadt uprising, set within a short fictional frame. This rebellion against Communist rule by the Kronstadt naval base, one of the locales conventionally celebrated as the cradle of the October Revolution, has long remained a forbidden chapter of Soviet history. But Kuraev's literary debut broke the stubborn silence on this volatile topic. Playful, digressive, and self-reflexively ironic in tone, Kuraev's text nonetheless offers a serious meditation on the nature and meaning of history. For Kuraev, the master narrative of history has disintegrated. A temporal sequence neither guarantees nor implies a teleological ordering, for history consists of random phenomena that become organized into a meaningful design only through subsequent perspective. According to this destabilized view, historical "facts" cannot exist independently of their later, constellating representation. Hence

Kuraev's predilection for diverse, often contradictory points of view on historical events, which, however, are highly particularized. If that technique communicates the accidental nature of history, Kuraev's self-conscious mode of narration in the framing portions of the novella likewise underscores the extent to which a constructed perspective determines the fictional organization of materials. Whereas Rybakov, Grossman, Solzhenitsyn, and other practitioners of historical retrieval credit both the necessity and the possibility of learning the Truth about the Past, Kuraev confronts the truism that the past is marked not by simple facticity or continuity but by rupture, breaks in identity, changes in name, and gaps in narration. Russia, like Kuraev's protagonist Igor' Ivanovich, underwent a fantastic series of transformations—in name, government, culture, and identity—accompanied by equally fantastic explanations of these metamorphoses. Thus the novella's subtitle of "a fantastic narrative" refers less to Kuraev's fictional mode, which evokes Gogol' and Dostoevskii, than to the course of Russia's history, which Kuraev conceives in Tolstoian terms. Kuraev's originality consists not only in perceiving contingency where others have claimed inevitability but also in revealing how the contingent and fantastic constitute so-called history.

Temporality and perception, sequence and causality, ends and beginnings—and the zigzags connecting and separating them—likewise fascinate Vladimir Makanin and Andrei Bitov, who share a reputation as difficult, intellectual writers. The artist's relationship to history, the need for cultural continuity, and the processes shaping the individual psyche are minutely explored in their highly self-conscious narratives, complicated by the interplay of layered spatial and temporal planes, multiple perspectives, and a knotted, loôped, and loosened narrative thread. Bitov, especially, presupposes a reader with an instant recall of the entire span of Russian literature, whether in his endlessly intertextualized novel *Pushkin House* (1978) or in the superb story that could function as its epilogue, "Pushkin's Photograph (1799-2099)." In the latter, the science fiction convention of time travel literalizes Bitov's matrix metaphor for tracing cultural origins as he continues his profound and often hilarious pursuit of Russia's supreme cultural icon: Pushkin. Although Makanin's transgressions against an unbroken linear structure are less colorful than Bitov's, his deliberate omissions and unexplained juxtapositions force the reader to perform the very jointure that he urges in the name of humanism, yet eschews narratively (e.g., in *Left Behind* [1987], *Loss* [1987], and *A Man and a Woman* [1988]).[21] Both authors share Kuraev's passionate interest in process and his skepticism regarding History as an inert body of interconnected facts awaiting reclamation.

The necessarily subjective nature of memory also finds poignant expression in Gennadii Golovin's *Anna Petrovna*, made into a film for television almost immediately upon publication and shown in June 1989. Patience and hope, the title of Golovin's first collection of novellas (*Patience and Hope* [1988]), attend the lessons that his slowly dying protagonist Anna Petrovna has learned from her long life, which she resuscitates in kaleidoscopic fragments through recollections, dreams and fantasies in the course of the narrative. This flutter of incessantly shifting, haphazard impressions ranging over the sixty-odd years of Anna Petrovna's existence skillfully simulates the associative processes of memory, dream, and semiconscious reflection. The collective images transmit a palpable sense of an intensely rich life, one illuminated by Anna Petrovna's generous responsiveness to everyday occurrences, to small details, atmosphere, visual stimuli, and human needs. Those familiar with recent Russian history will be tempted to read Golovin's delicate portrait of the refined yet resilient protagonist as a homage to an entire generation of real-life heroines: women with Anna Petrovna's sensitivity and spiritual resources—some now dead, others in their eighties but still working—who under often inhuman conditions, in poverty, isolation, and sickness, have made the preservation of Russian culture their life's work: for example, Nadezhda Mandel'shtam, Emma Gershtein, Lidiia Ginzburg, I. Grekova, and Natal'ia Baranskaia.

Golovin's collage technique, which enables him to slip unobtrusively in and out of psychological and physical states in a succession of temporal frames, allows Anna Petrovna's life to speak through her thoughts and reminiscences, without omniscient authorial intervention. This use of quasi-direct discourse (*erlebte Rede*), and first-person narrative (both of which sometimes teeter on the stream of consciousness), as well as of multivoiced narrative, reflects the decentering or dissolution of authoritative perspective prevalent in alternative prose. Freedom from dogmatic pronouncements or from a single, unified center of consciousness that labors to orient readers' responses according to authorial convictions, marks the fiction of Fazil' Iskander, Valerii Popov, Bitov, Petrushevskaia, both Erofeevs, Tolstaia, recent Makanin, and Nikolai Shmelev. In Iskander's and Popov's satires, the dissociation of author from narrator displaces onto the latter any political and social criticism, which may be ascribed more to his personal idiosyncrasies than to objective conditions. It also confers a certain legitimacy on the lively oral delivery—full of colorful slang, regional proverbs, and other individualized peculiarities of speech—favored by contemporary fictional discourse.

Kuraev's second and more firmly controlled novella, entitled *Night Patrol* (1988),[22] exploits the advantages of first-person narrative in a Dostoevskian key as it recreates the past from a dialogized perspective. The lyrical musings of the authorial persona who (with the aid of Dostoevskii's *White Nights*) extols the charms of Leningrad provide a contrastive tonal background for, and an indirect rejoinder to, the self-revelations of Polubolotov, a former executioner of "enemies of the people"; hence the novella's pointed subtitle, "A Nocturne for Two Voices, with the Participation of Comrade Polubolotov, a Marksman for Internal Security." Kuraev permits Polubolotov's own discursive ruminations on the rigors and rewards of his profession to disclose his moral blindness. Unable to distinguish his occupation of politically sanctioned murderer from that of, for instance, a plumber, Polubolotov perceives both jobs as serving the community in their respective ways. Like Dostoevskii's underground man, Polubolotov confides more than he realizes, and no explicit recrimination on the author's part could communicate as starkly as Polubolotov's self-presentation the sheer horror of his activities and his imperviousness to that horror. A similar effect is achieved in Viktor Erofeev's and Petrushevskaia's stories, which have prompted several commentators who equate explicitness with presence to assume that no moral standards obtain in the fictional universe of these authors.

In like vein, a deliberate echo of the Underground Man's confession that he is "a nasty man, a sick man" opens Petrushevskaia's "Our Crowd." The story closes with the narrator's rhetorical insistence on her own cleverness; at several junctures, however, the events described by the narrator herself call that emphasized cleverness into question. Her gritty, mocking litany of the personal betrayals and compromises, the dissoluteness, and the vicious games played out by a group of "friends" from the intelligentsia—conventionally viewed as the conscience of Soviet society—derives its impact primarily from Petrushevskaia's skillful manipulation of her ambiguous reporting persona. The highly condensed narrative scatters tangential references to grim social and historical developments—hostile invasions, imprisonment in camps, persecution of "refuseniks," groundless police surveillance, and intrusive political meddling in research—throughout a vitriolic portrayal of the maimed milieu in which she has spent her entire adulthood. That the narrator herself is not exempt from either the base motives or the self-deluded posturing that she ridicules in the group's members may be deduced from the uneven rhythm of her unwittingly self-revelatory monologue, with its mixture of occlusion and logorrhea. Indeed, the onset of the blindness that is an early symptom of her fatal disease serves a metaphoric function in the story. While it connotes her Tiresias-like gift for detecting others' hidden desires, grasping the hidden significance of immediate circumstances, and to some extent predicting their eventual outcome, it simultaneously transfers to the physical plane her weightiest psychological failing: An incapacity to subject her own psyche and behavior to the merciless scrutiny that she brings to bear on others. Petrushevskaia's well-known penchant for chatty first-person narration is chiefly motivated by her protagonists' conflicting impulses and strategies of survival. Here, the heroine's psychological need to stress her position as an outsider *within* her close-knit circle finds an ideal formal solution: The subjective power inherent in the distanced narrating vantage point (Bitov's "superior rank of observer") is undercut by her inescapably disempowered role of the "insider" as an object of narration. Like Tolstaia and Erofeev, Petrushevskaia takes scrupulous care to withhold her authorial voice and unmediated judgment from her fictional texts, which camouflage the essential with the incidental.

Authorial attitudes and allegiances, which are trumpeted forth in both standard Soviet fiction and the exposé branch of glasnost literature, are challengingly elusive in alternative prose. With her customary astuteness, Natal'ia Ivanova has remarked on the emergence of a new genre in Soviet literature—"discourse" or "the word" (*slovo*),[23] which subsumes the disparate contents of a work under the overarching monological *profession de foi* that the author cannot resist conveying unambiguously. That mode is exemplified by Viktor Astaf'ev's *Sad Detective Story* (1986) and Vasilii Belov's *Everything's Ahead* (1986).[24] By contrast, the multiple perspectives, unexpected shifts in tone and lexical levels, startling juxtapositions, and frequent compression of material in "alternative prose" tend to dialogize or obscure even tentatively implied values and hierarchies. Whereas monologists wishing to "speak out" (*vyskazat' svoe slovo*) conceive of texts as soapboxes to be mounted, dialogists try to distance themselves from their works. And the warmly amiable humor of Iskander and Valerii Popov, like Petrushevskaia's mordant wit, Tolstaia's deflective irony, and Erofeev's macabre funniness in the midst of monstrosities, helps to achieve that distance.

A major factor contributing to the complexity and exuberance of "alternative prose" is its densely intertextual nature. Whether one defines intertextuality à la Roland Barthes, as a set of relevant presuppositions sedimented in the past, surfacing as a "mirage of citations" that prove evasive and insubstantial as soon as one attempts to grasp them, or à la Julia Kristeva, as a consciously ironic play of discourse that derives its very identity from a wholesale but noncommittal appropriation of existent discourses, the prose of Erofeev, Tolstaia, Kuraev, Bitov, and, to a lesser extent, Petrushevskaia and Viacheslav P'etsukh (e.g., in his *The New Moscow Philosophy*) teems with intertexts.[25] A comparison of Vladimir Tendriakov's "Donna Anna" with Erofeev's "Anna's Body, or the End of the Russian Avant Garde" clarifies not only the distinction between simple citation and intertextuality, respectively, but also the vast conceptual divide separating current authorial practices from more traditional Soviet writing.[26] Alexander Blok's poem *The Steps of the Commendatore* (1912) supplies the title and the lines cited in Tendriakov's story by the protagonist narrator, who directs readers to the poetic source by asking a fellow soldier, Galchevskii, whether he likes Blok (from whose poem *The Scythians* [1918] Galchevskii subsequently recites a quatrain). Given the hyperbolic nationalism of *The Scythians* and the centrality of betrayal and retribution in Blok's lyrical version of a fraught moment from the Don Juan legend, the two quotations serve chiefly to underscore Tendriakov's concern with the perils of unreflecting jingoism and the nature of treason, both subsumed by his focal theme of moral responsibility. The quotations are grafted onto a text that would lose relatively little by their omission. By contrast, the very foundation of Erofeev's story, its distinctive structure and rhythm, would disintegrate were its many Annas and the Blokian refrain of "Anna! Anna! Anna!" eliminated. Any meaning attaching to Erofeev's narrative hinges on all the Annas evoked by the unidentified allusions accumulated within the few pages that dramatize a comic tragedy of love, treachery, and retribution: Blok's/Mozart's violated Donna Anna; the eighteenth-century Empress Anna Ioanna, who reneged on a contract; the Anna of Tolstoi's *Anna Karenina*, with its appositely vengeful biblical epigraph; Anna Akhmatova, justly admired for her superb love lyrics and her scholarship on Pushkin's treatment of the Don Juan legend; and Chekhov's several lovelorn Annas—whether in the guise of a "Lady with a Dog" or an "Anna on the Neck" (the latter citation from Chekhov's story being a paronomastic reference to the medal the tsarist government awarded for state service).

Erofeev's Anna not only culminates two centuries of Russian heroines ruled by passion, but synecdochically reviews the very culture that produced them. The interstices in this network of allusions are filled by additional cultural metonyms in the form of truncated, enigmatic references: From French art, Borges, the Eiffel Tower, the Leaning Tower of Pisa, the Caucasus, and *Women's Day*, to traditional subjects of still-life canvasses and the folkloric literalization of cannibalistic metaphor. The bared device of the climactic finale reveals the loving, suicidal "murderess" Anna as Erofeev's creative alter ego. Just as she performs the ultimate act of possession by swallowing the object of her love/hatred ("the other"), so

Erofeev asserts and nurtures his own authorial self through his nihilistic assimilation of "other" sources. In other words, intertexts are the building blocks of Erofeev's self-reflexive narratives—and *a fortiori* of Narbikova's controversial exercises in wholesale citation. Although Kuraev and P'etsukh handle their sources more gently, the indispensability of Dostoevskii (especially his *Crime and Punishment*) for P'etsukh's *New Moscow Philosophy*, and of Gogol' and Dostoevskii for Kuraev's first two novellas, amply demonstrates the authors' fundamental reliance on intertexts.[27] Part of the appeal of both Popovs similarly stems from their clever "recycling" of available linguistic materials: Evgenii Popov's stories consist of an ironic interplay between poetic language and the banalities of overly familiar ready-made phrases (e.g., verbal formulas for daily occasions, political double-talk, vacuous rhetoric, vulgarisms, and jargon) that stresses the creative rather than mimetic potential of language.[28] "Alternative prose," unlike the stylistically naïve exposé novels of Rybakov, Grossman, and Dudintsev, makes its implicitly rebellious point through its highly self-conscious, richly subversive manipulation of discourse. By virtue of resuscitating past works, styles, and ideologies through intertexts, "alternative" prose engages in a linguistic version of historical reclamation. In short, the historical dimension of "alternative" literature involves transforming utterance into quotation.[29]

Tolstaia's luxuriously poetic prose likewise installs and subverts concepts, cultural myths, literary styles, and the very act of narration through ironic intertextuality. Recontextualized citations from multiple sources—poetry and prose, folklore, songs, slogans, and popular clichés—proliferate in her fiction. By embedding this panoply of voices in dialogue, description, commentary on plot developments, and characters, Tolstaia synecdochically packs mini-worlds so tightly into her prose that some readers feel overwhelmed by the wealth of verbal color and variety. In "The Okkervil River,"[30] for instance, Tolstaia orchestrates an extraordinarily sophisticated interplay among a seemingly endless array of voices from Pushkin, Lermontov, Gogol', and Blok; unfurls a series of extended, ornate metaphors that stretch into paragraphs; slides with lightning speed from scrupulously particularized fantasy into fantastic reality, and from comic ridicule to elevated lyricism; collapses and expands time; and anchors her plot in irreconcilable paradox. The sensual pleasure of reading her trope-saturated prose—which, in addition to its assonances and onomatopoeia, features rhythmic patterns inviting poetic scansion—matches the considerable intellectual challenge of understanding it. Of all contemporary prose, Tolstaia's is probably furthest removed both from canonical Soviet style and from the publicistic novels of glasnost.

However innovative and unconventional Tolstaia and other representatives of "alternative" literature may be, they nonetheless subscribe to a mainstream cultural myth: That of Pushkin as supreme poet. It is no accident that Aleksei Petrovich, the mentally retarded adult in Tolstaia's "Night,"[31] who cannot use the bathroom and eat breakfast without his mother's supervision, nevertheless knows Pushkin and wishes to imitate him; that Igor' Odoevtsev in Bitov's "Pushkin's Photograph (1799-2099)" follows the example of his forefather Lev Odoevtsev (of *Pushkin House*) in endeavoring to "capture" Pushkin's life (with the aid of futuristic technology and a camera), and has at his fingertips detailed recall of the minutiae of the poet's official biography; that Iskander has incorporated Pushkin into several short works and his *Eugene Onegin* into "Old Hasan's Pipe" (1987)[32]; and that the entire narrative of Valeriia Narbikova's "Running through the Run" presupposes intimate familiarity with all aspects of Pushkin's personal and literary life.[33]

Almost two hundred years after his death, Pushkin as both man and artist continues to inspire a plethora of fictions. In that sense, Pushkin's case contradicts Foucault's concept of the author as a "functional principle" "by which one impedes the free circulation, the free manipulation, the free composition, decomposition, and recomposition of fiction."[34] Current disillusionment with the credibility of virtually every former political idol has boosted the Russians' long-standing trust and admiration for authors of fiction as repositories of truth. Perceived as both fountainhead and peak of the national modern literary tradition, Pushkin for countless Russians is synonymous with Russian poetry and in that capacity enjoys tropological status. A fleeting mention of his name suffices to conjure up an artistic ideal and the aggregate of inestimable human virtues associated with his mythic persona. Writers as divergent as Zamiatin, Zoshchenko, Bulgakov, and Solzhenitsyn invoke Pushkin synecdochically in their works, confident in their readers' command of the Pushkin code.[35] That universal veneration accounts for the vituperation unleashed by Siniavskii's *Strolls with Pushkin*. Siniavskii's demythologizing separation of man from artist, which enabled him to laud Pushkin's poetic gift, yet at the same time point to his human weaknesses, was for many Soviets tantamount to desecration.[36] The uproar demonstrated that ambivalence and bifocal vision have yet to establish a foothold in the unilinear approach of many Soviets, who resist not only political but also philosophical and artistic pluralism.

Writers such as Tolstaia, Bitov, Kuraev, both Erofeevs, and P'etsukh, whose imaginations entertain myriad options, bring an ironic consciousness even to their most prized synecdoches. Their receptivity to manifold phenomena, which threatens institutionalized monolithic constructs, is at the heart of "alternative prose" in general. Like post-modernism in the West, that prose calls for decentering, detachment in the midst of involvement, and skepticism of closed systems; it installs unresolved contradictions and raises questions to which only provisional and contextually determined answers are posited.[37] Its basic premises about the role and nature of literature, in other words, run counter to the assumptions apparently ingrained in the majority of Soviet intellectuals, including editors of mainstream publications, literary and social commentators, and influential leaders in the professional unions. At this stage, "alternative" fiction is competing for a place in an overcrowded cultural forum more absorbed with investigative journalism than with stylistically sophisticated art. Once the stream of retrieved materials runs dry, as it inevitably must, perhaps the role of "alternative prose" in contemporary Russian fiction will undergo reassessment and its rich potential will gain wider recognition.

Back to the Future...

Creative habits that have been molded by monolithic ideology do not disappear overnight, and to expect sudden masterpieces from experienced writers who have operated by accommodation or through the adoption of an oppositional stance (two sides of the same, and, in this case, devalued, coin) is utterly unrealistic. To hope for an original, independent Russian literature within the Soviet Union, then, is to place one's faith in writers whose prose does not march in tune with glasnost but, rather, bows to the dictates of an inner vision. Dudintsev's *Not By Bread Alone* (1956) and Il'ia Erenburg's *The Thaw* (1955)—during the post-Stalinist Thaw the equivalents of today's exemplary glasnost novels—also captivated readers for extraliterary reasons. Their fate suggests that fiction steeped in journalism or written "to the occasion" may confer temporary glory but ultimately dooms its authors to membership in a passing parade. This is not to say that "alternative" literature is artistically beyond reproach and has nothing in common with canonical or glasnost-inspired Soviet fiction. Like the Soviet economy, which smacks of imbalance, dislocation, and waste, *most* works published in the last few years would benefit from radical cuts, from horizontal reduction (i.e., strict editing) and vertical development (i.e., denser texture). That applies above all to the "blockbuster" novels: But it also, to some extent, holds true for the better crafted, engrossing narratives by such gifted writers as Anatolii Genatulin, Golovin, Ivanchenko, Anatolii Pristavkin, Leonid Shorokhov, and Makanin. Tautological verbs and epithets, occasional overdetermined insights, repetitious descriptions, and overlapping casts of characters also bloat sections of their longer efforts. That slackness no doubt stems from a desire for better communication, while presupposing a public bypassed by modernism—readers initiated into a code largely conceived to outwit a neanderthal censorship, but deprived of the modern æsthetics of minimalism, of ludic interaction, of a language uncontaminated by unmediated and predictable ideology. Current Russian prose, in other words, needs to import an invaluable cultural concept embraced by only a handful of its authors: namely, that less can be more. The swiftly expanding traffic between the Soviet Union and the West today gives cause for measured optimism about the likelihood of such an importation into a country given to paying its writers by the page and the pound. As Henry James noted, however, "it takes a great deal of history to produce a little literature," and freedom from political and cultural constraints offers no artistic guarantees. In the meantime, instead of lamenting the dearth of instant literary masterpieces under glasnost, we might investigate "alternative fiction" not only for the substantial rewards it offers in its own right but also for its partly fulfilled promise of a "brave new word."[38]

Notes

I wish to thank the Kennan Institute for providing conditions that facilitated the writing of this essay during my tenure there as a visiting scholar; Rebecca Epstein for admirably fulfilling her job as my research assistant at the Institute; Vladimir Padunov for supplying me with several useful texts and responding with his usual perspicacity to an earlier version of this essay; and Brittain Smith for making a number of thoughtful suggestions.

1. "The Test by Glasnost," *Moscow News*, No. 45 (November 13-20, 1988), p. 11.

2. "Inflammable," *Moscow News*, No. 43 (December 3-10, 1989), 3.

3. "Our Aliens: The Destinies of Emigrants," *Moscow News*, No. 44 (November 5-12, 1989), p. 15.

4. In an interview Venedikt Erofeev announced that he detects nothing remarkable in today's fiction, but nominates Druk, Prigov and other followers of the Oberiuts as the most promising current poets. "I'll Die Before I Understand It . . .," *Moscow News*, No. 44 (November 5-12, 1989), p. 15.

5. Nora Buks, "Zhurnalistika ili literatura? O publitsisticheskoi tendentsii v sovetskoi proze 80-kh godov," *Cahiers du Monde Russe et Soviétique*, Vol. XXVIII, No. 2 (avril-juin, 1987), pp. 209-220.

6. Natal'ia Ivanova, "Ne khochu byt' chernoi krest'iankoi . . .," *Literaturnaia gazeta*, January 29, 1986. See also Natal'ia Ivanova, "Ispytanie pravdoi," *Znamia*, No. 1 (1987), pp. 198-220. More recently, in an afterward to a Soviet anthology of glasnost prose entitled *The Last Floor*, Igor' Dedkov stressed the "artistic

individualism" of the short fiction that comprises "alternative prose." Igor' Dedkov, "Metamorfozy malen'kogo cheloveka, ili tragediia i fars obydennosti," in *Poslednii etazh* (Moscow: Knizhnaia palata, 1989), p. 420.

7. Reported by Viacheslav Kondrat'ev in *Komsomol'skaia pravda*, October 20, 1988. For more on the episode, see Julia Wishnevsky's "Censorship in These Days of *Glasnost*," Radio Liberty *Report on the USSR*, 495/88 (November 1988), pp. 1-3.

8. See *Sovetskaia kul'tura*, October 15, 1988, and Wishnevsky, p. 4.

9. *Ogonek*, No. 11 (1988), p. 8; No. 14 (1988), pp. 2-9; No. 26 (1988), p. 26; *Sovetskaia kul'tura*, June 16, 1988; and Wishnevsky, p. 6.

10. Michael Massing, "How Free is the Soviet Press?", *New York Review of Books* (September 28, 1989), pp. 55-58.

11. See Venedikt Erofeev's *Moskva-Petushki* (Paris: YMCA Press, 1981), pp. 105-111. The novel was published first in Jerusalem in 1973.

12. Compare Liudmila Petrushevskaia, "Svoi krug," *Novyi mir*, No. 1 (1988), pp. 116-130, with *Bessmertnaia liubov'* (Moscow: 1988), pp. 196-218. Citations refer to the collection and are identified by page number in the body of the text. For a translation of "Svoi krug," see *Glasnost: An Anthology of Russian Literature Under Gorbachev*, Vol. I, edited by Helena Goscilo and Byron Lindsey (Ann Arbor: Ardis, 1990), pp. 3-24.

13. Interview with the author in Moscow, May 1988.

14. Alexander Ivanchenko, "Tekhnika bezopasnosti I," *Ural*, No. 1 (1988), p. 64-90, translated in Goscilo and Lindsey, Vol. II.

15. See Leonid Heller, "Restructuring Literary Memory in the USSR," *Survey*, Vol. 30, No. 4 (June 1989), pp. 47-49.

16. Mikhail Kuraev, "Kapitan Dikshtein," *Novyi mir*, No. 9 (1987), pp. 5-80, translated in Goscilo and Lindsey, Vol. I, pp. 59-185.

17. Petrushevskaia finally succeeded in publishing her first two stories, "Rasskazchitsa" and "Istoriia Klarissy," in *Avrora*, No. 7 (1972), pp. 11-15.

18. For the notorious polemic between Urnov and Sergei Chuprinin, see their two articles, respectively titled "Plokhaia proza" and "Drugaia proza," *Literaturnaia gazeta*, No. 6 (8 February 1989), pp. 4-5.

19. Viktor Konetskii, "Koshkodav Sil'ver," *Znamia*, No. 5 (1987), translated in S. Zalygin, ed., *The New Soviet Prose* (New York: Abbeville Press, 1989). Konetskii's narrative style here departs dramatically from the rather mundane prose of the several collections of seafaring stories he had produced since the late 1950s.

20. Andrei Bitov, "Fotografiia Pushkina (1799-2099)," *Znamia*, No. 1 (1987), translated in Zalygin.

21. Vladimir Makanin, "Otstavshii," *Znamia*, No. 9 (1987), pp. 6-59, translated in Goscilo and Lindsey, Vol. I, pp. 195-270.

22. Mikhail Kuraev, "Nochnoi dozor," *Novyi mir*, No. 12 (1988), pp. 80-114.

23. Ivanova, "Ispytanie pravdoi," p. 201.

24. Readers' reactions to *A Sad Detective Story* included an astute observation by a certain Aleksandr Kucherskii from Khar'kov, which echoes Ivanova, that Astaf'ev's novel is essentially "a monologue with additional voices that constitute

a sort of personification of the author's opinions, comments, and tendencies. These voices, hurried and agitated, are prompted by the desire to say everything all at once and are characterized by extreme arrogance and deliberate crudeness." See "Diskussionnaia tribuna: 'Pechal'nyi detektiv' V. Astaf'eva: Mnenie chitatelia, otkliki kritikov," *Voprosy literatury*, No. 11 (1986), pp. 73-112, translated in *Soviet Studies in Literature* (fall 1988), pp. 8-9.

25. Viacheslav P'etsukh, "Novaia moskovskaia filosofiia," *Novyi mir*, No. 1 (1989). For P'etsukh's own comments on the work, see "Moskva, Sankt-Peterburgskii variant . . .," *Literaturnaia panorama*, No. 20 (May 17, 1989), p. 7.

26. Vladimir Tendriakov, "Donna Anna," *Novyi mir*, No. 3 (1988), pp. 43-61, one of Tendriakov's four first-person narratives devoted to different phases of Stalin's era, translated in Goscilo and Lindsey, Vol. II; Viktor Erofeev, "Telo Anny, ili konets russkogo avangarda," *Panorama*, No. 400 (December 9-16, 1988), p. 26, translated in *Glasnost*, Vol. I, pp. 379-382.

27. See also Mikhail Kuraev, "Malen'kaia semeinaia taina," *Novyi mir*, No. 3 (1990).

28. As Wendy Steiner notes, "[Modernism's] true means of representing reality was not to *re*present at all, but to create a portion of reality itself. And the way to do so was to stress the properties of the æsthetic media in question, since these are palpable, thinglike." Wendy Steiner, *The Colors of Rhetoric* (Chicago: University of Chicago Press, 1982), p. 17.

29. For a subtle, complex analysis of intertexts and banalization in recent conceptualist literature within the broader framework of the (post-)avant-garde, see Mikhail Epshtein's "Iskusstvo avangarda i religioznoe soznanie," *Novyi mir*, No. 12 (1989), pp. 222-235, followed by a counter-view in A. L. Kazin, "Iskusstvo i istina," pp. 235-245. The two articles were published together under the general heading of "Postavangard: Sopostavlenie vzgliadov."

30. Tat'iana Tolstaia, "Reka Okkervil'," *Avrora*, No. 3 (1985), pp. 137-146, reprinted in Tat'iana Tolstaia, *Na zolotom kryl'tse sideli* (Moscow: Molodaia gvardiia, 1987), pp. 16-28, translated in Tatyana Tolstaya, *On the Golden Porch* (New York: Alfred A. Knopf, 1989), pp. 17-29.

31. Tat'iana Tolstaia, "Noch'," *Oktiabr'*, No. 4 (1987), pp. 95-99, translated in Goscilo and Lindsey, Vol. I, pp. 187-194.

32. Fazil' Iskander, "Dudka starogo Khasana," *Oktiabr'*, No. 4 (1987), pp. 68-88, translated in Goscilo and Lindsey, Vol. I, pp. 25-58. Iskander's admiration for Pushkin has assumed a variety of forms, including essays on his work, e.g., "Motsart i Sal'eri," *Znamia*, No. 1 (1987), pp. 125-131.

33. Valeriia Narbikova, "Probeg–pro beg," *Znamia*, No. 5 (1990), pp. 63-87. Reaction to Narbikova's prose–a playful, closely sewn quilt of citations from philosophy, literature, and slogans–has ranged from admiration to disgusted denunciation. Her first publication, *Ravnovesie sveta dnevnykh i nochnykh zvezd* (*Iunost'*, No. 8 [1988], pp. 15-29), was awarded the Boris Polevoi prize in 1988 by the journal *Iunost'*. Whereas Bitov's preface to the story commended the debut of an original, gifted voice from the "mute generation," Urnov (who termed Erofeev's *Moscow to the End of the Line* "clumsily done gibberish") dismissed Narbikova as

incapable not only of wielding language, but of even describing what she set out to−sexual intercourse (Urnov, p. 4). Narbikova's other publications include "Okolo ekolo . . .," *Iunost'*, No. 3 (1990), pp. 10-25, and "Plan pervogo litsa. I vtorogo," in *Vstrechnyi khod*, edited by V. I. Pososhkov (Moscow: Vsesoiuznyi molodezhnyi knizhnyi tsentr, 1989), pp. 118-156.

34. Michel Foucault, "What Is an Author?", in *The Foucault Reader*, edited by Paul Rabinow (New York: Pantheon Books, 1984), p. 119.

35. Specific examples of submerged and overt references that play a crucial role in the thematics and values of the texts in question include Zamiatin's *We*, several stories by Mikhail Zoshchenko (e.g., "Speech About Pushkin"), Bulgakov's *Master and Margarita*, Solzhcnitsyn's *First Circle*, Vladimir Nabokov's *Ada*, and Sasha Sokolov's *Astrophobia*. On Pushkin's significance for Bulgakov, see Helena Goscilo, "His Master's Voice: Pushkin *Chez* Bulgakov," in *Memorial Volume to Honor J. Daniel Armstrong* (Columbus: Slavica Publishers, forthcoming, 1991).

36. Symptomatic of the persistent Pushkin cult is the recent heated exchange between *Voprosy literatury* and *Panorama* regarding the publication of Pushkin's *Secret Jottings of 1836-37*. See "'Treteiskii sud' nad 'Tainymi zapiskami'," *Voprosy literatury*, No. 10 (1989), pp. 256-261.

37. See Linda Hutcheon, *A Poetics of Postmodernism: History, Theory, Fiction* (New York & London: Routledge, 1988).

38. Anyone interested in translations of glasnost literature should consult *Michigan Quarterly Review*, Vol. XXVIII, No. 4 (fall 1989), entitled *Perestroika and Soviet Culture*; Zalygin; and Goscilo and Lindsey, Vols. I and II.

8

Gorbachev and Europe:
An Accelerated Learning Curve

Angela Stent

The first five years of perestroika in Soviet policy toward Europe suggest that Gorbachev learned a great deal—considerably more, one suspects, than he initially bargained for. This implication is particularly noticeable in Soviet policy toward the Eastern half of Europe, of which Gorbachev was a reluctant student forced to accept the bitter lessons of imperial defeat. The West has also learned much about Soviet-European relations, but it has always been a step behind Gorbachev. For a scholar of Soviet affairs, what emerges quite clearly from the first five years of perestroika is that Western specialists had too easily accepted the Soviet view of East European realities: The status quo would continue, not because the populations of Eastern Europe supported their régimes but simply because the Kremlin would hang on to its empire however great the political and economic price. Gorbachev surprised the West—and quite possibly himself—by recognizing that the costs of empire were simply too high if the Soviet Union itself was to survive.

The collapse of the Soviet empire in Eastern Europe was caused primarily by the disintegration of imposed Communist régimes that had never been accepted by local populaces. Gorbachev's moves within the Soviet Union to dismantle the apparatus of the repressive, bureaucratic Communist system also hastened the demise of Soviet-style socialism in Eastern Europe. Yet there was a third factor that contributed to the East European revolutions of 1989—the subversive impact of the Soviet-West European, especially Soviet-West German, détente of the Brezhnev era that ultimately helped to undermine Soviet power in Eastern Europe. One

139

major lesson that Gorbachev has learned since 1985 is that the Soviet Union's policy toward Europe can no longer be bifurcated, as it was during the Brezhnev era. Soviet policy toward both halves of Europe in fact became increasingly interconnected during the 1970s.

In the pre-Gorbachev era, Western scholars who examined either the connection between Soviet policies toward Western and Eastern Europe or the impact of Soviet West European policy on Soviet East European policy usually came up with rather meager results.[1] The whole subject was considered marginal to the study of Soviet policy toward Eastern Europe. Before Gorbachev took power, the Kremlin consistently sought to keep the two halves of its European policy discrete. This was particularly true of its relations with the two German states, although Brezhnev used the promise of closer inter-German relations to seek concessions from the Federal Republic of Germany (FRG). In general, Soviet policy sought to control Eastern Europe and to influence Western Europe.[2] Under Brezhnev and in the early Gorbachev years, the Kremlin tried to calibrate its policies toward both halves of Europe. But it was quite unable to calculate the effects of policy toward one part of Europe on the other. In retrospect, what was advantageous for Soviet Westpolitik (policy toward the West) proved to be disadvantageous for Soviet Blokpolitik (policy toward Eastern Europe). Today, as the Soviet Union struggles to exert any kind of influence on Eastern or Western Europe, it cannot separate the two halves of its European policy. One can discuss Gorbachev's policy toward Western Europe, but the question is whether the Soviet Union indeed has a distinct policy toward Eastern Europe.

This chapter analyzes the learning process in Soviet policy toward Europe by examining three areas: First, the Brezhnev era and the legacy of the interaction between Soviet policy toward both halves of Europe that Gorbachev inherited; second, Soviet policy during the first four years of the Gorbachev era, when the Soviet leader essentially tried to continue the more successful aspects of Brezhnev's policy toward Europe with a more active West European policy than that of the waning Brezhnev and interregnum years; and third, Soviet policy since the *annus mirabilis* of 1989, focusing on Soviet policy toward German unification, which symbolizes the demise of a dualistic Soviet policy toward the two halves of Europe.

The Brezhnev Legacy

It is virtually impossible in the Soviet Union today to find one positive word written about the Brezhnev era, the "era of stagnation." This is true of both domestic policy, inasmuch as immobility increasingly characterized the latter years of Brezhnev's rule, and foreign policy, in which there was in fact much greater mobility.[3] Yet an examination of Brezhnev's policies in Western Europe suggests that the Soviet Union, at least until 1979, reaped considerable benefits from its activities in Western Europe before détente began to undermine Soviet control over Eastern Europe.[4]

From the standpoint of Eastern Europe, détente between the Soviet Union and the Federal Republic was the single most important aspect of Brezhnev's Westpolitik affecting his Blokpolitik. Initially, the Soviet Union's international position was considerably enhanced by the rapprochement between the FRG and the USSR.[5] After all, the government of Chancellor Willy Brandt and Foreign Minister Walter Scheel normalized relations essentially on Soviet terms by accepting the boundaries of postwar Eastern Europe. As a result of the 1970 West German-Soviet Renunciation of Force Treaty, the Soviet Union's international status improved, its economy was strengthened by the significant improvement in Soviet-FRG trade, and the West German public, more and more favorably inclined toward the Soviet Union, developed a stake in the continuation of détente. In the eyes of most FRG citizens, détente with the Soviet Union brought concrete results.[6] Brezhnev's image became much more benign and there was a growing disinclination in the FRG to follow the United States in adopting a harsher policy toward the Soviets under the Carter and Reagan administrations.

The single major reason for the West German perception that détente had worked was also the ultimate cause of the undoing of socialism in East Germany—namely, the improvement in inter-German ties. The promise of closer ties between the FRG and the German Democratic Republic (GDR) was the major quid pro quo that Moscow offered Bonn in return for the recognition of the postwar European status quo. The Inter-German Basic Treaty of 1972 undoubtedly enhanced the GDR's external legitimacy, as it was now, for the first time, recognized by the world community and no longer an international pariah. But détente with West Germany ultimately challenged the GDR's already fragile domestic legitimacy by facilitating the penetration of East German society by the West German media, despite the policy of *Abgrenzung* (demarcation) that Erich Honecker so assiduously pursued.[7] The undermining of East German society was the most dramatic result of Soviet-West German rapprochement. But European détente also facilitated West German contacts with other East European states and contributed to the breakdown of both the real and the symbolic walls between the two halves of Europe.

This development was also reinforced by the evolution of the Conference on Security and Cooperation in Europe (CSCE) process. CSCE was initially viewed in the West as a Soviet triumph, inasmuch as Moscow had been calling for the convening of an all-European conference that would legitimize the division of Europe since 1954. Yet despite the fact that Basket One of the Final Act of 1975 recognized the current borders of Europe and Basket Two pledged both sides to increase economic cooperation, which was clearly more in the USSR's interest than in the West's, the Soviets ultimately paid a price for CSCE. Even though they observed Basket Three more in the breach than in its original spirit, it legitimized the claims of dissident groups in the USSR and Eastern Europe that were becoming increasingly critical of communism. Ultimately, CSCE contributed greatly toward the opening up of Eastern Europe to the West.[8]

The desire to avoid the destabilizing political impact of thorough economic reform in the Soviet Union led Brezhnev to seek détente, calculating that the USSR could import economic modernization from the West rather than tackle it domestically. Initially, it seemed as if the increase in economic ties with Western Europe, especially with the FRG, had brought significant gains to the Soviet economy, especially when the post-1973 oil price rises brought windfall hard-currency gains to the Soviet Union, thereby increasing its ability to import Western technology. Ultimately, however, the Soviets backed away from incurring too great a hard currency debt with the West and also began to realize that, without domestic economic reform, Western imports had limited effectiveness in improving Soviet economic performance. Moreover, Eastern Europe acted as a brake on the full realization of Soviet-West European economic ties because of the USSR's need, for political reasons, to supply Eastern Europe with cheap, soft-currency energy supplies that it could have sold for hard currency in the West.[9]

At the end of the Brezhnev era, therefore, growing restiveness in Eastern Europe was fueled by closer contacts with Western Europe. The impact of Soviet-West European détente on Eastern Europe had proved impossible to contain. In the interregnum years, from 1982 to 1985, when the Kremlin was partially paralyzed in its ability to conduct foreign policy, these trends were exacerbated. As U.S.-Soviet relations deteriorated, Eastern Europe became increasingly concerned that it would lose the economic and political benefits of détente, and cooperative efforts between such unlikely partners as East Germany and Hungary began to challenge Soviet foreign policy.[10] When Gorbachev came into office, he faced an empire that was determined to restore better ties to Western

Europe—a Western Europe that shared the same interest. He responded by emphasizing the theme of the USSR's European-ness early in his administration.

Gorbachev's First Four Years

When Mikhail Gorbachev became general secretary of the CPSU, he was already aware that Europe had become a rather different place from the Europe depicted in official Soviet pronouncements and writings. Indeed, he had begun this learning process well before becoming the Soviet leader. As a result both of his discussions with specialists at the various institutes of the Academy of Sciences and of his own personal travels in Western Europe, his understanding of European developments was considerably more sophisticated than that of his aging predecessors. He knew that the unprecedented military buildup under Brezhnev, out of all proportion to reasonable Soviet security needs, had significantly damaged Soviet interests in both halves of Europe and that this aspect of Soviet policy had to be addressed immediately.[11]

Gorbachev also recognized the significance of European integration and the success of the European Community (EC), despite official Soviet disparagement and nonrecognition of the EC as an institution. Since 1957, Soviet commentators had been predicting the imminent demise of the Community, and Brezhnev's grudging recognition of the EC in 1972 and the subsequent desultory and intermittent talks between CMEA and the EC had done little to change Soviet policy. Gorbachev viewed the EC as a potential model for the Soviet Union and Eastern Europe in two ways. First, the success of economic integration, despite tensions within the Community, was a striking contrast to the weakness of CMEA. Second, the prospect of a thriving single market of 320 million people after 1992 made him aware that the USSR and its partners would become increasingly isolated both from West European economic developments and from the revolution in high technology if the relationship between the Soviet Union and the EC did not improve. Gorbachev also viewed the EC as a political model, thus demonstrating that countries which for centuries had been adversaries could reconcile politically. France and Germany were the obvious candidates in this respect, in sharp contrast to the festering national hatreds within and between the CMEA nations.

Gorbachev apparently learned a third lesson before he became the leader of the Soviet Union: that the attempts under Brezhnev to drive wedges between the United States and its European partners, especially over the issue of intermediate nuclear forces (INF) deployments, had failed. Despite all the endemic tensions within the Atlantic Alliance, it was much stronger than its Communist counterpart.

From his discussions with specialists at the various institutes and Soviet officials in Eastern Europe, Gorbachev was apparently well aware of both the economic plight of these countries and the growing restiveness of their populations. He did not realize just how thin was the veneer of Communist legitimacy nor how weak was the sense of national identity in East Germany, but he did recognize that the Soviet Union's relations with its East European partners had to undergo serious perestroika. In 1985, neither he nor, one assumes, any of the East European leaders would have dreamed that socialism would collapse by the end of 1989.

In one of Gorbachev's first pronouncements on European questions, he stressed that the Soviet Union is a European power and used a phrase taken from Brezhnev, "our common European home." The concept of a common European home has elicited much analysis in both the East and the West, as well as some hyperbole, particularly in Soviet writings.[12] It has also evolved over the past five years, showing a definite Soviet learning curve. In the first few years, the Soviets viewed the concept as a means of encouraging Western Europe to contribute to the economic development of Eastern Europe, implying that there would be a gradual rapprochement between both halves of Europe that might culminate in the unification of Germany. Initially, the Soviets were ambivalent on the question of the United States' role in this common home. As events in Europe unfolded, however, officials' statements on the United States changed and in July 1989, during his landmark speech to the Council of Europe, Gorbachev declared, "The USSR and the United States are a natural part of the European international political structure. And their participation in its evolution is not only justified, but historically conditioned."[13] Moreover, his chief foreign policy adviser, Aleksandr Yakovlev, had hinted even earlier that he could foresee a time when the Eastern rooms in the common home might have "Finnish furnishings."[14]

To some extent, the events of 1989 have rendered moot the question of how the common home will develop. German unification has preceded European unity, and Eastern Europe—at least the Northern tier—has moved beyond Finlandization. Poland, Hungary, and Czechoslovakia are more interested in a common European security pact than in bilateral neutrality treaties with the Soviet Union, and East Germany no longer exists. Nevertheless, the common home metaphor did appeal to West Europeans in the early Gorbachev years and helped legitimize greater East European contacts with the West before the fall of communism.

In his first four years in office, Gorbachev pursued an active policy toward Western Europe, seeking to undo much of the harm done in the late Brezhnev era and under his two immediate predecessors. His policy toward Western Europe was much more active than that toward Eastern Europe and, as it became more flexible, demonstrated his learning process at work. The major successes of his policy toward Western Europe were (1) the conclusion of the treaty eliminating intermediate-range nuclear forces in December 1987, in which the Soviet Union, in order to achieve an agreement with the West, made major compromises on questions of verification, decoupling INF from the question of strategic defense, and the inclusion of British and French nuclear forces, hitherto viewed as non-negotiable issues; and (2) bilateral rapprochements with France and Great Britain and the CMEA-EC Treaty of June 1988, followed by a Soviet treaty with the EC in December 1989 that fully reversed the thirty-year-old Soviet disregard of the Community and demonstrated how seriously Gorbachev took the process of European integration – a fact underscored by his appearance at the Council of Europe in July 1989. Gorbachev's policy toward the Federal Republic of Germany was more cautious; it began to gain momentum in 1987, although he waited until June 1989 to visit Bonn. By the summer of 1989, Soviet-West German relations had greatly improved and were arguably closer than at any time since the heyday of the early Brandt-Brezhnev détente.

As the situation in Eastern Europe deteriorated, Gorbachev became more actively involved in the search for closer economic ties with Western Europe and between Western and Eastern Europe. Despite the changes in Soviet foreign trade law that encouraged joint ventures and much greater West European interest in the Soviet market, economic ties between the USSR and Western Europe did not develop as fast as the Soviets had hoped they would. Hundreds of joint venture deals were signed, but the difficulties in implementing them were considerable. The decline of the Soviet economy and the problem of hard currency revenues as energy prices remained depressed acted as barriers to greater West European economic involvement.

By the summer of 1989, Gorbachev had in essence put his West European house in order. He had substantially improved Soviet bilateral ties with the major West European countries; he had begun the process of developing a multilateral policy toward the EC; economic ties with Western Europe had been strengthened; and, because of the concessions made in the INF treaty, the Soviet Union's image as a country sincerely dedicated to defusing tensions in Europe and pursuing arms control had been enhanced.

But the crumbling East European house proved impossible to put in order. Gorbachev's learning process vis-à-vis Eastern Europe was much slower and far more painful than the learning process in Western Europe, for the obvious reason that the Soviet stake in Eastern Europe was much greater. Learning meant, in effect, giving up Soviet control and reversing a forty-year-old definition of Soviet security. In the first four years, the Soviet leadership correctly perceived that whereas it had everything to gain by changing its relationship with Western Europe, it had much to lose by redefining its ties with Eastern Europe.

Initially, Gorbachev's comments on the relationship between the Soviet Union and Eastern Europe were cautious. Then in February 1986, at the Twenty-Seventh Party Congress, Gorbachev by implication indicted the systems in Eastern Europe as he criticized the Soviet system. He failed to mention "socialist (or proletarian) internationalism" in his speech, emphasizing "unconditional respect in international practice for the right of every people to choose the paths and forms of its development."[15] Nevertheless, until the middle of 1987, Soviet policy toward Eastern Europe continued along traditional lines. By then, Gorbachev apparently understood that his own hopes of restructuring the Soviet economy could not succeed unless his allies began to implement similar measures. During his April 1987 visit to Prague, where he was celebrated as a hero by the disaffected population, he reiterated that although the Soviet Union recognized each socialist country's right to pursue its own path of development, it was necessary that the entire socialist alliance system be restructured. This point was emphasized in his book *Perestroika*: "It goes without saying that no socialist country can successfully move forward in a healthy rhythm without understanding, solidarity and mutually beneficial cooperation with other fraternal nations, or at times even without their help."[16]

From 1987 to 1989, the political, military, and economic situation in Eastern Europe deteriorated as the old leaders, fearful that Gorbachev-style reforms would undermine their power, refused to liberalize and their economies became crisis-ridden. Economic problems and growing ethnic difficulties within the Soviet Union increasingly occupied Gorbachev's attention. Under these circumstances, the Soviet Union had little choice but to move from its commitment to controlling Eastern Europe to the realization that Eastern Europe would either have to reform or face the danger of civil war. Moscow was no longer willing to use its military to keep unpopular governments in power.

In the fall of 1989, Foreign Ministry spokesman Gennadii Gerasimov somewhat disingenuously termed this new outlook the "Sinatra Doctrine," implying that the Soviets would now permit any Eastern European country to develop "its way." In fact, Gorbachev himself intervened at a number of strategic points in Eastern Europe—in Poland during the formation of the Mazowiecki government; in Hungary during September, when the Hungarians decided to open their border with Austria to allow 15,000 East German refugees holed up in the West German embassy to emigrate; and in East Germany itself, to push reluctant Communists toward reform. He was not willing to allow his allies to go "their way" if that meant continued repression and adherence to Brezhnev-style rule. By the end of 1989, the Soviet Union had both passively and actively allowed the old régimes in Poland, Hungary, Czechoslovakia, Bulgaria, East Germany, and Romania to be overthrown by popular movements. Gorbachev did not engineer the revolutions of 1989, but neither did he take a hands-off policy toward them.

By the spring of 1990, after the elections in the GDR, Hungary, and Czechoslovakia, Gorbachev had learned yet another lesson, possibly the most difficult and important lesson of his entire time in office. Soviet-style communism had failed so badly in Eastern Europe that it could not be salvaged. And if communism could not be reformed, it would have to go. As Eduard Shevardnadze said in his remarkably frank address to the Twenty-Eighth Party Congress in July 1990, "Is the collapse of socialism in Eastern Europe a failure of Soviet diplomacy? It would have been if our diplomacy had tried to prevent changes in the neighboring countries. Soviet diplomacy did not and could not have set out to resist the liquidation of those imposed, alien and totalitarian régimes."[17] How far the Soviet Union had come since 1986!

Germany and the Future of Soviet European Policy

Despite Gorbachev's role in facilitating the fall of communism in Eastern Europe and the opening of the Berlin Wall, no one in the Soviet Union—or, for that matter, in any other part of the world—ever dreamed that German unification would be completed a year after the Wall came down. In seeking to understand how Soviet policy toward Germany has evolved since November 9, 1989, we must remember that Moscow was essentially reacting to events that, to a great extent, moved beyond its control.

Although much remains unknown about the developments leading to the fall of Erich Honecker, the USSR's role in this event certainly transcended benign neglect. The revolution that deposed Honecker was indigenous—a product of decades of resentment at living under a repressive system that literally imprisoned its population. But at the decisive moment in early October—when Honecker had decided to use force against the burgeoning demonstrations in Leipzig and other cities—the Red Army was instructed not to assist this repression. The Soviets could have supported a GDR crackdown on dissent but chose not to, as it became increasingly clear that significant numbers of National Peoples' Army (NVA) officers had also decided not to support repression. When Egon Krenz replaced Honecker on October 18, 1989, Gorbachev's congratulatory telegram voiced the hope that the new leadership would be "sensitive to the demands of the time."[18] Soviet Foreign Ministry spokesman Gennadii Gerasimov implied that Gorbachev had warned the GDR leadership during his visit to East Berlin for the fortieth anniversary of the founding of the GDR that they had to "go with the times."[19] This understatement indicates what others have confirmed—namely, that during his visit, Gorbachev, who was the object of adulation by many demonstrators in East Berlin, gave his approval to the ouster of the old régime. However, he anticipated that reform communism would replace the Stalinist system and that the GDR would remain a separate state.

There is every indication that no one around Gorbachev believed that unification would come as quickly as it did. Indeed, the Soviets were surprised by the opening of the Berlin Wall and were not directly involved in that decision. The initial Soviet belief seems to have been that reform communism, in the person of Hans Modrow (who replaced Krenz in December) would survive in the GDR for some time. When FRG Chancellor Helmut Kohl proposed his ten-point plan for unification on November 29, envisaging a three-step process of contractual community, confederative structures, and finally federation, the Soviet reaction was negative, and Shevardnadze stressed that two German states were necessary for the security of Europe.[20] The official Soviet view began to soften in late January, and by February 10 Gorbachev had assured Kohl that he would do nothing to block German unity.[21] Nevertheless, the Soviet leadership reluctantly adopted this position only when it realized that the rapid movement toward unification was unstoppable.

The initial negative reaction to the prospect of German unity and continuing Soviet vacillation on future security arrangements for Germany are quite comprehensible given that, for forty-five years, the Soviet Union had justified much of its foreign policy in terms of the need to prevent Germany from ever again threatening Soviet security, following the two invasions of Russia by Germany in this century and the more than 27 million deaths in the last war. One can debate whether, for the past two decades at least, the fear of renascent German expansionism has indeed had any basis in fact, or whether the Soviet leadership itself believed it.

After all, how could a non-nuclear country of 60 million people pose a threat to a nuclear superpower with 250 million people? Whatever the Brezhnev leadership really believed, the German danger was the major justification for Soviet foreign policy; it was also used to justify all the domestic sacrifices that the Soviet population had made. During the Chernenko administration, the Soviet Union launched a major propaganda offensive against West Germany, alleging that it harbored new "revanchist" designs.[22] When Gorbachev and his generation came to power, one began to see the waning of the obsession with Germany in official propaganda. Yet this obsession remained a major pillar of the older generation's world view. Thus, Gorbachev's former chief conservative critic within the Politburo, Egor Ligachev, expressed a common outlook among members of the older generation and parts of the Soviet military when he warned against the "new danger" of a reunified and powerful Germany.[23]

After the March 18 election in the GDR when, contrary to the predictions of observers in both West and East, the center-right parties defeated the social democrats, it became clear that the pace of unification would again accelerate. Kohl's ten-point plan was rapidly overtaken by events and on May 18 the two German governments signed a state treaty outlining the terms of an economic and monetary union that went into effect on July 1. Germany was unified on October 3 and the first free all-German elections since 1932 were held on December 2, 1990. The Soviet Union was unable to delay the internal processes of unification, however disagreeable the prospect was. The decision in October 1989 not to let Soviet soldiers in the GDR become involved in internal affairs essentially removed Soviet leverage in this situation.

The one area in which the Kremlin did retain some leverage, however, involved the external aspects of German unification, particularly Germany's place in the alliance system. There was clearly disagreement within the Soviet leadership on this issue. The initial Soviet position, reiterating past arguments, stressed that a united Germany had to be neutral. During Kohl's February trip to Moscow, Foreign Minister Shevardnadze said that Germany must be neutral and demilitarized; then, referring back to Stalin's 1952 note proposing a reunified, neutral Germany, he observed that this was "a good old idea that started in the 1950s."[24] Subsequently Shevardnadze modified his position and dropped references to neutrality. Valentin Falin, chief of the CPSU Central Committee's International Department, proposed that a unified Germany remain in both NATO and the Warsaw Pact for a period of five to seven years after unification. Following the first round of the "Two Plus Four" talks between the two Germanies and the Four Occupying Powers held in May, Defense

Minister Dmitrii Yazov reiterated Soviet opposition to NATO membership for a united Germany.[25] Nongovernment spokesmen, however, were somewhat more flexible. Viacheslav Dashichev, a German expert and military historian who serves as a deputy to Academician Oleg Bogomolov at the Academy of Science's Institute for the Study of Comparative International Systems (formerly the Institute for the Economics of the World Socialist System) and who has been an outspoken critic of Brezhnev's policies, gave an interview to the mass-circulation *Bild Zeitung* published on the day of the GDR elections in which he said that the Soviet Union would accept a united Germany in NATO.[26] He later claimed that Moscow's opposition to German membership of NATO was only a negotiating ploy, prompting a Foreign Ministry spokesman to issue a disclaimer: "Professor Dashichev and his political allies are not among the circle of experts who participate in the formation of Soviet foreign policy."[27]

As German unification neared, the negotiations between the four occupying powers and the two German states over future security arrangements intensified. The West insisted that a united Germany must be a full member of NATO, although no Bundeswehr troops assigned to NATO would be stationed on the former territory of the GDR until Soviet troops had withdrawn from East Germany. By the summer of 1990, the NATO card was the one "German card" that Moscow still held, and the Soviets were able to exert leverage because the West Germans wanted to move toward unification by the end of the year. The West Germans offered the USSR considerable economic incentives for a concession on NATO. They agreed in principle to take over all the GDR's economic obligations toward the Soviet Union for the 1991-1995 Five-Year Plan Period, although there are questions as to how a capitalist united Germany will fulfill contracts originally signed between two state-trading countries.[28] On June 22, 1990 (the anniversary of the Nazi invasion of the USSR), the West German government announced that it had extended a 5 billion DM bank credit to the Soviets, the largest ever extended by Western banks to the USSR. The Federal Republic was also willing to make certain security guarantees to the Soviets, including a reduction in the size of their armed forces and a promise that NATO would be restructured to emphasize political, as opposed to military, tasks.

Finally, in July 1990, during Chancellor Kohl's visit to Stavropol', Gorbachev officialy accepted the West's demands: a United Germany would remain in NATO and Soviet troops would withdraw from the GDR by 1994. The Germans subsequently pledged 12 billion DM to help repatriate and retrain Soviet troops, and pledged to reduce the size of their armed forces within a united Germany to 370,000 within four years. Thus, the Soviet Union ultimately helped create a situation that, at least officially, was always depicted as its worst nightmare—a united, capitalist Germany, allied to the United States and firmly anchored in the European Community. That Gorbachev accepted this dénouement is an indication of how much he has been forced to learn.

Conclusion: Europe After Unification

In the next few years, the major benefit that the Soviet Union hopes to reap from the fall of its empire and the unification of Germany is German economic largesse, ranging from credits and joint ventures to technology transfer and management training for the new Soviet entrepreneurial class. Whether this deepening German-Soviet economic relationship can rescue the Soviet economy from its current crisis will depend largely on the Soviet leadership's willingness to introduce more radical economic reforms and accept the inevitable shock therapy for the economy. For the foreseeable future, German entrepreneurs will remain wary of investing in the increasingly crisis-ridden Soviet economy.

One earlier model of Soviet-German relations has little relevance for the future—the 1922 Rapallo Treaty between Germany and Russia, an alliance between two international pariahs that produced closer economic cooperation and also includes secret military ties. The idea of a strong, neutral Germany in alliance with Russia may have a certain appeal in the Soviet Union. But the Federal Republic would have no interest in such an alliance. It would have to leave NATO and the European Community, and be allied to an economically ailing nuclear superpower. By agreeing that a united Germany could remain in NATO, Gorbachev in essence has admitted that he prefers to have Germany firmly anchored in the Western alliance, rather than an unrestrained major power in Europe.

Nevertheless, public opinion within Germany is increasingly questioning the FRG's NATO membership. After all, the East German revolution of 1989 was about self-determination and liberation from foreign domination. The majority of former East Germans favors a demilitarized Germany. And a significant number of West Germans have always supported neutrality. No one is sure what the psychological impact of unification in the long run on the German population will be; but it is likely that many Germans will question why they need any foreign troops on their territory, since for them unification means that they have finally overcome the stigma of World War II and foreign occupation. It is quite conceivable that a future German government before the end of the century, particularly a Social Democratic one, may yet review the whole NATO question.

The security structure of Europe as we have known it for the past four decades may have to change radically because of a shift in German policy. Indeed, the Soviet Union views a united Germany as its entrée into Western Europe, both politically and economically, and it hopes to collaborate with Germany to institutionalize a security system that eventually will make NATO—like the Warsaw Pact—obsolete.

Even if NATO were to disappear, however, the Soviet Union's ability to benefit from this outcome and to assert its power and influence in Europe may be very circumscribed. Some have attributed to Gorbachev a grand strategy in which the fall of the empire was a conscious decision ultimately designed to increase Soviet leverage over Central Europe through the neutralization of Europe.[29] But it is far more likely that the Soviet leader has no blueprint for either part of Europe; that he has been trying to exercise damage control in a situation over which he has decreasing influence. Indeed, it is quite probable that during the next decade the Soviet Union will be so preoccupied with its own internal decline and potential for ethnic civil war that it will play a diminishing role in Europe. The "common home" may include only a small apartment for the Soviet Union, which will be an absentee tenant unable to pay the rent. Even though the Soviet Union will remain a formidable military force in Europe, its political and economic ability to be a major player in the emerging architecture of a new Europe may be reduced over the next few years. Thus, the dream of Rapallo may be replaced by the reality of increasing isolation from Europe, as the new Germany helps the emerging democracies of Central Europe to become viable pluralist states with market economies.

If Gorbachev has learned just how circumscribed Soviet power in Europe may become, what has the West learned? In the past five years, Western opinion on Gorbachev—at both ends of the political spectrum—has moved from skepticism and initial disbelief to the point where many politicians and members of the public believe that his survival is the only hope for the West. Among the vast majority of observers and specialists who believed that the Communist Party's monopoly of power and the immutability of Soviet-style systems were iron laws of postwar history, the recognition that there are no eternal truths, even in the Communist world, has finally sunk in. The comfortable, rather static field of Soviet studies has been revolutionized. As recently as 1989 books were published on Soviet-East European relations which insisted that the USSR could never give up its empire. Now, no self-respecting specialist would venture to give predictions on what might happen within the Soviet Union or, indeed, in Soviet foreign policy within a period of months. The only predictable thing about Gorbachev is his unpredictability.

The fall of the Soviet empire and developments within the Soviet Union have also taught us that the power of Marxist-Leninist ideology pales in contrast to the power of nationalist sentiment in Eastern Europe and the Soviet Union. Take away the veneer of communism, and you are left with raw national and ethnic rivalries, hundreds or even thousands of years old, that modernization has not attenuated. Such persistent ethnic conflict should indeed prompt some major rethinking among social scientists.

The experience of the first five years of Gorbachev in power should humble those who believed that they understood well the systems within the Soviet Union and Eastern Europe. It should encourage us to revise our entire outlook on these countries and their histories, and make us more wary of future predictions. Indeed, it is difficult to imagine what Europe will look like in the next millennium. The future role of Soviet power in Europe will be greatly influenced by the policies that the new unified Germany pursues, once its Eastern sector has been transformed into a fully functioning democracy and market economy. But the future German role in Europe is also impossible to predict.[30] Thus, if Gorbachev has learned anything, he would be well advised to cooperate with the West in designing new structures for Europe—structures which embed Germany in an effective security system that will ensure a constructive German international role in the next century.

Notes

1. The best example of such scholarship is Pierre Hassner, "Soviet Policy in Western Europe: The East European Factor," in *Soviet Policy in Eastern Europe*, edited by Sarah M. Terry (New Haven: Yale University Press, 1984), pp. 285-314.

2. See Hassner, p. 285.

3. See Viacheslav Dashichev, "Vostok-Zapad: Poisk novykh otnoshenii o prioritetakh vneshnei politiki sovestkogo gosudarstva," *Literaturnaia gazeta*, May 18, 1988.

4. See Angela Stent, "Western Europe," in *Areas of Challenge for Soviet Foreign Policy in the 1980s*, edited by Gerrit W. Gong, Angela Stent, and Rebecca Strode (Bloomington: Indiana University Press, 1984), pp. 1-51, 131-133.

5. Angela Stent, "The USSR and Germany," *Problems of Communism* (September-October 1981), pp. 1-33, and Roland Smith, *Soviet Policy Towards West Germany*, Adelphi Paper No. 203 (London: International Institute for Strategic Studies, 1985).

6. See Angela Stent, *From Embargo to Ostpolitik: The Political Economy of West German-Soviet Relations, 1955-1980* (Cambridge: Cambridge University Press, 1980).

7. See Angela Stent, "Soviet Policy Toward the German Democratic Republic," in Terry, pp. 33-60.

8. See Vojtech Mastny's *Helsinki, Human Rights, and European Security* (Durham: Duke University Press, 1980).

9. See John P. Hardt and Kate Tomlinson, "Soviet Economic Policies in Western Europe," in *Soviet Policy Toward Western Europe*, edited by Herbert Ellison (Seattle: University of Washington Press, 1983), pp. 159-208, and Angela Stent, "Economic Strategy," in *Soviet Strategy Toward Western Europe*, edited by Edwina Moreton and Gerald Segal (London: Allen and Unwin, 1984), pp. 204-238.

10. See Ronald Asmus, "The Dialectics of Détente and Discord: The Moscow-East Berlin-Bonn Triangle," *Orbis*, Vol. 287, No. 4 (winter 1985), pp. 743-774, and A. James McAdams, "The New Logic of Soviet-East German Disputes," *Problems of Communism*, Vol. 34, No. 5 (September-October 1988), pp. 47-60.

11. Mikhail S. Gorbachev, *Perestroika* (New York: Harper and Row, 1987), Chapter 3.

12. For a discussion of the evolution of this concept, see Neil Malcolm, "'The Common European Home' and Soviet Policy," *International Affairs*, Vol. 65, No. 4 (autumn 1989), pp. 659-675; and Gerhard Wettig, "The Soviet Concept of Security in a Common European Home," *Bundesinstitut fuer Ostwissenschaftliche und internationale Studien, Bericht*, No. 13 (1990).

13. Speech to the Council of Europe, July 6, 1989, reported on Moscow TV, in *FBIS-SU*, July 7, 1989, pp. 89-129.

14. Aleksandr Yakovlev interviewed in *Die Zeit*, May 12, 1989.

15. "Political Report of the CPSU Central Committee," delivered February 25, 1986, by Mikhail S. Gorbachev, in FBIS-SU-111, February 26, 1986, pp. 1-42.

16. Gorbachev, p. 161.

17. *The New York Times*, July 4, 1990.

18. Cited in Radio Free Europe *RFE Report* 14, No. 42, October 20, 1989, p. 10.

19. Radio Free Europe *RFE Report* 14, No. 43, October 27, 1989, p. 7.

20. Radio Liberty *Report on the USSR*, No. 49, December 8, 1989, p. 20.

21. *The Washington Post*, January 31, 1990 and February 11, 1990.

22. See G. Kirillov's "FRG: Reviving the 'Ewig Gestrige'," *International Affairs (Moscow)*, No. 10 (1984).

23. *The Washington Post*, February 8, 1990.

24. *The Washington Post*, February 11, 1990.

25. Interview in *Rabochaia gazeta*, cited in Radio Liberty *Report on the USSR*, Vol. 2, No. 20, May 18, 1990, p. 31.

26. *Bild Zeitung*, March 18, 1990.

27. Radio Liberty *Report on the USSR*, Vol. 2, No. 15, April 13, 1990, p. 37.

28. Heinrich Machowski, *Aussenwirtschaftliche Verflechtung zwischen der DDR und der UdSSR* (Berlin: April 1990). Report for the Federal Economics Ministry.

29. See Eugene V. Rostow's "Beware of Soviet-German Friendship," *The Wall Street Journal*, June 27, 1990.

30. For a discussion of Germany's future international role, see Angela Stent, "The One Germany," *Foreign Policy*, No. 81 (winter 1990-1991), pp. 53-70.

9

Perestroika and U.S.-Soviet Relations: The Five-Year Plan No One Devised

Robert T. Huber

The first five years of perestroika produced myriad lessons for scholars and policymakers, particularly with respect to the conduct and study of Soviet foreign policy and U.S.-Soviet relations. Several generally accepted U.S. and Soviet assumptions about each other's foreign policy changed to an astonishing degree in the five years between 1985 and 1990. Not all of these assumptions were universally accepted by scholars or policymakers five years ago. Indeed, many scholars have suggested that they neglect a number of important and evolving factors that could modify dominant clichés and frames of reference, including generational change among U.S. and Soviet foreign policy élites, and the complex, variegated character of international politics that limits the usefulness of analysis focused primarily on state-to-state relations.

As of March 1985, Washington "mainstream" official assumptions (as well as many in the scholarly community) about Soviet policy toward the United States and the international system included the following tenets: (1) While necessary steps must be taken in conjunction with the Soviet Union to reduce the risk of nuclear war, the Soviet Union has been the most critical threat to U.S. interests both in Europe and in developing areas. (2) U.S. military power has needed to be modernized and maintained in the face of a growing Soviet military capability, and friends and allies of the United States have had to be bolstered through increased amounts of military collaboration and assistance. (3) Pro-Soviet governments, particularly in developing countries, have threatened both U.S. global interests and regional stability, and must either be contained or, if possible, overthrown by means of support for internal opposition forces or direct military intervention. (4) Free market economic systems are preferable to state socialist economic systems or even free-market systems with a large state sector. The encouragement of free-market systems through assistance and the use of the structures of the international economic system has been essential to counter Soviet exploitation of the grievances of developing countries toward industrialized countries. And (5) international disputes and domestic unrest in developing countries can be resolved through the application of liberal democratic principles including basic human rights, orderly change, compromise, and the building of stable institutions; but the use of power and force against the Soviet Union and its allies is a valid principle if used for self-defense against the perceived greater evil of totalitarianism.[1]

In Moscow, conversely, the basic assumptions about U.S. foreign policy toward the Soviet Union and the international system in general included these tenets: (1) The eventual triumph of socialism over capitalism, despite its setbacks in the early 1980s, will eventually take place; hence the adversarial nature of U.S.-Soviet relations is a permanent feature of the international system and has actually intensified. (2) Although ideological differences have not obviated the need for negotiations with the West where benefits could be obtained, the aggressive nature of U.S. policy under the Reagan administration made successful negotiations far more difficult. (3) The U.S. military modernization program, particularly the Strategic Defense Initiative (SDI), was designed to achieve military superiority over the Soviet Union; hence additional Soviet military modernization has been necessary. (4) The Soviet Union has an obligation, as the socialist superpower, to support national liberation movements seeking to overthrow repressive capitalist control; moreover, it has reserved for itself the role of supporting such movements as well as established pro-Soviet states in the developing world. And (5) the principle of inviolability of borders, as established in the Conference on Security and Cooperation in Europe (CSCE), was threatened by U.S. efforts to undermine the stability of socialist states in Eastern Europe through economic and ideological warfare; the Soviet Union has reserved the right to protect the socialist character of those states.[2]

Even a cursory examination of these assumptions five years later, in 1990, reveals how irrelevant most of them have become. Rather than seeking further advances in its military arsenals, the Soviet Union has thoroughly revised its military doctrine (including force structures and the nature of equipment), and cut back its defense budget. It has also considerably reduced its support for national liberation movements and even pro-Soviet governments in the Third World. Indeed, a disillusioned consensus has developed among Soviet foreign policy specialists concerning revolutionary prospects in the Third World, as well as the strategic and political value of a large foreign policy commitment to existing allies.

Similarly, the profound U.S. policymaking concern about the Soviet Union as a source or instigator of regional instability has been dramatically diminished by the Soviet Union's willingness to withdraw its troops from Afghanistan, to play a constructive role in both the removal of Cuban troops from Angola and the transition to a liberal democratic structure in Namibia, and to play a tacit role in efforts to reduce the prospect of another regional war in the Middle East. Moreover, its interest in participating in the International Monetary Fund (IMF), the General Agreement on Trade and Tariffs (GATT), and the World Bank, as well as their acquiescence in the collapse of the Council for Mutual Economic Assistance (CMEA) amounts to a tacit acknowledgement of the failure of state socialist economics.

Likewise, the Soviet perspective on U.S. foreign policy, which had exhibited a clear-cut pessimism about U.S. intentions toward the Soviet Union with respect to security issues, was built on dubious assumptions. Unprecedented nuclear and conventional arms reduction agreements have been concluded as of 1990; and the perceived U.S. quest for nuclear superiority has proved unfounded, given the growing difficulty that various nuclear weapons delivery systems are likely to encounter in upcoming budget cycles. In addition, the expected U.S. onslaught of aggressive behavior in the Third World, while not without some validation in the conduct of U.S. foreign policy, has not occurred. The United States' support for the anti-Communist forces in Afghanistan did not produce the expected overthrow of the pro-Soviet government, and its support for similar forces in Nicaragua and Angola was unfocused and largely ineffective.

In short, what seemed so clear and convincing just five years ago now seems out of touch with reality. How could both U.S. and Soviet policymakers have been so wrong? How could decades of scholarship, which to a considerable degree helped build the foundations of official policy, have produced a paradigm of Soviet foreign policy with such poor predictive capability? What did Gorbachev learn about U.S. foreign policy and the making and conduct of Soviet foreign policy? What are the lessons for both scholars and policymakers in the years ahead? The following discussion attempts some preliminary responses and proposes corrective measures.

Soviet New Thinking

Soviet foreign policy in the first five years of perestroika has been described as "new thinking" — a misnomer as "new thinking" in fact becomes established thinking. It is difficult to ascertain whether such new thinking is a function of Gorbachev's own reformulation of the basic assumptions of policy, or a response to what he and his supporters in the foreign policy establishment regarded as a foreign policy not well served by conventional assumptions in 1985.

Perestroika in foreign policy has not emanated from the top alone but has also involved the assumptions, concepts, and policy initiatives proposed by various foreign policy specialists. The changes that have developed have been largely uncalculated but are often the results of experiments in policy formulation that solidified into stated policy objectives. Some policy initiatives have become even bolder as the response to those initiatives has demanded a faster pace of change.

The results of perestroika have been a dramatic revision of Soviet foreign policy pronouncements and implementation, both of which, to varying degrees, have shifted throughout the period of Soviet rule, especially since the Twentieth Communist Party Congress held in 1956. Gorbachev's foreign policy direction is more starkly rooted in change than in continuity. His new thinking has included a number of elements: (1) An intensified integration of domestic and foreign policy objectives, with the latter subordinated to the former but mutually reinforcing whenever possible; (2) an expansion of the scope of peaceful coexistence and a deemphasis on militarized, bipolar correlation of force calculations in order to enable much greater degrees of superpower cooperation in economic trade, even when such cooperation implies the failure of socialism and actively undermines the political fortunes of pro-Soviet political movements and systems; (3) a rejection of the concept of class struggle as a principal factor explaining the conduct of foreign relations by capitalist states; (4) an emphasis on the destabilizing influence of the possession of nuclear weapons, a rejection of traditional notions of deterrence, efforts to achieve security primarily through unilateral military procurements and a balance of power calculus, and a stress on the necessity for security to be achieved through coordination of deescalation and disengagement in Europe and elsewhere; (5) a corresponding doctrinal revision of requirements for Soviet force structures ("equivalence in terms," "reasonable sufficiency," and "defensive defense") as well as a raised threshold of likely Soviet military intervention through the calculated abandonment of past pronouncements on the defense of pro-

Soviet regimes, including those in Eastern Europe; (6) a corresponding emphasis on global security and the peaceful resolution of conflicts through economic and political means and mechanisms such as the United Nations and its agencies, the World Bank, GATT, the IMF, and other ad hoc arrangements, as a consequence of perceptions of growing global economic and environmental interdependence; (7) the de-ideologization of Soviet history, including the history of Soviet foreign policy, so as to challenge the legitimacy of previous foreign policy assumptions and its domestic components, and to encourage the delimiting of policy alternatives.[3]

It was to be expected that the increasingly radical revision of Soviet foreign policy would meet with basic skepticism among Washington policymakers. Not surprisingly, the political establishment in the United States enshrined the "watch his deeds, not his words" dictum as a cardinal principle of interstate relations that even to this day strikes a resonant chord. Nonetheless, with each passing year, that supposedly wise policy prescription has increasingly become the prescription for a reactive U.S. policy at best, and a destructive policy paralysis at worst.

Soviet foreign policy decisionmakers under Gorbachev have in fact been more than willing to match revolutionary pronouncements with revolutionary transformations. The so-called zero-option proposal, which prompted an earlier Soviet government to walk out of intermediate-range nuclear weapons negotiations, became the basis for an eventual agreement with respect to those weapons. The Soviet troop presence in Afghanistan, once considered to be part of a calculated military strategy for securing access to the Persian Gulf oilfields, was withdrawn in orderly fashion. And military assistance to national liberation movements and pro-Soviet governments in the developing world, regarded as a critical element of influence-building in Soviet foreign policy, was scaled back. Indeed, Soviet disarmament proposals with respect to chemical weapons, conventional weapons, and nuclear testing have not only matched U.S. initiatives but have included even more comprehensive measures in terms of both levels of reduction and verification procedures.

What led Gorbachev and other Soviet foreign policy decisionmakers to undertake such revolutionary transformations? Why did the more marginal foreign policy adjustments typically undertaken by political leaders prove insufficient? These questions have numerous possible answers; but there is a growing consensus that Gorbachev reached the conclusion, as did a number of his advisers even prior to his accession to general secretary, that past foreign policy practices had been an abject failure and that the agenda Gorbachev had established in domestic policy would by its very nature require unprecedented changes in foreign policy.[4]

As Gorbachev surveyed the foreign policy landscape in 1985, the outlook was dim. Only nine years earlier, at the Twenty-Fifth Party Congress, then General Secretary Leonid Brezhnev expounded with exuberance on the natural link between emerging developing nations and the Soviet Union, the intensification of the class struggle in the Third World in favor of national liberation movements and radical social changes, the growing success of the "revolutionary democratic, anti-imperialist movement," and the doomed failure of counterrevolution and international imperialism.[5] The declaration of victory over capitalism in the struggle for influence in the developing world was indeed premature. The disastrous invasion of Afghanistan and increasingly costly assistance programs in Cuba, Ethiopia, Vietnam, Kampuchea, and Angola made Brezhnev's pronouncements seem ludicrous. Indeed, over the course of the early 1980s Soviet foreign policy specialists had become increasingly doubtful that political upheavals in the developing world served Soviet foreign policy interests. Instead, arguments about the likelihood of military confrontation with the United States as a result of such upheavals were occurring more frequently, while rising costs strained an increasingly burdened Soviet economy.[6]

Soviet policy in the Third World, based on Brezhnev's formulation, provoked reactions among U.S. policymakers that not only undermined the success of Third World gains but also led to increased U.S. activism intended to reverse those gains. As a result, necessary levels of accommodation with the United States were threatened, particularly with respect to arms control. Beginning with the Angolan civil war and culminating in the Soviet invasion of Afghanistan, U.S.-Soviet relations became increasingly antagonistic, radically altering the political environment under which arms control negotiations were conducted and producing a growing consensus for rearmament in U.S. domestic politics. The collapse of the SALT II agreement in the Senate, major increases in defense spending, and the formulation of the Reagan Doctrine reflected an aggressive assertiveness in U.S. foreign policy that was more disadvantageous from a Soviet foreign policy perspective than the illusory gains of additional, expensive Third World allies.

The disadvantage of U.S. assertiveness was particularly acute in light of the state of the Soviet economy at the time of Gorbachev's selection as general secretary. Declining economic growth rates, worsening living standards in both consumption and health, poor quality goods, and abysmal market distribution systems added up to a litany of Soviet economic failures, which intensified in the late 1970s and early 1980s. In the face of massive economic problems at home, official foreign policy rhetoric on the collapse of capitalism and the need to support national liberation movements in the Third World to hasten that collapse looked surrealistic.

Given the perceived urgency of change, Gorbachev and his advisers moved with remarkable speed and sense of purpose to reform the infrastructure of diplomacy.[7] The postwar generation of Soviet diplomats, well trained by Soviet standards, began assuming positions of authority as part of a conscious perestroika of the diplomatic corps. Increased focus on efficient diplomatic procedure, questions about the cost-effectiveness of foreign policy funds, creativity and flexibility in negotiations, and forthright responses during discussions of Soviet compliance with internationally recognized standards of human rights—all became elements of the day-to-day implementation of new thinking.[8]

Since 1985, cadre turnover rates in the Ministry of Foreign Affairs have reached unprecedented levels. In a manner typical of Gorbachev's personnel strategy in dealing with foreign and national defense bureaucracies, his new foreign minister, Eduard Shevardnadze, was not a veteran diplomat but, rather, the first secretary of the Georgian Communist Party. And his first choice for the International Department of the Central Committee, Anatolii Dobrynin, was not a party official but a veteran diplomat from the Ministry of Foreign Affairs, a long-time institutional rival of the International Department. In addition, Gorbachev replaced ten of twelve deputy foreign ministers as well as nearly all key ambassadors. He also made structural adjustments in order to give greater priority to arms control and human rights considerations in an obvious bow to the goal of increased accommodation with the United States.[9]

Moreover, Foreign Minister Shevardnadze's public remarks to diplomatic audiences put the diplomatic service on an entirely different professional footing. Perestroika in the Ministry was not to be the typical one-time reshuffling of the cadre deck but, rather, an ongoing process in which all topics and problems could be discussed, protectionism and favoritism would be rooted out, accountability to the Soviet people and their elected legislature enforced, and openness in dealing with the public (including explanations of its policies to domestic and foreign audiences) demanded. Intensified efforts have also been undertaken to coordinate and increase funding for foreign policy research at scientific institutions and within the Ministry of Foreign Affairs. These structural changes, while not complete (and not ever likely to be completed fully), became a critical tool in giving operational meaning to new thinking. Gorbachev either already knew or came to learn shortly after coming to power that to transform Soviet foreign policy he had to transform the diplomatic corps as well, through an infusion of personnel ready to accept and advocate radical departures of policy.

Similarly momentous changes were under way with respect to security policy. Gorbachev's decision in February 1987 to launch a major revision of Soviet military doctrine had the clear-cut purpose of justifying "less stringent force requirements . . . that make it possible for Moscow to launch new initiatives in foreign policy."[10] The doctrine of reasonable sufficiency reduced the requirement for offensive nuclear and conventional weapons, which in turn complemented unprecedented Soviet proposals for the reduction of such weapons, particularly in Europe. Accompanying these proposals were equally dramatic verification proposals, also unprecedented in their intrusiveness. The arms control proposals, if accepted, would facilitate defense expenditure reductions that could be used for other economic purposes such as investment in consumer goods and civilian machine-building.

The doctrinal change was more than rhetorical. Like past changes in doctrine, the shifts determined both military objectives and the forces and equipment needed to meet them.[11] Major unilateral force reductions were announced and are being implemented. A ceiling of 195,000 Soviet and U.S. troops has been tentatively agreed to in the ongoing Conventional Forces Talks. And significant reductions in armed forces have been proposed by the government to be approved by the revitalized and increasingly skeptical Soviet legislature.

In achieving this shift in military doctrine, Gorbachev appears to have learned another lesson, although hardly a new one for Soviet leaders: If defense expenditures are to be reduced, military doctrine must be revised. A related lesson, one rather more distinctive and far-reaching in its implications, was also learned: Propose arms control measures greater in scope and depth than those proposed by the United States and its NATO allies, and fall back if necessary on the framework of the U.S./NATO measures. This lesson reflected a situation in which the West was hard-pressed not to accept a positive Soviet answer on its own proposals. In the process, doctrinal changes and other reforms aimed at reducing defense expenditures were further energized.

Yet another lesson learned by Gorbachev during his first five years in power was the need for a public posture that would advance rather than weaken existing Soviet foreign policy positions. In an unprecedented manner, Gorbachev has improved not only the style of official foreign policy communications but also the openness of foreign policy debate. In keeping with the objective of increasing governmental accountability and improving the political climate in which Soviet journalists must operate, open debates about the invasion of Afghanistan, the decision to deploy the SS-20, and even the value of Marxism-Leninism as an organizing framework for the conduct of foreign policy have been conducted.[12] To be sure, not all of the opinions expressed in the Soviet press represent official views. However, the dramatically widened range of views presented to domestic and foreign audiences reflects favorably on the credibility of more official statements of policy emanating from the Party press and the Ministry of Foreign Affairs.

In addition, Gorbachev's team has undertaken conscious efforts to build media relations with the foreign press. Press conferences at the Ministry of Foreign Affairs have been regularized. A press information section has been established with the Ministry in order to routinize and familiarize Soviet leaders and diplomats about the need to be sensitive to media coverage of Soviet foreign policy. And the foreign press corps has been cultivated through the circulation of position papers, press releases, photo opportunities, and the infamous background interviews with Soviet officials. Soviet media relations have taken on a character rather different from the stiff, combative style of the past.

At home, foreign policy coverage has also been upgraded. Radio and television programming not only gives increased attention to the current state of foreign affairs but features in-depth discussion of policy options and past policy failures as well. Increasing numbers of Western policy-makers and scholars are granted the opportunity to speak to Soviet audiences without censorship. While glasnost in media coverage of foreign policy issues is not complete, and not as extensive as coverage of domestic policy issues,[13] Gorbachev has learned what his predecessors would never have accepted: That increased openness about the substance of Soviet foreign policy has the potential to alter the perceptions of Western leaders and their publics about the objectives of Soviet foreign policy.

To summarize briefly, Gorbachev has learned the following lessons about Soviet foreign policy and U.S.-Soviet relations during the first five years of perestroika: (1) Given the apparent shortcomings of Brezhnev's foreign policy and the need to subordinate foreign policy to domestic policy objectives and requirements, policy assumptions and actions had to be radically transformed, rather than marginally adjusted. (2) The transformation of Soviet foreign policy could not have been conducted with existing senior foreign policy cadres. A major turnover was required, as were major revisions in the operational environment of the foreign policy establishment. (3) The security aspects of Soviet foreign policy, if they were to be subordinated to domestic policy requirements, have necessitated major doctrinal change. Sustained support for doctrinal change, in turn, required expansion of the parameters of arms control positions so as to improve the prospects for success. (4) Soviet foreign policy was unsuccessful not merely because of "objective" policy mistakes. Both the type and level of discourse in which foreign policy issues were considered had to be overhauled, with far greater emphasis on public discussion, accountability, and accessibility to both domestic and foreign policy audiences.

Obviously, the making and conduct of Soviet foreign policy toward the United States is a complex international process within the larger environment of states, nonstate actors, and global economic and environmental structures. Included in that environment are U.S. foreign policymakers and scholars, who must relate not only to their Soviet counterparts but to the complex international environment as well. It is therefore appropriate at this juncture to address the second major question of this volume: What have *we* learned from the first five years of perestroika?

Lessons for American Policy

The Reagan administration took office in 1981 with a world view concerning the international system and the Soviet Union that was more clearly and sharply defined than its predecessor. In many respects that world view represented a mirror image of the Soviet world view during the Brezhnev period. Focusing on military power as the primary determinant of influence in international politics, convinced that the Soviet Union sought military dominance and the demise of the U.S. political system, and viewing Soviet-style socialism as a morally bankrupt form of social, economic, and political organization, the Reagan administration spent most of its early years correcting what it saw as insufficient attention to the military elements of U.S. foreign policy. It scuttled past agreements in the security field that it perceived as unfavorable and dangerous to U.S. interests. It put arms control negotiations in a different conceptual framework, seeking deep and asymmetrical reductions in Soviet nuclear and conventional forces. It experimented with a transition from reliance on nuclear deterrence to nuclear warfighting and strategic defense. And, finally, it tended to see political upheavals in the developing world largely through the prism of ideological struggle between socialism and capitalism.

By the time Gorbachev came to power in the Soviet Union, the advantages of a renewed emphasis on U.S. ideology in conducting relations with the Soviet Union had come into serious question. The new arms control framework produced not agreements but walkouts and a stalemate, as well as increasing domestic skepticism about the validity of the new approach, its credibility, or both. As relations continued to worsen in the face of events in Central America, Eastern Europe, and the Middle East, both the Soviet Union and the United States narrowed the definition of what was considered to be an acceptable outcome of any given negotiation.[14] With the shooting down of KAL 007, relations reached their worst point in twenty years, and active negotiations were either suspended or became moribund.

In an effort to break the ice on a "frozen diplomatic landscape partly of its own making,"[15] the Reagan administration in late 1984 commenced a tactical retreat from militarized, ideologized foreign policy. Shortly before Gorbachev's succession, a newly revised framework for arms control negotiations was put into place. Concomitant with Gorbachev's radical revisions of Soviet foreign policy assumptions was the administration's willingness to acknowledge and put into practice the maxim that "ideological conflicts brook no compromises, while power and influence are negotiable commodities."[16] The evolving tendency toward tactical compromise on the Soviet side (indeed, if not wholesale accommodation with respect to the conduct of arms control negotiations) was eventually complemented by a growing pragmatism among U.S. policymakers, who accepted the need to take mutually beneficial approaches to various issues in U.S.-Soviet relations.

Given the Reagan administration's rather clear-cut sense of mission with respect to U.S. foreign policy, its accession to power by an electoral landslide, and the sense of disarray that permeated domestic political opposition, the administration conducted foreign policy with the sense that restoring U.S. military power, challenging pro-Soviet governments in the developing world, and shoring up U.S. friends and allies through dramatically increased amounts of military assistance were urgent priorities that could be successfully met. Though not openly described as such, the international environment and domestic influences on that environment were thought to be malleable and amenable to reinvigorated U.S. military power. The immediate objectives were defense modernization, a commitment of military assistance to friends and allies, and restoration of the perception of a strong presidential leadership.

In fact, the Reagan administration gradually came to realize that the assumed ability of the United States (or for that matter the Soviet Union) to manipulate international relations to achieve its objectives was a dangerous oversimplification. Many conflicts in the developing world (e.g., the Iran-Iraq War, the Arab-Israeli conflict, the war in Lebanon, chronic political upheavals in Africa, and the crisis in South Africa) simply lacked any identifiable cold war tint, despite the rather strained rhetorical attempts by some administration policymakers to color them as such. Although U.S.-Soviet cooperation in reducing political conflict in the Third World was still at a nascent stage, the administration came to recognize that Soviet willingness to confront U.S. interests was more and more limited and, in fact, had become less than U.S. willingness to confront Soviet interests. In the case of Afghanistan, even a reversal of Soviet political fortunes was met with acquiescence. With both powers increasingly aware of the limits of their influence, both sides began the process of devising strategies that would lower the levels of their confrontation and open the way for settlement of regional disputes.

Equally mistaken was the assumption that the U.S. Congress, an often underestimated force in U.S.-Soviet relations, would acquiesce to Reagan's policy toward the Soviet Union. The legislative branch, which had grown in staff size and had undergone a generational change that helped to alter the foreign policy outlook of its membership, experienced a renaissance of activism in foreign policy beginning in the late 1960s, when the Vietnam War produced the first major foreign policy disagreement between the president and the Congress since the interwar period. Although the composition of the Congress became dramatically more conservative after the 1980 election, this development in no way represented a major attitudinal change with respect to institutional activism.

The Democratic opposition in Congress, as well as selected conservative Republicans, used the rather considerable constitutional powers at their disposal to limit, alter, or oppose administration policy, and even, on occasion, to propose the broad outlines of virtual alternative foreign policies. Assistance to the non-Communist forces in Nicaragua became the subject of a long-running battle between the president and Congress, resulting in superheated rhetoric, policy stalemates, and executive branch circumvention of legislative restrictions on assistance. Nagging doubts about the credibility of the Reagan administration's arms control policy led to repeated attempts by Congress to use appropriations power to force new policies with respect to nuclear testing, antisatellite weapons, chemical weapons, the suspended terms of the SALT II agreement, and the amount of funds and operational flexibility allocated to the Strategic Defense Initiative. While most of these restrictions were eventually dropped, they did provide a constant source of pressure on the administration with respect to its arms control negotiating positions in Geneva. The outlines of the negotiating proposals were sensitive both to Congressional opposition, particularly with regard to SDI, and to the continuation of the limits of the SALT II agreement. The administration, against its own preferences, did agree to a prohibition on funds for antisatellite weapons; and production of binary chemical weapons was delayed for several years. In short, the 1980s demonstrated that the flexing of legislative muscle in the formulation of foreign policy was not merely a phenomenon derived from the political aftermath of the Vietnam War. Rather, legislative activism has been institutionalized as a more or less permanent feature of U.S. foreign policymaking. As a result, the making and conduct of policy became more complex and difficult than had been envisioned in the Reagan administration's early foreign policy strategy.

This institutionalization has also been closely observed by both scholars and policymakers in the Soviet Union. Both the scope and the intensity of attention given to congressional activity on international relations issues has increased.[17] Gorbachev has met personally with the entire Democratic and Republican leadership of the U.S. House of Representatives and Senate, and has demonstrated a fairly clear working knowledge of Congress's activities. And hundreds of members of Congress have visited the Soviet Union. A wide number of other interactions—including ongoing contact with the Soviet Embassy, parliamentary exchanges, policy discussions via satellite, participation in arms control and other negotiations through the appointment of House and Senate observer groups and the executive-legislative Commission on Security and Cooperation in Europe, and testimony by Soviet diplomats, military officers, and politicians before congressional committees—demonstrate the richness of what might be called Soviet-U.S. Congress relations. The more dire predictions of a legislature duped into supporting Soviet positions on issues of foreign policy, against the wishes of the White House, have clearly not been borne out by the facts. However, the deepening of discourse and means of interaction between the Soviet leadership and the Congress does provide an alternative channel of communications in superpower relations. This channel, which has endured through both good and bad periods of U.S.-Soviet relations, adds to the complexity of those relations.

The Reagan administration came to power with a profound mistrust of personal diplomacy in U.S.-Soviet relations, and as late as Gorbachev's accession continued to exhibit this mistrust. The famous "backchannel negotiations"—which led to the conclusion of the SALT I Treaty by the Nixon administration, the fear that "deadline diplomacy" and the political pressure to "agree to something" would produce premature concessions, and perhaps the indelicate possibility that President Reagan might not fare well in face-to-face encounters with his Soviet counterpart—were factors that contributed to this mistrust. Accordingly, the administration formulated conditions that would have to be in place before a leadership summit could occur. The entrenchment of its suspicion was reflected in the fact that, although there were no leadership summits between the United States and the Soviet Union from 1979 to November 1985, a string of Soviet general secretaries met with the entire leadership of the U.S. Congress during this period.

In light of what has occurred in the intervening five years, it is clear that American presidents, no matter how conservative, have become rather zealous converts to the value of summitry, which consists in the occasional need to demonstrate political commitment and overcome bureaucratic resistance, the opportunity to negotiate one's way out of a policy cul de sac, and the inculcation of personal acquaintance into the policy calculations of leaders. Conversion to the value of summitry in turn has reduced the impulse to close off channels of communication. The creation of a "known quantity" in the adversary was an important hallmark in all of the Reagan-Gorbachev and Bush-Gorbachev summits: In 1983, the Soviet Union was called "the focus of evil in the modern world"; after the Geneva summit just two years later, President Reagan referred to the new Soviet leader as "our kind of guy."

Furthermore, the fears about "deadline diplomacy" and the pressure to "agree to something" seem to have been removed completely from U.S. negotiating strategy. After five years of a no-summit policy, President Reagan wound up holding more leadership summits than any of his postwar predecessors. The agreements concluded at some of these summits were rather meager. Indeed, the Reykjavik summit produced no tangible agreements at all. Yet the inclination to see the benefits of small agreements seems to have been stronger than the fear that such agreements were only cosmetic and thus ineffective in addressing the serious issues facing the United States and the Soviet Union.

In sum, U.S. policymakers (and, in an indirect sense, scholars of foreign policy) have learned these principal lessons from Gorbachev's first five years: (1) The advantages of a renewed emphasis on U.S. ideological hostility in conducting relations with the Soviet Union were outweighed by its disadvantages, particularly while the prospects for reducing tensions between the United States and the Soviet Union were improving. (2) The conduct of foreign policy in a framework dominated by East-West considerations overestimated both U.S. and Soviet influence in the international environment, particularly in the developing world, and thus led to unproductive uses of military power that actually may have undermined U.S. foreign policy objectives. (3) The president's ability to obtain domestic consensus on the conduct of relations with the Soviet Union has become increasingly difficult. Such a consensus requires the active support of the legislature, which in the 1980s did not endorse many of the president's strategies for achieving his articulated foreign policy goals. Congress' own analytic capabilities, as well as its willingness to exercise broad foreign policy powers, extended to dealing directly with Soviet foreign policy élites. (4) Personal diplomacy between U.S. and Soviet leaders is an important element in the resolution of differences and the expansion of possible parameters of cooperation. If formal policy objectives are to be more fully achieved, a network of leadership communication is required.

A New Framework for Foreign Policy Analysis

The lessons learned from the first five years of perestroika have demonstrated the humbling reality that official policy assumptions on both sides (as well as the scholarship that helped build those assumptions) were a questionable guide to policy formulation and implementation. In terms of predictive capability, such assumptions were virtually useless. Remarkable changes in Soviet foreign policy easily outpaced the ability of policymakers and scholars either to anticipate them or deal with them effectively. In short, public policy and scholarship have in large measure been witnesses rather than participants in a five year "plan" that no one devised.

Where do we go from here? What new directions should be taken by policymaking and scholarly analysis? Can the track record of scholarship in advising policymakers be improved? Will policymakers listen and shed increasingly outdated policy assumptions?

A productive way to deal with these admittedly contentious and difficult questions is to recognize that a more flexible analytical approach to anticipating the future direction of Soviet foreign policy is long overdue. Excessive energy has been expended in the search for the "operating principles" or "permanent characteristics" of Soviet foreign policy. On the whole, this search has not proved a reliable means of achieving an understanding of the Soviet Union's policy actions.

The limits of such an approach have become increasingly apparent over the last five years. We have watched somewhat helplessly as one supposed operating principle or permanent characteristic after another has proved to be neither. "The Soviet Union will never accept the zero-option"; "the Soviet Union will never conclude a strategic nuclear forces agreement without U.S. compromises on SDI"; "the Soviet Union will not support asymmetrical reductions in conventional forces"; "the Soviet Union will not

tolerate the political collapse of Communist states anywhere in the world";
"the Soviet Union will not remove its troops from Afghanistan without an
elimination of U.S. military support for the non-Communist resistance
forces"; "the Soviet Union will never allow East European governments to
be controlled by non-Communist political parties." Given this long parade
of limiting maxims during what has clearly been a delimiting period in
Soviet foreign policy, scholars and policymakers alike would do well to
"never say never again."

Perestroika has shattered the paradigm of a rigid, ideologically driven
Soviet foreign policy. Soviet debates about the mistakes of the past and
the direction of future policy initiatives no longer need to be read only
between the lines. Such debates now occur in the popular as well as the
specialist press and on the screens of millions of Soviet televisions.
Scholars now have access to the daily internal operations of the Soviet
Ministry of Foreign Affairs. Far-reaching exchange agreements are being
negotiated with foreign policy élites and their institutional affiliates. The
revitalized Supreme Soviet, both through its committee structure and by
means of floor debate, is rapidly expanding its oversight activities, seeking
technical assistance on how to build the infrastructure of a contemporary
parliament, and increasingly demonstrating its power to reject or modify
the government's foreign policies. The Ministry of Foreign Affairs, in turn,
has established formal structures to conduct ongoing liaisons with the
Supreme Soviet.

Furthermore, the liberalization of the Soviet foreign policy process
represents a potentially revolutionary breakthrough in the means by which
scholars can conduct their research, thus pointing the way to a different
kind of scholarship in which normal scientific activity is possible. Full
utilization of this opportunity requires that the United States abandon the
rigid formulations and theoretical straitjackets stressing characteristics of
Soviet foreign policy that cannot be replicated elsewhere. Indeed, the
United States' tenacious defense of uniqueness must be replaced by a
comparative examination of foreign policy processes drawn from the
experiences of other states and other processes in the international
environment. Fortunately, some interesting research stressing such
comparisons is beginning to surface.

One such approach is to place Soviet foreign policy in the comparative
context of states or empires in decline. In this way, Soviet foreign policy
initiatives during the first five years of perestroika can be seen as a
response to costly policies of the past, as an attempt to reduce defense
expenditures, as an effort to advance foreign policy objectives with more
prudent use of existing resources, and, above all, as a need for "breathing

space" in which to resolve chronic and continuing domestic economic and political instability. Indeed, analogies to other states—such as Egypt under Anwar Sadat, the United States under Richard Nixon,[18] and especially Ottoman Turkey during the nineteenth and early twentieth centuries—can be studied in an effort to offer hypotheses about the future direction of Soviet foreign policy.

The "Ottomanization" metaphor points to the attempt by Soviet foreign policy to deal with "a long, slow process of imperial decline in the course of which one would see an unplanned, piecemeal and discontinuous emancipation, both of the constituent states from the imperial center and of societies from states."[19] The decline of influence in other states occurs "mainly by uncoordinated independent action, whether individual, collective, or national, by pressure from below or from outside, in an overall context of growing relative backwardness."[20]

Much like the Ottoman empire, the Soviet Union is seen as a Eurasian power with considerable military capability and a repressive political system. Similar to the rapid collapse of Ottoman control in Eastern Europe after a long period of domination, Soviet political and military control of that region has also dissolved. The dilemmas faced by various nineteenth- and early twentieth-century states in "propping up the sick man of Europe" are roughly analogous to the current political debate about whether the West should "help Gorbachev."

Adherents of the Ottomanization metaphor generally have a pessimistic outlook on the future of the Soviet Union.[21] A corrupt party and government apparatus, riddled with nepotism and elitist privileges, limits and vitiates efforts at systemic change through radical reform. The elimination of the prevailing system of government through either peaceful or violent means is required to bring foreign policy commitments in line with resources, and this outcome in turn requires a reduced role for the Soviet Union in the international system.

A different comparative approach sees the Soviet Union and its foreign policy as undergoing a transition from an authoritarian regime to a more relaxed, democratic and liberalized political system, integrated more fully into the international market economy. This approach points to the experiences of southern Europe and Latin America, and seeks comparative similarities in foreign policy formulation during the transitional period.

Thus, the frequent calls in Soviet foreign policy for the creation of a "common European home" and the Soviet Union's stated interest in joining international economic institutions can be compared with post-Franco and post-Salazar Spanish and Portuguese foreign policy, which sought to integrate those countries more fully into West European economic, political, and military institutions. The benefits perceived by the Soviet Union as likely to accrue from its cooperation with international economic institutions can be compared to the benefits that post-fascist Italy expected as a result of its participation in the Marshall Plan.

In addition, the new emphasis on global interdependence and the utilization of the United Nations in resolving regional disputes and global economic and environmental problems is regarded in this computative analytical approach as an effort to reduce rigid isolationist or dogmatic tendencies—a process that also took place in the transitional phases of Spanish, Portuguese, and Greek foreign policy.[22] Italy's decision to join NATO because the international climate had forced the consolidation of military blocs may be likened to the Soviet Union's interest in a more accommodationist foreign policy so as to loosen such blocs. Tight bipolarity and high levels of confrontation in the international environment are also seen as constraining the domestic political struggle, thus limiting the acceptable political parameters of socioeconomic transformations.[23] Changes in Soviet military doctrine and defense expenditures, subjection of the defense establishment to public accountability, and a decreased political role for the military are seen as roughly analogous to efforts to deal with these issues by transitional regimes in Latin America and southern Europe.[24]

Supporters of the "transition" metaphor stress the effects of modernization, industrialization, education, and generational change on shaping attitudes toward domestic and foreign policy. They posit a differentiated pattern of élite interests and objectives among the establishment, held together by the consensus that changes in foreign policy direction are needed. The postwar Soviet foreign policy establishment has had the benefit not only of a relatively calm period but also of a learning curve in foreign policy that its predecessors did not have.

The ability of supporters of new thinking to draw upon the experiences of past failures and propose new approaches seems far more in keeping with the dynamism of the foreign policy process under way in the Soviet Union than the image of a desperate Ottoman despot lurching from one concession to another in an effort to buy time. The transition to a more democratic political system indicates not decline so much as the possibility of a transformed foreign policy that gives meaning to Gorbachevian rhetoric concerning the rule of law, common human values, and socialist democracy. Soviet foreign policy has both the opportunity and the means to silence quickly any self-congratulatory rhetoric about the West's victory in the cold war by portraying the USSR as "more willing to run risks for a safer and less militarized international order, more committed to strong and effective international institutions, and more ready to free us from the contests of the past."[25]

In addition to explicit comparative research, major challenges lie ahead with respect to the rigorous, piece-by-piece inductive contributions being made to the study of Soviet foreign policy. Relatively little research has been conducted on the role of the Supreme Soviet in defense and foreign policy. The Presidium of the Supreme Soviet contains advisers with considerable foreign policy experience. The chairman of the Council of the Union is an Americanist. The joint International Affairs Commission has three active subcommittees, two of which are headed by Americanists. The committee is staffed with foreign policy experts who are actively participating in rewriting the Soviet Constitution, including a crucial portion dealing with the war powers of the Soviet government. And active hearings on foreign policy issues, including testimony by Secretary of State James Baker and former President Reagan have been conducted. The Supreme Soviet has not only rejected nominees for foreign policy positions, but has also debated a whole range of foreign policy issues including arms reduction agreements and other aspects of relations with the United States, relations with Eastern Europe, the situation in Afghanistan, foreign trade policy, and legal parameters for joint ventures with foreign firms. An important symbol of the growing importance of the Supreme Soviet in foreign policy has been the establishment of a legislative liaison office in the Ministry of Foreign Affairs.

Given the growing amount of legislative activity, attention to literature about the U.S. Congress and other parliaments will be needed if we are to understand more fully the future direction of Soviet foreign policy. The formal and informal sources of foreign policymaking in the Supreme Soviet, the nature and effect of rules and procedures for the consideration of foreign policy issues, executive-legislative relations and coalition-building among foreign policy élites in the government and the legislature, the development and intensity of legislative involvement in foreign policymaking, the role of elections in the making and conduct of Soviet foreign policy, the effects of ethnicity and ethnic groups on foreign policy, and the role of the media and public opinion in affecting legislative decisions in foreign policy—all are major foreign policy processes requiring further investigation.

But comparative research is not without its problems. There clearly exists no model for the transition of a state socialist political system to a system combining a market-oriented economy, a more democratized form of government, and a fundamentally different foreign policy. Given past experiences with models and operating principles, the effort to anticipate and explain the future course of Soviet foreign policy may be better off without such models. Nonetheless, comparative research does offer exciting opportunities for cross-national analysis of foreign policy that previously has not been possible. Such research potentially allows us to ask new questions, posit new explanations, and steer clear of past research mistakes with respect to Soviet foreign policy.

The implications of "never say never again" are also significant in relation to the future actions of U.S. policymakers. As a consequence of the dramatic expansion of the arms control agenda, "unprecedented" arms reductions agreements could soon look obsolete. Already Soviet arms control experts are exploring the benefits of a "minimum deterrence" strategy in which nuclear weapons are viewed as a useful transition to nonnuclear deterrence. Such a proposal, according to perestroika in Soviet foreign policy, is certainly well within the range of possible Soviet proposals. One such proposal is to reduce current stockpiles not by 50 percent, but by 95 percent. In Europe, political leaders still advocate a U.S. troop presence, but the magnitude of that presence—195,000 troops—may not be politically sustainable either in Western Europe or in the United States. Comprehensive agreements to ban chemical weapons production and stockpiles in both the United States and the Soviet Union, as well as a major reduction if not a ban on nuclear testing, will undoubtedly be within reach given the current political climate for greater U.S.-Soviet arms control agreements and the general Soviet acceptance of on-site verification measures.

German reunification has also moved to the center of the European political agenda. To date, the member-states of NATO have been willing to support reunification if the new German state remains a member of that organization. The Western position is based on the traditional but politely understated ancillary purpose of NATO: to deter and harness German military power.

But the comfort that U.S. and West European political leaders derive from a NATO solution to German reunification may be short-lived. The 1990 elections in the German Democratic Republic led to a vote in that country to join the Federal Republic of Germany. A remarkably rapid political reunification has taken place. But what are the implications of reunification for German internal stability? How will problems of economic dislocation be dealt with? As Soviet internal economic problems mount, will a reunified Germany be drawn toward the traditional exercise of *Schaukelpolitik*, positioning itself, even if it remains a member of NATO, toward both East and West depending on the advantages of the moment?

The NATO structure itself will undergo considerable examination in the years ahead. The underlying trans-Atlantic bargain, in which U.S. predominance in both the making and the burden of security policy conduct has been evident, will be increasingly challenged as troop and equipment reductions as well as new political alignments fundamentally transform the security environment in Europe. The doctrinal justification for a whole class of nuclear weapons—short-range tactical nuclear weapons—evaporated in the course of a few months in 1989 as a result of the political upheaval in Eastern Europe. As economic cooperation under the framework of the European Community draws the economies of West European states closer together, the already established EC framework for cooperation on political matters could be expanded to include security decisionmaking and defense procurement. Decisions on future defense commitments could well drift away from the NATO structure and toward the EC. In addition, as the urgency of the disarmament agenda eases, the domestic political priorities inherent in Soviet foreign policy could shift attention away from security-based Soviet relations with the United States and toward economic-based relations with EC member states.

All such possible future directions will have to be at least considered by U.S. scholars and policymakers. And the actual developments will fundamentally test our abilities to move beyond earlier foreign policy assumptions about the Soviet Union. How the United States responds to the accelerating pace of change and to the increasingly popular calls for a much more ambitious disarmament agenda and a transformed framework for the conduct of international security is a question that will acquire greater importance with the passage of time. Advancing U.S. foreign policy objectives and scholarship after the first five years of perestroika will require more than simply waiting for a declining Soviet empire to make the next concession on major issues of international affairs. Moreover, if the United States frames its responses based on assumptions of a Soviet foreign policy thought to be rigidly ideological and immutable in the pursuit of its interests, it will reveal the rigidity and lack of imagination in its own foreign policy. New approaches to the study of the future direction of Soviet foreign policy will require that policymakers be properly informed. The policymakers in turn must recognize that new thinking must emanate not only from Moscow but from Washington as well.

Notes

1. For a full discussion of official U.S. policy assumptions about Soviet foreign policy, see United States Congress, House of Representatives, Committee on Foreign Affairs, *Soviet Diplomacy and Negotiating Behavior—1979-1988: New Tests for U.S. Diplomacy*, by Joseph G. Whelan of the Senior Specialists Division, Congressional Research Service, Library of Congress (Washington, DC: U.S. Government Printing Office, 1988), pp. 163-167, 208-210.

2. For discussion of official Soviet policy assumptions about U.S. foreign policy, see Whelan, pp. 204-208.

3. For a more complete discussion of the various tenets of "new thinking" in Soviet foreign policy, see Whelan, pp. 635-650; also see Robert Legvold, "The Revolution in Foreign Policy," *Foreign Affairs*, Vol. 68, No. 1 (1988-1989), pp. 84-91, and George W. Breslauer, "Thinking About the Soviet Future," in *Can Gorbachev's Reforms Succeed?*, edited by George W. Breslauer (Berkeley: Berkeley-Stanford Program in Soviet Studies, Center for Slavic and East European Studies, 1990), pp. 1-2, 14-17, 22-24.

4. For further discussion on the linkage between domestic and foreign policy objectives in "new thinking," see Whelan, pp. 644-646, and Legvold, p. 83.

5. For a complete analysis of Brezhnev's foreign policy report at the Twenty-Fifth CPSU Congress, see U.S. Congress, House of Representatives, Committee on Foreign Affairs, *The Soviet Union in the Third World: An Imperial Burden or Political Asset?*, by Joseph G. Whelan of the Senior Specialists Division, Congressional Research Service, Library of Congress (Washington, DC: U.S. Government Printing Office, 1985), pp. 18-25.

6. For a full discussion of the debates among *mezhdunarodniki* concerning Soviet foreign policy in the Third World, see Whelan, *The Soviet Union in the Third World*, pp. 33-53; for a sampling of such debates, see E. Khristich, "Programma 'kollektivnoi opory na sobstvennye sily," *Mirovaia ekonomika i mezhdunarodnye otnosheniia*, No. 6 (June 1982), pp. 120-128; I. Zorina, "Razvivaiushiesia strany i politicheskaia struktura sovremennogo mira," *Mirovaia ekonomika i mezhdunarodnye otnosheniia*, No. 8 (August 1982), pp. 80-91; and Iu. S. Novopashin, "Vozdeistvie real'nogo sotsializma na mirovoi revoliutsionnyi protsess: Metodologicheskie aspekti," *Voprosy filosofii*, No. 8 (August 1982), pp. 3-16.

7. For an analysis of the structural and personnel changes in the Soviet Ministry of Foreign Affairs, as well as the postwar training and work environment for Soviet diplomats, see Whelan, *Soviet Diplomacy and Negotiating Behavior*, pp. 587-595; Teddy J. Uldricks, "The Tsarist and Soviet Ministry of Foreign Affairs," in *The Times Survey of Foreign Ministries of the World*, edited by Zara Steiner (London: Times Books, 1982), pp. 514-535; and Vernon Aspaturian, *The Soviet Foreign Policy Apparatus*, The Woodrow Wilson Center, Kennan Institute for Advanced Russian Studies, Report of Meeting on November 16, 1987.

8. See, for example, Foreign Minister Shevardnadze's speech to the Ministry of Foreign Affairs, *Vestnik Ministerstva inostrannykh del SSSR*, No. 1 (August 5, 1987).

9. Whelan, *Soviet Diplomacy and Negotiating Behavior*, pp. 601-602.

10. Michael MccGwire, "Update: Soviet Military Objectives," *World Policy Journal*, Vol. 4 (fall 1987), p. 723.

11. For more on the importance of doctrinal changes to Soviet force procurements, see MccGwire, pp. 723-725.

12. For a thorough analysis of the "politicization" of the Soviet media and its effects on career advancement, see Thomas F. Remington, "Politics and Professionalism in Soviet Journalism," *Slavic Review*, Vol. 44 (fall 1985), pp. 489-503. For more on debates about foreign policy issues, see Stephen Sestanovich, "Gorbachev's Foreign Policy: A Diplomacy of Decline," *Problems of Communism*, Vol. 37 (January-February 1988), pp. 2-7, and David Holloway, "'New Thinking' Abroad and the Military's Stake in Reform at Home," in Breslauer, pp. 113-117.

13. For more on the scope of foreign policy debates, see Holloway, pp. 113-114.

14. The phenomenon of narrowing parameters in negotiations so as to preclude agreement during periods of poor U.S.-Soviet relations is described in full detail in Strobe Talbott, *Deadly Gambits: The Reagan Administration and the Stalemate in Nuclear Arms Control* (New York: Alfred A. Knopf, 1984).

15. Whelan, *Soviet Diplomacy and Negotiating Behavior*, p. 239.

16. William G. Hyland, "East-West Relations," in *Gorbachev's Russia and American Foreign Policy*, edited by Seweryn Bialer and Michael Mandelbaum (Boulder: Westview Press, 1988), p. 445.

17. For a full discussion of Soviet analysis of the role of the U.S. Congress in American foreign policy and the myriad of interactions between Soviet policymakers and social scientists and the Congress, see Robert T. Huber, *Soviet Perceptions of the U.S. Congress* (Boulder: Westview Press, 1989).

18. For further discussion of such comparisons, see Sestanovich, pp. 1-2.

19. John Evans, *Exploring the "Ottomanization" Metaphor*, The Woodrow Wilson Center, Kennan Institute for Advanced Russian Studies, Report of Meeting on February 5, 1990.

20. See Note 19.

21. Breslauer divides views of American scholars with respect to the future evolution of the Soviet Union into two basic categories: optimists and pessimists (see Breslauer, pp. 4-32). Pessimists generally use words like "decline" and "monolithic ideology," and do not regard the ruling structure as differentiated and composed of conflicting views on society's problems. Such an outlook is fully consistent with the Ottomanization metaphor. See, for example, Kenneth Jowitt, "Soviet Neo-Traditionalism: The Political Corruption of a Leninist Régime," *Soviet Studies* (July 1983).

22. For three excellent articles on the transition from authoritarianism in Spain, Portugal, and Greece, see respectively Jose Maria Maravall and Julian Santamaria, "Political Change in Spain and the Prospects for Democracy," Kenneth Maxwell "Régime Overthrow and the Prospects for Democratic Transition in Portugal," and P. Nikoforos Diamondouros, "Régime Change and the Prospects for Democracy in Greece: 1974-1983," all in *Transitions from Authoritarian Rule: Southern Europe*, edited by Guillermo O'Donnell, Philippe C. Schmitter, and Laurence Whitehead (Baltimore: The Johns Hopkins University Press, 1986), pp. 71-108, 109-137,

138-164. For a Soviet discussion that touches on similar issues, see E. Shevard-nadze, "Diplomatiia i nauka: Soiuz vo imia budushchego," *Kommunist*, No. 2 (January 1990), pp. 14-22.

23. For a more detailed discussion of this point and its effects on Italy's foreign policy decisionmaking during its postwar transition from fascism, see Gianfranco Pasquino, "The Demise of the First Fascist Régime and Italy's Transition to Democracy: 1943-1948," in O'Donnell, p. 70.

24. For a discussion of policy changes designed to reduce the involvement of the Greek military in political life, see Diamondouros, pp. 145-162. For a Soviet discussion that touches on similar issues, see the exchange between V. A. Korotich and Marshall S. F. Akhromeev, "Kakie vooruzhennye sily nuzhny sovetskomu soiuzu," *Ogonek*, No. 50 (December 1989), pp. 6-8, 30.

25. Legvold, p. 97.

10

Lessons for Western Theories of International Security and Foreign Relations

Jerry F. Hough

This volume has focused on the implications of the last five years for our understanding of the Soviet Union, and the contributors have dealt with developments during the period in some detail. The current chapter will take the major changes of the last five years in Soviet foreign and security policy for granted and ask a broader question: What are the implications of these developments for the way that we in the United States look at international relations and national security?

Reflection on our fundamental assumptions in light of perestroika is an enterprise to which theorists of international relations must give the greatest attention. Our theories of international relations have emphasized the response of governments to changing lines of force, levels of threat, and balances of power. Our theories have suggested that countries, in the words of Lord Palmerston, have "no eternal friends, no eternal enemies, but only eternal interests" and that they change their alliances in response to changing circumstances.

If Gorbachev's policies are examined from the perspective of theories stressing rational interests, they make eminently good sense. Indeed, Gorbachev's actions seem quite predictable in light of the theories that have dominated our thinking about international relations. Yet most Americans were continually surprised by the changes in Soviet foreign policy that occurred in the last five years.

Such a paradox requires explanation. Events will force us—indeed, have forced us—to rethink Soviet foreign policy. If we don't ask why we were surprised by Gorbachev when our theories should have led us to correct predictions, we are likely to make similar mistakes in our thinking about other foreign policy questions in the future.

In addition, such an analysis can help us to better understand the past. Although our theories of international relations actually help us to explain developments in the *last* five years of the 1980s, we previously thought that they explained the foreign policy of the *first* half of that decade. Obviously, one explanation cannot do both. Thus any rethinking of the underlying causes of Soviet foreign policy in the past five years leads to a rethinking of the nature of Brezhnev's foreign policy as well.

The Rationality of Gorbachev's Foreign Policy

I believe that Gorbachev's foreign policy behavior has been quite rational. In fact, to the extent that I predicted his policy accurately, it was because I assumed that the traditional U.S. theory of international relations is correct and that Gorbachev would behave as a rational actor. To the extent that I was behind the curve—and I was, to some extent, on Central Europe and Germany—it was because I assumed that subjective, "irrational" factors would prevail over rational considerations. The logic of Gorbachev's policy is absolutely compelling, given the basic postulates of our theories of international relations and the realities of the modern world, and Gorbachev is unusual only in that he has had the coolness of judgment, the power, and the ruthlessness to be led by the logic of his situation.

What are the dominant facts to which Gorbachev is reacting? There are five major considerations underlying Gorbachev's foreign policy:

1. Colonies have proved to be economically unprofitable in the modern world. At best, the home country must conduct its relations with its colonies on the basis of market prices; at worst (as happened in the Soviet-Central European relationship), the colony requires subsidies to prevent popular unrest. Estimates of the difference between the market value of Soviet energy sent to Central Europe and manufactured goods sent to the Soviet Union in return may be as high as $10 to 15 billion a year. Even if market prices prevail, the administrative and military costs associated with control of the colonies make the relationship less profitable than a pure market one and more of a political hassle.

2. Allies or colonies have become a much more dubious security asset for a nuclear superpower than they were in the prenuclear age. This is particularly the case if the allies are not vital for the protection of crucial raw materials (e.g., oil from the Persian Gulf). As Robert Tucker has pointed out, even Western Europe matters only marginally to the basic

security interests of a United States with intercontinental missiles and nuclear warheads. Indeed, he correctly suggested that alliance with Western Europe actually detracted from U.S. security on balance. The major consequence of the NATO alliance from this perspective was to increase the number of conflicts in which the United States might feel obligated to utilize its nuclear weapons and in which U.S. cities might be jeopardized.[1]

3. The geostrategic realities of Western Europe have changed radically for the Soviet Union in the postwar era. From the time that the Mongol threat ended in the fifteenth century, Russia has reacted predominantly to the fields of force in Europe. Of course, it filled a power vacuum in the relatively unpopulated steppes to the east of Muscovy and then had to worry about Japan in the first half of the twentieth century. Primarily, however, Russia reacted to the changing power configurations to its west. Now a range of circumstances (including Soviet policy itself) have ended 400 years of war in Western Europe. As a consequence, the Soviet Union faces no threat from Western Europe other than British and French nuclear weapons.

Among the many results of the end of the European threat to Russia is a radical reduction of the geostrategic significance of Central Europe for the Soviet Union. Central Europe was always a worthless buffer in the defense against nuclear missiles from the United States or even Western Europe, but if there is no conventional threat from Western Europe—and no politics that is likely to produce one—then Central Europe is also no longer a useful buffer against a conventional attack. Clearly the Soviets fear the introduction of major foreign forces into Central Europe, let alone the introduction of foreign nuclear weapons, but the likelihood of such a development is remote.

4. The most probable long-term geostrategic threat to the Soviet Union comes from Asia, specifically from China or India. Each has a billion people, each has nuclear weapons, and each is growing rapidly. While we can hope that the domestic political development of each country will be benign and that the already-existing tension between the two will not express itself in a deadly struggle for supremacy in Asia, the realist theory of international relations focuses on capability and potential danger. It is pessimistic about the perfectibility of mankind. Indeed, the worries expressed about Saddam Hussein obtaining nuclear weapons in Iraq, with only 17 million people, reminds us that the potential threat is not limited to the most populous states.

Imagine that Canada on the northern border of the United States had a billion people and nuclear weapons and was growing rapidly. Imagine that the United States simultaneously had a rapidly growing Mexico on its southern border, also with a billion people and nuclear weapons, and that Mexico was asserting with some justice that the United States had stolen Texas, Arizona, and half of California. Imagine that the U.S. economy was functioning poorly and that the United States had hostile relations with Japan and Western Europe. And, finally, imagine that America had been conquered by a Genghis Khan from Mexico, had experienced more than 200 years of Mexican domination, and remembered 1492 as the year in which the last vestiges of that control were finally broken. Americans would be extremely nervous, and that is how the Soviets feel about the situation on their southern border.

Certainly, however, any Asian threat to the Soviet Union is a long-term one. Over the last decade, China—the most worrisome Asian power—has actually reduced its troops unilaterally. Especially if Soviet nationality problems stimulate national independence movements within India (and, indeed, the timing of the renewal of troubles in Kashmir is probably not an accident), an extremist nationalist régime in India is a more likely threat in the near term, but it will probably not be anti-Soviet in its immediate policy.

Thus, the Soviet Union does not need to increase its direct defense expenditures to meet any potential Asian threat. Instead it needs to reform its economy so that it will be able to produce the most technologically sophisticated weapons for any future threat. It needs to ensure that its Moslem rural youth know how to use computers in order to function in a technologically advanced army. International security in the most direct, military sense of the word requires a transfer of resources from the production of tanks to the computerization of the civilian sector.

5. Integration into the world economy is vital for bringing the Soviet economy toward the world level. A fatal flaw of the communist model is that the autarchy that was designed to protect workers from the world business cycle, from the inegalitarianism of the market, and from unemployment, simultaneously protects Soviet manufacturers from world competition. The very nature of the planning system guarantees manufacturers—especially manufacturers of capital goods—a market for all their goods. Even when foreign goods were imported, Soviet manufacturers lost no business and did not need to raise the quality of their goods to world levels. Unlike major Japanese manufacturers, who have often been protected at home but have had to meet foreign competition abroad, Soviet manufacturers have no need to export to market economies because they have a captive domestic market. Total protectionism had precisely the kind of economic consequences that Western economic theory predicted:

low quality goods, inefficient production, slowness of innovation, and lack of responsiveness to the consumer.

Many still think in terms of Brezhnev's policy of the 1970s and assume that integration into the world economy means no more than the purchase of foreign technology. However, the Soviet Union simply does not earn enough hard currency to purchase significant quantities of technology, and an importation of technology that neither causes local manufacturers to lose business nor forces them to meet foreign competition serves few useful purposes for the huge Soviet economy. If the Soviet Union is to integrate into the world economy, it must adopt an export strategy such as that utilized by South Korea and Taiwan, which export their low quality goods at cheap prices and force their manufacturers to compete in foreign markets. The Soviet Union must attract massive foreign investment and become part of the network of the international sourcing of components for the industrial world. Huge amounts of foreign capital are needed to meet this objective. In 1988, Spain—a country emerging from a period of dictatorial rule and becoming a modern industrial nation—received $17 billion net in foreign investment. Poland has approximately the same population as Spain and needs investment on the same scale. The Soviet Union has eight times the population of Spain and Poland. A few billion dollars of investment, let alone trade, are not going to have an significant impact.

Real integration into the world economy implies a far more intimate technological relationship between the Soviet Union and the capitalist world than Brezhnev ever sought. Investors will want the right to continually update both products and production processes. But this intimacy and a large-scale investment will never be possible if the West feels militarily threatened. It turns out that the realist theory was right: A strong threatening force did serve to maintain the countervailing NATO alliance, and the way to "Finlandize" Europe is to reduce Soviet military strength.

Others may want to emphasize alternative geostrategic imperatives. Some may insist that the five geostrategic imperatives of the Soviet Union presented here have been postulated with excessive starkness. But regardless of the weight accorded specific factors, the main outline of the analysis still holds.

The only major consideration omitted from the equation is the danger of nuclear proliferation. In the European framework, this question basically concerns the possible consequences of an independent Germany, especially a reunified one, that is no longer part of the NATO military command structure and no longer has U.S. nuclear weapons on its soil.

Given the fact that Great Britain and France have nuclear weapons, would an independent Germany soon be under serious major domestic political pressure to acquire nuclear weapons of its own? Or, alternately, would the fear of the potential nuclearization of an independent Germany lead to a rapid political unification of Western Europe and a centralization of its nuclear weapons that would be dangerous to the Soviet Union?

Analysts may differ regarding the weight of the danger of nuclear proliferation in Soviet calculations relative to its other geostrategic considerations. They may differ on the degree to which Gorbachev has actually been driven by the logic of the Soviet geostrategic imperatives as I have defined them. Nevertheless, it is striking how well the five geostrategic considerations presented here would have predicted Gorbachev's policy in Europe. Indeed, these five considerations so outweigh the danger of nuclear proliferation to Germany that they explain why Gorbachev so willingly accepted the process of German reunification.

In the long term, Gorbachev is moving his country back into the broader European community, including that in North America. If the great achievement of the last forty years has been the creation of a common European home of 600 million Europeans from the Elbe River to California—that is, people of European language and culture in Western Europe and North America—then Gorbachev wants to join Central Europe and the Soviet Union to this "home" to make a common community of a billion Europeans from Vladivostok to California across the Atlantic. The Soviet Union is integrating into the global economy; it is adopting the same relationship to the Third World as other members of the European community; it is moving increasingly into open military alliance with the United States and Western Europe, at least initially in the name of preserving European stability during German reunification. This military alliance is what President Bush calls "a new world order," and Saddam Hussein's fundamental blunder was in failing to recognize how useful he was in symbolizing the general threat that is producing it.

Some continue to think that "the Soviet national interest will continue to be defined as a search . . . for ways of buffering the transition to a diminished world role."[2] But this is a profound misreading of what is going on. Indeed, the Soviet Union is ending its period of isolation from the rest of the world and is moving toward the kind of active role that a country of its size should assume.

The movement toward military alliance with the United States and Western Europe is precisely what the realist theory would predict as power relations and the character of the potential threat change. The United States reversed its attitude toward Germany and Japan very quickly after World War II. If the future threat to the Soviet Union comes not from the West but from a future Khomeini in some Third World country, then it is natural for the Soviet Union to change its alignments. And, of course, if the Soviet Union changes its policy in this direction and ends the threat to the West, then the greatest potential threat to the West also comes from a future Khomeini. The West, too, would have a natural interest in the coming together of the Europeans—"the North," it is hoped, with Japan joining in—in the interests of long-term common defense.

The Mystery of Leonid Brezhnev

If the analysis presented here is correct, then the events of the last five years require us to rethink U.S. security policy in the 1990s, but not the fundamental assumptions of our theories of international relations and international security. But if Soviet policy in the second half of the 1980s corresponded to the postulates of the realist school of international relations, then clearly the Soviet policy of the first half of the 1980s did not, for nothing happened during the decade to change the geostrategic environment for the Soviet Union. If Gorbachev's foreign policy is rational in terms of the Soviet Union's national interests, then Brezhnev's must have been irrational in these terms, at least toward the end of his life.

If Brezhnev's foreign policy did not advance Soviet geostrategic interests, what factors were, in actuality, driving his policy? In analyzing Brezhnev's foreign policy, one must draw a distinction between the periods of 1965-1972 and 1973-1982. Although many of the same factors influenced policy in both periods, the Soviet military buildup in the former period actually makes much more sense than Western observers were willing to concede at the time. One can argue that in the broader perspective, the interests of the Soviet Union would have been better served by refusing to support North Vietnam in its effort to reunite the country and by following a Gorbachev-like policy in Europe. (Indeed, Brezhnev could have refused military support of Vietnam on the grounds that intervention might have set a precedent threatening stability in divided Germany and Korea.) Nevertheless, it was logical for him to conclude that the split with China was the result of Khrushchev's impulsiveness, and that a cooperative policy with China in Vietnam might restore a very important alliance for the Soviet Union. It was also logical for him to think that the rigidity of Soviet-West German relations in the early 1960s and the bitterness of Russian memories about World War II meant that the development of detente with West Germany—and, therefore, with the West—was going to take a number of years.

Brezhnev's subsequent military policy is quite explicable against the backdrop of military escalation in Vietnam. The U.S. Minuteman program and the decision to install multiple warheads on intercontinental rockets required a very expensive expansion of Soviet nuclear delivery systems. The U.S. conventional buildup associated with Vietnam created the potential danger that the United States might become frustrated enough with Vietnam to think of serious "horizontal escalation"—the application of force elsewhere to induce a change in Soviet policy in Vietnam. On another level, the revolutionary situation among the youth in Western Europe might spread to the youth in Central Europe—indeed, it did so in Czechoslovakia in 1968—and require a number of interventions, some of them far more difficult than the bloodless invasion of Czechoslovakia. And, finally, the Soviet Union was absorbing U.S. debates on deterrence far better than we understood, and it concluded that, perhaps, war in Europe might not inevitably become nuclear. If so, the Soviet Union needed modernization of its conventional forces to correspond with this possibility.

The great mystery about Brezhnev concerns his policy after 1972. By that time, both the Soviet Union and the United States were reaching levels of nuclear overkill that implied a leveling off of strategic military spending. The United States had clearly decided against escalation of the Vietnam War beyond the boundaries of Vietnam and instead was bringing both the war and its own conventional buildup to an end. With the United States obviously in no mood for another major intervention, the cooperation of the Soviet Union and the United States in ending the 1973 Arab-Israeli conflict seemed to suggest that the Middle East would be less likely to provoke a dangerous U.S.-Soviet confrontation. The Soviet Union had reason to be offended by its exclusion from the Camp David peace process, but any process reducing the possibility of war between Israel and Egypt had to be reassuring to the Soviet Union from a purely military point of view. The revolutionary situation in Western Europe quieted down, and, even though it took years to prepare the public for a warmer relationship with Germany, that process was completed by the early 1970s.

The time seemed ripe to move beyond political detente to military detente. Thirty years after the end of World War II, the danger of war in Europe seemed minimal and the threat to the Soviet Union even less. A mutual build-down of the huge military armadas in Europe seemed not only desirable but inevitable. In actuality, it didn't happen. The expensive modernization of both Soviet and U.S. forces continued, and the relationship between the West and the Soviet Union came to be dominated by a major dispute about the installation by both sides of quite meaningless and unnecessary intermediate range nuclear missiles in Europe.

What went wrong? Why was there not a major reduction in the huge military forces on both sides of European borders that were becoming quite stable? Part of the answer is to be found in the United States. The Vietnam period was a major shock not only because of the loss of the war but also owing to the turmoil the war caused at home. The anti-war demonstrations were disturbing enough, but even worse was the appeal to a substantial portion of American youth of an attack on traditional values in the realm of culture, sexual behavior, drugs, and law-and-order.

In the international sphere, Americans feared that the attraction of communism in Vietnam might be contagious in the rest of the Third World, a fear further fueled both by the election of Salvador Allende as president of Chile and by the radicalization of his policy. Americans feared that the oil blockade of 1973 presaged a general loss of control in the Third World. Some also worried that U.S.-Soviet cooperation in the 1973 Arab-Israeli war might be followed by further cooperation that would force a settlement in the Arab-Israeli conflict detrimental to Israel. In Europe, Americans feared that the Soviet detente with West Germany might lead to the reunification and neutralization of Germany. The older-generation officials within the foreign policy establishment shared Henry Kissinger's understanding that the Soviet threat had been very useful in ending the conflicts among Britain, France, and Germany; they also feared that the end of a military Soviet threat might increase the strains within the West that had been made manifest during the Vietnam war.

For all these reasons U.S. policymakers were determined to ensure that the end of the Vietnam War did not lead to a general attack on national defense values and military spending. They were determined to demon-strate to the Soviet Union (and to others) that defeat in Vietnam and the 1973 oil boycott did not mean a loss of American will or of the capability to function as a great power in the Third World. The United States was seeking an issue on which its policymakers could induce the West Europeans in general and the West Germans in particular to reaffirm their support of the NATO alliance. And since the West European élite also was eager to end the revolt among its youth, to retain U.S. defense of the supply of petroleum from the Persian Gulf, and to prevent a return to the old conflicts among Britain, France, and Germany, they too found the maintenance of a Soviet threat very useful.

Nevertheless, as Gorbachev demonstrated in the last five years, it is not possible for Western leaders to maintain a perception of a Soviet threat if the Soviet Union is determined to prevent it. Whatever other judgments may be made about Brezhnev's motivation and behavior, one thing is absolutely incontrovertible: Brezhnev did not act in a way that would relieve anyone's perception of threat. In retrospect, the United States probably overreacted to Soviet policy in Angola, Ethiopia, and Nicaragua, but the overreaction was certainly predictable given the defeat in the Vietnam War. Even at the time, few took seriously the charge that the invasion of Afghanistan meant a drive toward the oil of the Persian Gulf, but the revolutionary turmoil in Iran at the same time necessitated a strong U.S. response. The informal Soviet explanations for the invasion of Afghanistan—the dangers of the spread of Islamic fundamentalism, the strategic threat on their border—applied even more to Iran than to Afghanistan, and a radical coup against Khomeini was quite conceivable. Whereas the Soviet invasion of Afghanistan posed no strategic threat to the United States, a Soviet response to an appeal for help from a radical régime in Iran was another matter altogether, and Brezhnev must have known that the Afghanistan precedent would be seen as very threatening.

Soviet behavior in Europe was even more provocative. The only defensive justification for the large Soviet forces in Europe was the need to control Central Europe. Yet, even if we forget (which we should not) that domination of Central Europe was no longer important to the Soviet Union from a geostrategic point of view, the Soviet Union behaved in a way that maximized Western concerns.

First, despite the diminishing threat of war and the increasing economic difficulties in the Soviet Union, Brezhnev made no moves to reduce his military spending. Even in arms control negotiations, he focused all of his attention on strategic arms talks that had few budgetary implications, and no one even hoped that progress was possible in the conventional arms control negotiations in Vienna.

Brezhnev also made no attempt to reassure the West about his intentions. Even if he had been determined to maintain an army of the same size, he could have reduced the sense of threat by adopting a defensive military doctrine, by holding defensive-oriented maneuvers, or by deploying his troops and equipment in a defensive posture. When he introduced intermediate SS-20 rockets into Europe, he could have quite openly—and legitimately—said that the Soviet Union had the right to replace the already-existing but aging SS-4 and SS-5 intermediate missiles in Europe. If he had announced what he was doing and had guaranteed that the number of warheads would not rise, his action would have created little alarm.

Instead, Brezhnev maintained a level of secrecy about his military policy that inevitably led to exaggerated fears in the West. The SS-20s were installed secretly, with no indication that the number of new missiles would be limited. The number of warheads actually increased. When the Central Intelligence Agency—as it was later to admit—overestimated the rate of increase in Soviet military spending in the late 1970s, Brezhnev took no steps to correct the misperception.

The actual configuration of Soviet troops in Central Europe—especially in East Germany—gave the West no assurance that the control of Central Europe was the primary consideration in the minds of the Soviet leaders. Gorbachev would eventually proclaim a defensive doctrine and begin to position troops and conduct maneuvers in accordance with this doctrine. Under Brezhnev, by contrast, official Soviet military doctrine for war in Europe featured a counterattack that drove to the English Channel. Not only were Soviet troops in East Germany poised to launch such a counterattack, but all their maneuvers until 1981 were exclusively limited to practice for such a move. Even after 1981, defensive actions constituted only a small proportion of military exercises. As the preparation for an all-out counterattack and that for a surprise offensive strike were essentially identical—and the possibility of a Western attack seemed remote—Soviet doctrine and behavior were bound to alarm the West—or, at least, to strengthen greatly the hand of those in the West who were alarmist about a surprise Soviet attack and who wanted to increase U.S. and European defense expenditures.

What, then, explains Brezhnev's policy? The rate of growth of the Soviet economy was declining in the 1970s, and especially after 1975 Brezhnev faced excruciating choices between investment and consumption. Why did he not accelerate conventional arms control negotiations so that he could reduce military spending drastically? Why did he act in a way that was certain to increase the pressures for growth in Western military expenditures?

A number of explanations exist, and all require qualifications to the realist theory of international relations. One possible explanation is that Brezhnev was living at least partially in the past. As Ernest May has argued, people disproportionately absorb the "lessons of the past" that were learned in their youth or early adulthood. Generals proverbially plan for the last war, but May suggests that this is a general human phenomenon.[3]

For Brezhnev and his generation, there was only one overwhelming international lesson from the past: Germany and Japan were dangerous. The soldiers in the losing Russo-Japanese War had essentially been the fathers of the Brezhnev generation, and they had certainly told their children often about the "perfidious" Japanese and their surprise attack on

Port Arthur. (As Gromyko reported in his memoirs, his father actually had fought in that war.[4]) The first international memory of the Brezhnev generation was World War I, especially the enormous danger to Russia from Germany in 1917 and 1918. (Brezhnev was 12 years old in 1918 and Gromyko was 9.)

As members of the Brezhnev generation were drawn into college at the end of the 1920s and moved upward during the 1930s (spectacularly during the Great Purge of 1937-1938), they did so against a constant drumbeat of regime propaganda about the danger of war and capitalist encirclement, and then about the danger of fascism specifically. During the 1930s the propaganda came to reflect reality. Japan was extremely expansionist, and 1938-1939 had been years of major incidents—really war—between Soviet and Japanese troops on the Manchurian-Soviet border. Had Soviet troops under Georgii Zhukov not defeated the Japanese on this border in 1939, the Japanese might have decided to go north in 1941 to dismember Russia in conjunction with Germany rather than turning south. There was, of course, nothing hypothetical about the threat of Hitler in the second half of the 1930s, and the Soviet Union was devastated in the German attacks of 1941 and 1942. Brezhnev himself spent the entire war as a political officer in the army at the front.

If Ernest May is correct, then we should expect to discover that memories of the threat from Germany and Japan would be a dominant factor in the thinking of the Brezhnev generation. Whether intentional or not, Stalin and Khrushchev adopted policies that led to U.S. control over Japan and the once-warring countries of Western Europe, and Soviet control of the areas in Central Europe that had been the source of the conflicts that led to World War I. (However, when Yugoslavia broke away in 1948, Stalin surely remembered the role of Serbia in the origin of World War I and did not intervene.)

When Brezhnev came to power, he had strong reasons to want at least some partial detente with Western Europe. The question was the closeness of the relationship and the degree to which the Soviet military threat would be reduced. As the United States hardly wanted a close technological tie between Western Europe (and Japan) and the Soviet Union during the Vietnam War, the development of such a relationship would have required major Soviet concessions in an attempt to break the Western alliances. A major reduction in the Soviet military threat would have been one such step.

If the "lessons of the past" argument is accurate, however, one would hypothesize that Brezhnev and Gromyko would have been very nervous at the thought of an independent Germany and Japan that were no longer being controlled by the United States. In fact, they acted with great caution in their negotiations with West Germany. Soviet-Japanese relations were so rigid that it is difficult to avoid a historical memory argument on both sides as part of the explanation.

The desirability of U.S. control of Germany and Japan was expressed in the censored media was through the use of the codewords *German revanchism* and *Japanese militarism*. These phrases did not reflect any irrational paranoia about the current danger from Germany and Japan. Rather, Soviet rhetoric implied that if Germany or Japan became independent, the two countries retained aggressive tendencies and would become dangerous. Sometimes the point was made more explicitly, if still indirectly. For example, a scholar at the Institute of the USA and Canada analyzed China's purported interests vis-à-vis Japan in a way that was obviously meant to apply to the Soviet Union as well: China had no interest in Japan becoming independent of the United States, for it would soon then acquire nuclear weapons of its own.[5]

Indeed, if there was no concern about Soviet economic performance and long-term power interests, if there was no possibility that the Soviet Union might want to ally with Germany and Japan against a greater threat from, say, China or India, then there was real sense to this argument and to Gromyko's policy. If the geostrategic alignment of Western Europe is really irrelevant (that is, if it doesn't really matter whether Western Europe is allied to the United States, allied to the Soviet Union, or is neutral), then the Soviet Union should prefer U.S. control to prevent the possibility of either Germany or Japan acquiring nuclear weapons, for nuclear proliferation would not be in the Soviet Union's interests.

A second explanation for Brezhnev's behavior can be found in the attitude of his generation toward contact with the outside world. If one considers Soviet foreign relations in 1982 (or earlier), the distinctive feature of those relations was not Soviet policy towards arms control, Japan, or even Afghanistan. The really peculiar fact about Soviet relations with the outside world was that the capital of the world's largest country did not have a single French or Italian restaurant. The essence of the communist system was the construction of two Iron Curtains—one against foreign economic forces and the other against modern culture and ideas. Even with the partial opening of the Soviet Union in the post-Stalin era, the degree of isolation remained astonishing.

The theory of totalitarianism suggests that at certain periods a large proportion of a country's population can become so insecure that it seeks to "escape from freedom"—that is, it responds to authoritarian, xenophobic leaders. In Germany the insecurities produced by the collapse of the old régime, the defeat in war, the Versailles treaty, runaway inflation, and then the depression were said to have produced the rise of Hitler. Communism, for its part, was seen as the "disease of the transition"—the product of the insecurities of newcomers to the city whose old world was collapsing and who were terrified by their exposure to new "satanic" urban values (to use the vocabulary of the right-wing totalitarian movement in Iran that was also a disease of the transition).

Any revolution is carried out by two generations—one, the leaders and activists (who themselves are often quite young), and the other, the teenagers who provide the mass of the guerilla fighters, demonstrators and rock-throwers. The Brezhnev generation comprised the teenagers of the Russian Civil War, and as he aged, Brezhnev still retained many of the values of his youth. He simply could not accept the kind of exposure to Western ideas, especially the concept of market forces, that Gorbachev was able to tolerate. Brezhnev and his generation felt insecure, as often was said in the West, but it was an insecurity that came from the character of the West, not its foreign or military policies.

Brezhnev did not need a near-term alliance with Western countries for military reasons—although detente with West Germany was consciously or unconsciously a useful signal to Mao Zedong about a potential Soviet option. Movement toward a long-term alliance, a real integration into Europe, would have required a fundamental change in the economic relationship and a real receptiveness to European culture and ideas. Brezhnev did not want this.

A third explanation of Brezhnev's behavior can be found in his personal political interests. Communist régimes that have been imposed from the outside have long been known to be unstable. In 1989, it was surprising that Gorbachev decided not to use Soviet troops to preserve communist régimes in Central Europe, but conservatives and liberals alike had long assumed that only Soviet troops were preserving Central European stability. The result of the withdrawal of military support should not have been surprising. By contrast, communist régimes that have come to power by their own efforts have been quite stable, and there never has been the need for Soviet troops to keep communist régimes in power in countries such as China, Cuba, and Vietnam. None of these régimes fell in 1989, and the great surprise of the year was actually the durability of the Afghan régime once Soviet troops had withdrawn.

The explanation for the difference in stability of communist régimes that were imposed and those that came to power on their own clearly is to be found in their different relationship to nationalism. Communist régimes that were imposed entailed a loss of national independence for their countries, whereas Communists who seized power on their own have managed to identify themselves with local nationalism in one way or another.

Certainly the Communist Party in the Soviet Union had long identified itself with Russian nationalism. Lenin's one-party system had implied Moscow's control over the non-Russian regions, and the revolution itself had overthrown an élite that was westernizing Russia. Lenin linked his opposition during the Civil War with foreign intervention, and Stalin then spoke of socialism in one country and asserted that only his industrialization program would defend the country from outside threat. The victory of the Soviet Union in World War II, the adoption of the communist model by the Chinese, and early successes in space all seemed to validate these claims.

In the 1970s, however, Brezhnev was in danger of losing this link between Russian nationalism and the Communist Party. Russia and Japan had begun to industrialize at approximately the same time, but Japan began to surge ahead. Worse than that, Leninist doctrine had claimed that isolation from the world capitalist economy was necessary if a newly industrializing country was to avoid deformed, "semicolonial" development, but the experience of the Pacific countries was suggesting that integration into the world economy was actually the secret to success.

In these circumstances Brezhnev found it useful to justify if his secretiveness and his military buildup created a sense of threat in the West. If the West was continually saying that the Soviet Union had achieved military superiority and was threatening to Finlandize Europe, if the United States in its rhetoric was talking about summits between the two superpowers and according the Soviet Union a recognition of equality that it did not deserve, Brezhnev's opponents found it very difficult to argue convincingly that he had been presiding over a decline in Soviet power.

In other words, it was precisely because Brezhnev was not maintaining Russia's power and position in the world that he wanted to create the false impression that he was. The clearest evidence of his calculation came when the CIA revised its estimates of growth in Soviet military spending from 5 percent a year to 2 percent, with no growth in expenditures on weapons procurements. One might have thought that the Soviet media would have trumpeted this change as proof of the peace-loving character of the Soviet Union and the tendency of the United States to exaggerate. Instead, the Soviet media never reported the change in the CIA's estimate. Brezhnev did not want the Soviet public to know that economic difficulties were having an impact on Soviet military power.

Soviet Foreign Relations
and International Relations Theory

A major intellectual problem remains. Mikhail Gorbachev was 26 years younger than Leonid Brezhnev, and there was no reason to expect that he would think in World War II terms. He came to power at the age of 54 and clearly hoped to rule at least until the end of the century. He had to worry about the long-term impact of both Soviet economic decline and threatening Soviet behavior toward the West. His time perspective and the requirements of maintaining his personal power were congruent with the policy implied by the geostrategic imperatives of the Soviet Union. Why, then, were most foreign policy specialists so surprised by the Soviet policies of the last five years?

Part of the explanation is that the majority of Western specialists judged Gorbachev's domestic political interests differently than he did. Clearly, long-term national interests demanded radical economic reform and an opening to the West. A majority of analysts, however, believed that such reform would require steps (e.g., the raising of subsidized meat prices) that would destabilize the Soviet Union and, therefore, that Gorbachev would not take them.

Another part of the explanation, however, lies in the way that U.S. analysts used—or did not use—their theories of international relations. When Brezhnev's policy did not correspond to the assumptions of their basic theory of international relations, they should have concluded either that Brezhnev's behavior was irrational (and might well be reversed by his successors) or that some of the fundamental assumptions of their theory required modification.

For a series of reasons (primarily the close relationship of political science analysis and the needs of policy), modifications in the model did not occur. Instead, the theory was retained and people unconsciously began to assume that Brezhnev's policy corresponded to it. Thus, for example, when Brezhnev continued to build up his forces in the 1970s—indeed, to increase his already high level of military spending by 5 percent a year according to the CIA estimates that were widely believed—it was assumed that this was what the realist theory predicted. The realist theory was often unconsciously reinterpreted to equate overall power with military power and to imply that the distribution of nuclear weapons required more or less the kind of confrontation and type of bipolar system of alliances in Europe that had characterized the postwar period.

Similarly, as realist theory assumed that adversaries seek to break up each other's alliances, it followed that Brezhnev must be trying to break up NATO. And because Brezhnev was building a threatening force, it followed that this policy might Finlandize Europe, not hold a countervailing alliance together. We sometimes recognized that Soviet actions actually did solidify Europe, but this was attributed this to the incompetence of the Soviet foreign minister, Andrei Gromyko. We feared that the next time the Soviet Union might be successful. Those who did have an accurate sense that a Soviet threat was useful for NATO generally were committed to NATO and either kept silent or followed the dictates of policy as they saw them and made the opposite case in public.

Clearly we must make at least some qualifications in the realist theory.

1. We must go beyond simple focus on governmental policy to talk about the relationship of society to the outside world. In relations within the Western world, this factor tends to wash out. But in some circumstances it becomes quite significant. This fact was recognized in the discussion of "ideology" in Soviet foreign policy, but the discussion was fundamentally misleading because "ideology" is an intellectual category and the phenomenon that was being discussed is an emotional, psychological one. It refers to a desire for security from disturbing cultural forces, not just military danger.

2. The factor of time and the variability associated with it must be given greater emphasis. It is a truism that people and states react to threats. The question is, How do they define their threats? These threats may come at a very individual, psychological level. But even if threats are defined in a purely military manner, the definition of the nature of the threat can be subjective. How should a Soviet policymaker have defined the threat in 1975? If by the concentration of force that was capable of destroying the Soviet Union, then clearly the U.S. nuclear capability was all that mattered. If leaders took a longer-term perspective, they could then paradoxically either return to their youth and assume that the problem was the prevention of the conflicts that led to World War I and World War II, or they could look to the twenty-first century and assume that the problem will come from the "South"—most likely from China, India and Iran—and that they need to take the steps (both in economic reform and reconciliation with the West) that would position the Soviet Union to meet this problem.

3. Finally, the differences between the interests of those actually making decisions and the interests of the "state" are often crucial. Mancur Olson's work has had an enormous impact on political science in the last quarter of a century, especially in the realm of U.S. and formal theory. It is striking, however, how little the analysis has been applied in the study of foreign countries or international relations. Few ask about individual rationality when revolution in areas such as Lithuania is analyzed, but talk about the desires and interests of the "Lithuanians" or "Lithuania." The focus in international relations is upon the interests of the nation or of the state, and Mancur Olson's analysis is applied only at the level of individual nations in alliance relationships.[6]

In reality, decisions are made by individuals, and they may reflect the interests (or nonrational factors) of the individual decisionmakers. Other actors try to structure the incentives so that the decisions of policymakers correspond to collective interests, but this effort is often unsuccessful. The essence of a dictatorship is precisely that the leader has a particularly strong ability to ensure that his individual interests are served by policy.

4. In a larger sense, the lesson of the United States' analysis of the last decade is that political science is not a science—that international relations theory in particular is likely to be a handmaiden of policy. If so, only rarely will the international scene be marked by the kind of fluidity that is conducive to an open discussion of the basic principles of international relations theory. Fortunately, this is such a time.

Gorbachev's foreign policy corresponds to the rational interests of the Soviet Union today and, therefore, is unlikely to be reversed. It is crucial to understand that the threat to the Soviet Union from the "South" is also the key threat to the United States. The attempt of the Soviet Union to become a part of a common European home—a de facto military alliance from Vladivostok to California across the Atlantic—is a policy that the United States should support. Because the wars in the South in coming decades and centuries are likely to result from many of the same ethnic factors that tore Europe apart for four centuries, it is in the interests of the United States not to promote the principle of the absolute rights of ethnic and linguistic purity in the Soviet Union (or elsewhere) but, rather, to work toward ethnic peace in the Soviet Union. Governments—or intellectuals who seek governmental posts—may not find it politically advantageous to recognize these points publicly, but they need to understand them in private.

Notes

1. Robert W. Tucker, "The Nuclear Debate," *Foreign Affairs* (fall 1984).

2. Stephen Sestanovich, "Inventing the Soviet National Interest," *The National Interest*, No. 20 (summer 1990), 14.

3. Ernest May, *'Lessons' of the Past: The Use and Misues of History in American Foreign Policy* (New York: Oxford University Press, 1973).

4. Andrei Gromyko, *Memoirs*, translated by Harold Shukman (London: Hutchinson, 1989), p. 3.

5. M. G. Nosov, *Iapono-kitaiskie otnoshenie (1949-1975)* (Moscow: Nauka, 1978), p. 197.

6. Mancur Olson, "The Logic of Collective Action," *Journal of Soviet Nationalities*, Vol. 1, No. 2 (summer 1990), pp. 8-27.

11

The Soviet Union in 1990

Galina V. Starovoitova

During 1990, the pace of events in the Soviet Union accelerated. We began the year with great hopes, but very soon we suffered from a certain sense of loss. At the end of the year in Moscow, the exciting page of Soviet and world history called perestroika was turned. Now we are waiting to find out what the new page will be titled.

I would like to recall the events of the past year. First, 1990 began not on the first of January, but on the fourteenth of December, 1989, with the death of Andrei Sakharov. That particular date already had historical significance for Russia, marking the beginning of the Decembrist uprising in 1825. (That was the day the first Russian democrats, who were members of the aristocracy, took a stand against absolute monarchy and demanded a constitution.) At the beginning of December 1989, Sakharov, the great defender of human rights and opposition leader in the new Soviet Parliament, appealed to the nation to participate in a two-hour political strike against an impending new dictatorship. But only now, after hearing the resignation speech of Eduard Shevardnadze, has the West become aware of the reality of this threat. Two hours before his sudden and unexpected death, Sakharov said to me, "The battle will be tomorrow!" This was during the Second Congress of People's Deputies, and he meant that the sharp conflicts between reformers and conservatives would become apparent the next day. However, the Congress ended without Sakharov. Despite a particularly harsh snowstorm in Moscow, half a million citizens joined his funeral procession.

Perhaps it was at that Congress that for the first time high-ranking army officers felt under attack. The legislature condemned the dirty war in Afghanistan, the 1939 Molotov-Ribbentrop Pact (which paved the way for the annexation of the three hitherto independent Baltic states), and the slaughter of peaceful Georgian demonstrators in Tbilisi on April 9, 1989.

In February, with the abrogation of Article Six of the Constitution—which had guaranteed the Communist party's monopoly on power—the popular movement toward political pluralism gained in strength. The Party did not surrender its monopoly position willingly. The reformers and leaders of the parliamentary opposition—Boris Eltsin, Iurii Afanas'ev, Gavriil Popov, and Sergei Stankevich—called for a demonstration just outside the Kremlin walls. Hundreds of thousands of people gathered, demanding the repeal of Article Six—a demand CPSU General Secretary Mikhail Gorbachev took seriously. At the February Plenum of the CPSU Central Committee, Communist leaders finally agreed to rewrite the text of the Article Six. The change was ratified by the Third Congress of People's Deputies in March 1990. At the same time a new Soviet presidency was created. Gorbachev, the sole candidate, was elected with 59 percent of the votes. The uncontested election took place despite numerous protests from ordinary voters, who insisted that Gorbachev should have been challenged and that a nationwide vote should have been held to choose the head of state. The parliamentary opposition, reflecting the wishes of their constituencies, refused to participate in the presidential election under those conditions.

At this Third Congress, a majority of deputies condemned the separatist tendencies of Lithuania, a republic which was not represented. Who would have thought then that nine months later, the Fourth Congress would be boycotted by deputies from *five* Soviet republics?

The absence of an alternative candidate for the presidency and the attempts by the central authorities to threaten supporters of national self-determination were not accepted in the republics, contributing to the further breakdown of the center. Following the Third Congress, many republican parliaments elected their own presidents and declared sovereignty, although they still belonged to the Union. The spring elections to the republican parliaments took place on a multi-party basis, at least in the Christian republics. In the Central Asian republics, the hardliners, as before, remained in control, and even tried to use Islamic traditions to strengthen their position of power. In several republics, martial law and a curfew were enforced during the elections. In the streets of some republican capitals, tanks became a customary feature of the urban landscape. Nevertheless, five of the fifteen republics (Armenia, Estonia, Georgia, Latvia, and Lithuania) held the first free elections in 72 years. The Communist party lost power. Moreover, in Armenia and

Georgia the elected leaders were former prisoners of conscience. (The leader of the Armenian parliament, Levon Ter-Petrosian, was arrested in 1988, after Gorbachev came to power.) In the parliaments of the Slavic republics—Belorussia, Russia, and Ukraine—non-Communist factions emerged. These factions include up to one-third of the deputies and sometimes are able to persuade the majority to vote in favor of their proposals. This happened, for example, when Boris Eltsin was elected Chair of the Russian Parliament, despite Gorbachev's objections.

The election of Eltsin was warmly welcomed in Russia and other republics, but it marked a new stage in the long-running Gorbachev-Eltsin conflict. Their battle is fueled partially by jealousy: in the summer of 1990, Eltsin's approval rating stood at about 90 percent, while Gorbachev's was 21 percent. The conflict is not just a psychological one, nor does it reflect merely a difference in interpretation of democracy. It goes deeper.

A fundamental shift has taken place, as important political conflicts and power struggles no longer take place in the center, but in the republics. Apart from Gorbachev, no one is vying for the presidential post, because the Soviet Union as a state is losing credibility while the republics are gaining strength. Mutual economic interests and socialist ideology no longer serve as uniting factors in the Soviet Union, so that now the last empire in the world is following the path of its predecessors. The two distinguishing characteristics of the Soviet empire are that its colonies are not overseas, and that the center of the empire—Russia—is much poorer than its colonies. Moreover, Russia itself was a colony of Stalin's totalitarian regime, and needs to be decolonized and have its sovereignty restored just as much as the other republics. So, in losing power over the huge Russian Federation, the President of the USSR may lose power over the whole of the Union.

Here is the root of the conflict between Gorbachev and Eltsin. Like Winston Churchill in an earlier era, Mikhail Gorbachev does not want to preside over the breakup of the empire, but probably—also like Churchill—he will have no choice. I think Russia and the other republics may in the future create something similar to the Commonwealth. However, today, radical economic reform has been undermined by Gorbachev's attempts to keep the empire together by force. The West, reluctant to deal with fifteen new states, all with nuclear capability, and fifteen new presidents instead of one, tacitly supports central authority. When Gorbachev abandoned his short-lived alliance with Eltsin—just after they developed the radical 500 Days Plan for economic reform in September 1990—the alternative economic strategy became Western credits, which the President himself secured without consulting his parliament or his republics. But who is going to repay the debts?

The Soviet Union is being saved from hunger due to West Germany's redemption of East Germany (like a hostage) from the socialist camp, because of the repeal of the Jackson-Vanik Amendment in the United States, and finally as a result of the charity of ordinary well-intentioned people in Europe and the U.S.—charity that is for our rich country a national disgrace.

The year 1990 has shown that not all new political developments are progressive. In July, the Russian Communist party was founded as a new branch of the Communist party of the Soviet Union. With Gorbachev's blessing, hard-liner Ivan Polozkov was elected as its leader. Shortly before, he had been the unsuccessful competitor against Eltsin in the election for Russian republic leader. In the public's eyes, he replaced Egor Ligachev, as the leading extreme conservative. During the Twenty-Eighth CPSU Congress on July 11, there was a wave of miners' strikes throughout the country, featuring anti-Communist slogans. Many democrats left the Party, including Boris Eltsin, the mayors of Moscow and Leningrad (Gavriil Popov and Anatolii Sobchak, respectively) and dozens of people's deputies. Despite democrats' appeals for the President to suspend his membership in the Party during his term of office, Gorbachev chose to remain General Secretary. But I don't think anyone can succeed in being both the Pope and Martin Luther at the same time.

Gorbachev is evidently under pressure from the military-industrial complex and powerful Russian nationalists. But we should remember that the military today is not homogeneous. Many army and KGB officers have shown their willingness to promote democracy by serving in a new sovereign Russia. The famous example of KGB general Oleg Kalugin is not unique. Gorbachev, feeling the lack of stability and legitimacy of his presidency, decided to restructure the top of the Soviet political pyramid. He is trying to compensate for the decline in public confidence by vesting in himself sweeping new presidential powers: the right to impose direct presidential rule, to declare a state of emergency in unbending republics, to issue decrees having the force of laws, and to govern the Council of Ministers directly.

Obedient deputies recently satisfied Gorbachev's demands. As a result we have a freakish model of a presidency, unprecedented in history, which combines the huge body of presidential and legislative power. What took place was a "velvet counter-revolution" which many in the West did not immediately notice because it was packaged in parliamentary wrapping paper.

Gorbachev's victory over the Congress was clouded by Shevardnadze's warning about the threat of dictatorship and by the heart attack suffered by sacked Prime Minister Nikolai Ryzhkov. Indeed, it was a pyrrhic victory because it led to the ultimate disappointment of the newly politicized Soviet people. In this sense, I think Gorbachev is a tragic figure in our history. He managed to initiate perestroika, but he is incapable of carrying the reform process through. How does he intend to use his unlimited powers? Perhaps by introducing martial law in Georgia, Latvia, Moldova, or other republics? Having enjoyed the fruits of glasnost, a product of Gorbachev's efforts, people have started to believe in democracy. It is impossible now to turn them back into cogs of the Stalinist state machinery. The genie cannot be put back into the bottle. I remember seeing the happy faces of thousands of people who came to rallies held under the banner of democracy. Today the Russian winter days are filled with the search for bread and milk, and people's faces have become careworn. But many are beginning to understand the alphabet of democracy that was created long ago by the civilized states:

1. State power and the political system can only be replaced by means of free elections.

2. Democracy is the embodiment of the will of the majority with respect for the rights of all.

3. Democracy means that a political minority may fight for power openly.

During the course of the last year, as in our previous history, not one of these principles has been ensured in the Soviet Union. Just as we were about to liberate ourselves from a seven-decade heritage of totalitarianism, once again we stand under the threat of a new dictatorship. It turns out that our path to democracy is more difficult than it seemed one short year ago. But I hope we will overcome this. And it will be easier if the West understands us better.

Epilogue: The View in 1991

Harley D. Balzer

In March 1990, the dominant view of the Soviet future was optimism regarding the prospects for continued reform, possibly leading to a transition to some sort of democratic system. The optimism crested in spring and summer with the abolition of Article 6 of the Soviet Constitution (the passage that had codified the Communist Party's monopoly position in political life), victory by progressives in elections for local government in some fifty major cities, Gorbachev's apparent mastery of what many thought would be the last USSR Communist Party Congress, and expectation of the imminent adoption of some variant of the "500 Days Plan" (frequently called the Shatalin Plan) for rapid transition to a market economic system. Observers with good connections in Moscow spoke of new, genuinely representative elections, and serious market reforms.[1]

There were many cautionary voices, both in the USSR and in the West. Even those most strongly supporting democracy and elections warned that conservative forces would not relinquish power without a fight. Economic difficulties and national unrest offered opportunities for the "forces of order" to assert their indispensability. More pessimistic observers predicted an outright coup by the military, most likely in alliance with conservative factions of the Communist Party. A variant of this scenario portrayed Gorbachev becoming either the leader of or the figurehead for a conservative and military government.[2]

By early 1991, reformers were in retreat on every front. Virtually all of them were gone from top leadership positions. Having rid himself of the conservatives on his original team, Gorbachev now removed or lost the progressives, most notably Alexander Yakovlev and Eduard Shevardnadze. Vadim Bakatin was replaced as Minister of the Interior by Boris Pugo, and Afghan War figure General Boris Gromov was appointed as Pugo's deputy. Gennadii Yanaev was "elected" to the newly created position of Vice President.[3] A loyal *apparatchik*, Leonid Kravchenko, became head of a new broadcast media administration.

The pattern of personnel changes was too far-reaching to be considered a momentary blip or zig-zag. All of the new appointees were loyal Party men inclined to support a law-and-order regime. Conservative and reactionary forces became more assertive in public. Pugo and Minister of Defense Dmitrii Yazov presided over a crackdown on independence movements in the Baltic republics and an increased role for the military in preserving law and order throughout the USSR. Blood was shed in Lithuania and Latvia, and both the head of the KGB and a leader of the political right warned that there would be more. The Communist Party was again mentioned as an important institution, and opponents were accused of being "bourgeois" and seeking to "restore capitalism."

The economy appeared on the verge of a free fall, with the potential to belie judgments of Western economists who thought that an economy of Soviet proportions could not self-destruct. All of Gorbachev's most respected pro-market economic advisers resigned. The new Prime Minister, Valentin Pavlov, introduced a currency reform that amounted to an effort to confiscate the money he had just printed during his tenure as Minister of Finance. Then he compounded the damage by making absurd accusations of a Western economic conspiracy against the USSR.[4] Other measures cast a pall over the business environment and foreign economic relations, threatening to disrupt fragile new joint ventures and initiatives promoting international economic cooperation.[5] Fundamental principles of planning and the command economy were reasserted.

A Shift to the Right

What happened? The most plausible explanation is that Gorbachev peered into Janos Kornai's chasm and blinked.[6] Never a democrat and never intending to completely abandon "socialism," Gorbachev was not willing to pursue the changes he had set in motion beyond certain limits. No one, perhaps not even Gorbachev himself, could define the limits, but they appear to have been reached, at least for a time. A combination of economic, political, national and foreign policy considerations led him to resort to more traditional appeals and methods.[7]

Some have suggested that Gorbachev finally read the fine print of the Shatalin plan and realized that it meant too great a surrender of control over the economy, too much power for the republics, and too much buffeting by international economic forces over which the Soviet Union would have no control. It was safer to take the position that the USSR was not yet ready for a plunge into the market. When he was Prime Minister, Nikolai Ryzhkov had insisted that no major economic reform could be attempted until the government regained control over the disintegrating economy. Despite the irony that Ryzhkov proposed resorting to the very command-administrative techniques that caused "stagnation" and led to introducing perestroika in the first place, the chimera of regaining control continues to exert a powerful appeal.

Gorbachev's affection for the Shatalin plan could not have been enhanced by the fact that some of the strongest support for rapid transition to a market economy came from Boris Eltsin and other independent-minded leaders of the Russian Republic. Gorbachev found himself occupying a narrowing middle in the evolving political spectrum. The Communist Party and the conservatives chafed at his restraint, and began to find new leaders in the Russian Communist Party and the military. To many progressives, Gorbachev now appeared to be an obstacle to reform.[8] His position as the only reform leader not elected by the people became an anomaly undermining his authority vis à vis politicians who had successfully faced the voters.

It became evident that for Gorbachev, new thinking in international relations stopped at the borders of the USSR. Even if he could have accepted the overturning of fundamental economic and social beliefs and the shift of political power to more popular (in his mind irresponsible and demagogic) figures, Gorbachev and the conservatives could not accept the disintegration of the inner empire. The Soviet Union's security equation had already been drastically altered by the virtual disappearance of the Warsaw Pact. The military argued that it could not accept the loss of the entire Western buffer, acquired at such enormous cost in World War II. The argument that the USSR would be more secure with friendly democratic governments on its borders came up against emotional appeals to history, empire and *rodina* (motherland).[9]

Gorbachev found himself faced with an increasingly coherent conservative movement. Beginning with the Russian Republic Communist Party's founding Congress in mid-1990, dissatisfied groups from the Party, the military, the KGB, the defense industry, state farms, and the cultural world began to join in an informal but quite powerful conservative coalition. They are not a solid or united bloc, and they articulate a range of views from conservative to extreme reactionary. But they do represent a significant political force, claiming to speak for the Russian Party organization, the military-industrial complex, the food producing sector and the security services.[10] They have become increasingly vociferous, both in the media and on the floor of parliament.

By the end of January 1991, many democrats wished Gorbachev would go quietly. But he also still appeared to be a major force preventing a civil war. Colonel Viktor Alksnis followed his November warning that Gorbachev had thirty days to restore order with a threat in January that the military might have to switch to an "independent regime of work."[11] Thus many observers are drawn to the hope that political magician Gorbachev might pull yet another skittish reform rabbit out of his increasingly tattered hat.

Such hopes are not based solely on wishful thinking. Being the skillful politician that he has repeatedly shown himself to be, Gorbachev has sought to avoid becoming a captive of the conservatives. The personnel changes constitute a decisive shift, but policy has not been one-sided. The most serious change from the policies of perestroika, the resort to violence in Lithuania and Latvia, is still somewhat ambiguous. The precise origin of the events is not known. Gorbachev has denied direct responsibility, but his denial is not credible.[12] It seems to be part of an attempt to shift the discussion to "What did Gorbachev know and when did he know it," rather than admitting his approval of the decision to resist the independence movement by force if necessary. Unlike 1990, when economic pressures were used against Lithuania, in January 1991 the foreign media were not prevented from covering events in the region, which might suggest either that no violence was planned in advance, or that Gorbachev wanted it to be well-publicized. After the bloodshed, the special forces (OMON) units were removed from Vilnius, though they remain in Latvia.

There are other indications that Gorbachev does not intend a total reversal of course. The Ministry of Defense has announced that Vladivostok is to become an open city; a mass demonstration in Moscow took place without bloodshed; and Gorbachev has apparently accepted judgments overturning his edicts by the Constitutional Oversight committee. The right has complained bitterly that Gorbachev betrayed them by flinching when the Vilnius coup resulted in violence.[13] In attempting to remain in a shifting (and shrinking) middle, Gorbachev, perhaps inevitably, finds himself condemned by both sides.

In this situation, the literature on transitions from authoritarian rule to democracy remains relevant to the Soviet experience.[14] The difficulties being encountered are not the result of some cultural flaw that makes Russians unsuited for democracy. Nor are the problems due to the "totalitarian" as opposed to "authoritarian" nature of the USSR.[15] Of all the obstacles to successful transitions discussed in the literature, the multinational character of the USSR is probably the most significant.[16]

But political developments in the USSR are not theoretical; they are depressingly real. The most serious obstacles to a successful transition have been the mistakes and vacillations of the Soviet leadership. We will never know if the demands for complete independence by the Baltic and other republics were inevitable. We do know that failure to introduce genuine economic reform made it impossible for Moscow to offer positive inducements for them to remain in a restructured Union.[17] Resorting to repression, far from cowing the subject populations, has escalated their demands for separation. In 1987 or 1988 it might have been possible to maintain some sort of federation or confederation including all fifteen republics. In 1991, that prospect appears dim.

In the clash of two versions of security, those who viewed Lithuania as the first of what would be a devastating series of independent dominos won at least a temporary victory.[18] But, as in Tbilisi and Baku, the result of military repression may be to strengthen the resolve of those desiring complete independence. Just as the monetary reform may convince advocates of the market that they must escape the Soviet system if they are to improve their economic conditions, harsh repressions convinced even some of the Slavic population in the Baltic that independence might be a preferable solution.[19]

Gorbachev seems to understand that the forces of the old order have demonstrated their weakness as well as their power. They are incapable of solving the economic problems, or of holding the empire together by any means other than coercion. But they do have the power to impose martial law, concoct shadowy "national salvation committees," and disrupt the activities and food supplies of elected local governments.[20] They appear to be tenacious in their efforts to hang on to what remains of their power and privileges, in the name of preserving public order, socialism, and the Union.

Their negative power is far greater than their positive power. They can defer and disrupt market reforms, but cannot themselves create a viable economic system. They can threaten, arrest, or otherwise remove democratically elected political leaders, but cannot replace them with individuals enjoying popular authority and legitimacy. They can preserve the formal structure of the Union by force, but cannot convince the Baltic and Caucasus republics willingly to remain part of the empire. In short, they can obstruct, but they cannot create. Most important, they cannot do anything that offers a long term solution.

But just as Gorbachev was surprised at the lack of gratitude his reforms and the changes in Eastern Europe elicited, he may be surprised at the extent of the reaction that is being unleashed. Once again, his strongest supporters are those who wish to go a lot farther than he seems prepared to go. Gorbachev may have a limited agenda of restoring law and order and preserving the Union, but a great many Communists want to settle scores with their opponents.[21] And association with the Communists ties Gorbachev to forces that appear incapable of winning elections in most areas.

The conservatives, even in alliance with the reactionaries, are far from being a political majority in the USSR. Their electoral performance has been weak, despite a system rigged to enhance their chances. Might they try to seize power? Polling data suggest that a coup might be supported by 20% of the Soviet population.[22] But support for the idea in the abstract is very different from confronting the reality

The Question of a Coup

Pressures and threats from the right have once again raised the specter of a coup. While it may be within the realm of possibility that a coup will be attempted, it is important to remember that a coup *attempt* is not the same as a *successful* coup. The literature on transitions includes much discussion of coups.[23] The threat is always present, and coup attempts are attractive to military leaders who see themselves in the guise of saviors. But fear of a coup leads some observers—especially those in the USSR who would be the first targets of the perpetrators—to make the leap from a coup *attempt* to a government of colonels or generals in alliance with Russian nationalists and hard-line elements of the Communist Party. In the Baltic, an analogy is made to Bolshevik suppression of the elected Constituent Assembly in 1918.

Despite the danger of an attempted coup, even the most reactionary opponents of perestroika would have to think twice before trying to seize power. First, to do so would make them fully responsible for the economy, social problems, and whatever happens in the future. Second, the *threat* of a coup may be a much more attractive political technique than the coup itself. The right may be able to achieve policy goals such as preventing market reforms and maintaining the union by threats of what they will do if their wishes are ignored. Once the coup is attempted, however, it either succeeds or fails: it is less valuable as political capital, at least for a while.

And there is no guarantee that a coup would be successful. Machinations by the shadowy "Committees of National Salvation" in Lithuania and Latvia—considered by some to be the model for a reactionary-military-Party alliance that might attempt a coup in Moscow—provoked opposition not only from Baltic nationalists but also from the Russians and other Slavs in these republics.[24] While there is not much question that special forces units consistently do and will carry out orders to use their weapons, the behavior of the Soviet army in a civil conflict is less predictable. I doubt that anyone knows whether the result would be similar to that in Poland under Jaruzelski or that in Romania in December 1989.[25]

Given that a coup could lead to defeat or to civil war, are the potential gains from a seizure of power worth the risks? Would the military want to be responsible for what is left of the Soviet economy, in conditions where it would be regarded as a pariah by all of the world's economic powers? The prospect may not prevent misguided behavior by the reactionaries and generals, but it must certainly give them pause. In these circumstances, the advice given by O'Donnell and Schmitter is particularly apt:

> It follows that, contrary to the wishes of the soft-liners and the advice of almost everyone, the regime's opponents should increase their activity instead of prudently diminishing it, as the feared moment of the coup seems to approach. In particular, they should promote the diversification and extension of opposition throughout society, since that increases the perceived costs of repression for the hard-liners.[26]

Rumors of a coup circulated repeatedly during 1989 and 1990. The leader of the Moscow Party organization, Iurii Prokof'ev, has even suggested that Gorbachev should assume the sort of role Pinochet played in Chile—a ten- or fifteen-year authoritarian interregnum to prepare the nation for a market economy. Let us leave aside the question of whether planning and control types like Valentin Pavlov would know a market if it bit them, and the irony of Prokof'ev embracing a dictator reviled in the USSR since the death of Salvador Allende. What is truly important about Prokof'ev's proposal is that it is another variant of the "not now, not me" approach to reform. It is a way to keep things pretty much as they are, deferring hard choices and uncomfortable changes to an undefined future.

The argument for a strong power to guide the nation through difficult times is understandable, but misguided. Just before this volume went to press, Jerry Hough published a short article summarizing his argument that a coup is unnecessary because Gorbachev is already in full control and following the policies of a "modernizing autocrat."[27] The description may well be valid. However, I would question whether another Peter the Great or Stalin is what the Soviet Union needs (or wants). By most sociological definitions of "modernity," the USSR already qualifies.[28] It *is* a middle class society, even if it features what may be the most economically disadvantaged middle class we have ever encountered.[29]

The longing for order promises few genuine solutions. It is easy to forget just how great a role the perceived lack of order played in the formulation of Gorbachev's policies. As one keen observer wrote in 1985, a large portion of the Soviet population found the status quo "unacceptable" due to a pervasive "lack of order":

> "lack of order" is a widespread condition that permeates daily existence and causes deep disquiet. At its most literal, lack of order means that crime and corruption are—or are perceived to be, the statistics being a state secret—steadily rising. So too is the incidence of petty stealing, alcoholism, divorce, abortion, infant mortality, congenital defects in children, adult male mortality, and animosity between and within social classes. Moreover, the institutions charged with providing at least a measure of protection against such woes—the police, the courts, the soviets, the Party, the health services, and so on—are regarded as increasingly corrupt or ineffective... Chronic shortages of basic foodstuffs and the constant need to resort to bribery or the black market—both of which are illegal and expensive—have become more common ...[30]

It is important to remember how chaotic things had become by the mid-1980s, so that the current crisis can be kept in perspective. Perestroika did not create the difficulties, and few of the problems are susceptible to old-style solutions.The Baltics and other restive republics could be subjected to higher levels of repression; the independent press could be curbed; military patrols and even martial law could become a common feature of life in major cities. But these measures will do nothing to increase the popularity of the idea of the Union in the restive republics and will do even less to improve the economy. Resorting to the measures that created the mess will not get them out of it—such a course will only prolong the economic crisis and make a long-term solution that much more difficult.

More likely than a coup is imposition of martial law by Gorbachev himself. If those are the two choices, Gorbachev is probably a preferable candidate for the job than Gromov, Pugo, or Polozkov, and certainly a better choice than Alksnis. But have we been driven to pose the question in terms of these stark choices by a genuine lack of other options or by clever political positioning? During the first four years of perestroika, it was repeatedly asserted that there was no alternative to Gorbachev. It may have been true then: it is not necessarily accurate in 1991.

Pessimistic Progressives

Leading reformers have outdone each other in bemoaning the drift to the right. Many joke about living in a restored *gulag*. The only hopeful sign is that at least some of them are rallying around Boris Eltsin in the Russian Republic government and as informal advisers. Similar groups have also developed in other republics, and following their activities is an important agenda for research. But in general the retreat and disarray among the reformers is one of the most disquieting aspects of the current situation. Rather than remaining to fight from within, many are bailing out. Unless they can develop an alternative institutional locus of power, they will have no means of resisting counterreform short of overthrowing the system. Regime change might be the preferable outcome, but it will involve a much more serious conflict that could be more than just political.

The desolation among the democrats is a reflection of the most fundamental failure of perestroika—the lack of genuine political institutions. Gorbachev has created neither a functioning legislature nor a viable executive arm.[31] The impact of Gorbachev's failure to build institutions emerges clearly from a comparison with a Russian reformer who did create new institutional structures. The Great Reforms of the 1860s were not "great" because Alexander II sought to balance between reformers and conservatives. They deserve the superlative because lasting institutional changes were brought about: emancipation of the peasantry, an independent judiciary, University autonomy, a banking system, organs of local government, and a reserve-based army. The institutional position of the reformers was sufficiently solid to withstand or moderate the effects of most of the "counterreforms" in the 1870s and 1880s.[32] It is the lack of comparable institutional achievement that gives rise to my greatest uneasiness about the quality of Gorbachev's leadership. Thus far, the institutional legacy of perestroika consists of half-measures and hybrids. He has not overcome the autocratic tradition that makes written legislation subservient to the will of the ruler. In the choice between ends and means, he has thus far been a true Leninist, emphasizing ends. For the achievements to be lasting, at some point pragmatism in policy must be superseded by permanent institutional structures. And Gorbachev's time may be running out.

Mikhail Gorbachev has already been in power longer than the four American presidents who served between Dwight Eisenhower and Ronald Reagan. In an age of television and satellite communications, the political half-life of any leader may be limited. In late 1989 I began to suggest that if Gorbachev wished to be remembered as a hero in 100 years, it was time for him to resign and hold new elections. By early 1991 it is probably too late for Gorbachev to win a genuine popular vote, and even his referendum on the Union could be in doubt. The greatest tragedy involves the long-term prospects for change. All of the fence sitters who had to be convinced to support reform may now have had their direction determined, and it is not the direction of risk and restructuring. It took a decade of internal conflict and the ravages of World War II to create the Stalinist system. We should hardly expect its extirpation to be quick or easy. It is the work of a generation. That battle has only begun.[33]

Notes

1.   Giulietto Chiesa, "The 28th Congress of the CPSU," *Problems of Communism* XXXIX No. 4 (July–August 1990) pp. 24-38; also Kennan paper.

2.   See Peter Reddaway, "The Threat to Gorbachev," *New York Review of Books*, August 17, 1989, pp. 19-24.

3.   Yanaev was defeated on the first ballot, despite being the sole candidate put forward by Gorbachev. In behavior typical of his parliamentary style, Gorbachev then demanded a second vote, and this time Yanaev was approved.

4.   Hedrick Smith describes an incident in which Pavlov argued with Leonid Abalkin against allowing a foreign businessman to sell computers for rubles and reinvest the profits in the USSR. Pavlov's position was that the USSR could not permit any element of its economy to be controlled by outsiders. See *The New Russians* (New York: Random House, 1990), p. 275.

5.   For a summary of the economic as well as political atmosphere, see "The Trade Bonanza that Never Was," *Financial Times*, February 6, 1991, p. 18; and Quentin Peel, "KGB Tries to Reassure Foreign Investors," in the same issue, p. 20.

6.   I first heard the situation formulated in this way by Thane Gustafson.

In addition to a conversation with Gustafson, my thinking about these topics has benefitted from numerous conversations with Marjorie Mandelstam Balzer, and from discussions with jerry Hough and Blair Ruble. The issues are raised in a particularly valuable way by a series of articles in *Soviet Economy*. See George W. Breslauer, "Evaluating Gorbachev as Leader," *Soviet Economy*, Vol. 5 No. 4 (1989), pp. 299-340; and the three articles in Vol. 6, No. 1 (1990): Peter Reddaway, "The Quality of Gorbachev's Leadership," pp. 125-140; Archie Brown, "Gorbachev's Leadership: Another View," pp. 141-154; and Andranik Migranyan, "Gorbachev's

Leadership: A Soviet View," pp. 155-159. If continued, this discussion promises to provide a contribution as valuable as the articles in *Problems of Communism* in the mid-1960s. See Zbigniew Brzezinski, ed. *Dilemmas of Change in Soviet Politics* (New York: Columbia University Press, 1969).

7.   Gorbachev has frequently invoked the need for a combination of old and new methods.

8.   See the comments by Galina Starovoitova in Chapter 11; Seweryn Bialer, "The Last Soviet Communist," *U.S News and World Report*, October 8, 1990, pp. 53-54.

9.   The most publicized instance of pressure on Gorbachev came from the threat by Colonel Viktor Alksnis that the President had "thirty days" to reimpose order. Alksnis represents a reactionary fringe on the political spectrum, and is apparently very useful to the conservatives. Defense Minister Yazov meets with Alksnis, smiles as he delivers mild reprimands, and thereby encourages the right wing to put increased pressure on Gorbachev. The extreme right thus help to push the president into an alliance with the conservatives.

Gorbachev could not have reacted with equanimity to the Russian Republic's direct challenge to his foreign policy prerogatives. See Andrei Kozyrev, "Russia, in Its Own Voice," *The New York Times*, November 25, 1990, "Week In Review," p. 11.

10.   The degree of unanimity within the Party, the military and the KGB is a subject of much debate. Both left and right claim adherents in all the major institutions, with the divisions coming largely but not exclusively along generational lines.

11.   Quentin Peel, "Decline and Fall of Economic Perestroika," *Financial Times*, January 26, 1991, p. 8.

12.   Saulius Girnius, "Lithuania's 'National Salvation Committee'," Radio Liberty *Report on the USSR*, January 25, 1991, pp. 6-8; and Stephen Foye, "Gorbachev Denies Responsibility for Crackdown," pp. 1-3. A recent article in *Nezavisimaia gazeta* describes the plans for suppression of Lithuanian independence by the Communist Party in advance of the crackdown.

13.   David Remnick, "The Hard-Liners' Bad Boy Challenges Gorbachev," *Washington Post*, February 8, 1991, p. A1.

14.   Guillermo O'Donnell and Philippe C. Schmitter, *Transitions from Authoritarian rule: Tentative Conclusions about Uncertain Democracies*, Baltimore: (Johns Hopkins University Press, 1986, 1989).

15.   The classic formulation of the argument about the difficulty of transition from a totalitarian regime to democracy is Juan J. Linz, Totalitarian and Authoritarian Regimes," *Handbook of Political Science* Vol. III (Reading, MA: Addison-Wesley, 1975), pp. 259-264. It has been formulated for the USSR by Andranik Migranian, "Dol'giy put' k evropeiskomu domu," *Novyi mir*, No. 7 (1989), pp. 166-184); and "Gorbachev's Leadership: A Soviet View," *Soviet Economy* Vol. 6 No. 2 (1990), pp. 155-159.

Migranian recently reiterated his reasons for believing in the need for a strong hand to guide reform, but also made it clear that the sort of dictatorship he saw

Gorbachev introducing was not what he had in mind. See the interview under the rubric "Tak chto zhe s nami proiskhodit?" *Komsomol'skaia pravda* January 23, 1991, p. 2.

16.   Dankwart A. Rustow, "Transitions to Democracy: Toward a Dynamic Model," *Comparative Politics* Vol. 2 No. 3 (April 1970), pp. 337-363, particularly pp. 350-352. where he discusses national unity as the single necessary "background condition."

17.   The demands for sovereignty and then for independence involved far more than economics. However, it might have been possible for Moscow to use economic inducements to encourage membership in a reconstituted confederation. Lack of resources made that tack impossible.

Migranian has also stated that the economy should have been tackled first. (*Dol'gii put'*, repeated in *Soviet Economy*). However, he also notes that the democrats do not have the power to introduce radical economic changes. (*Soviet Economy*, p. 157). He would argue that this proves the need for a strong executive authority to push through the reforms.

18.   Gorbachev has consistently insisted that independence may only be achieved in conformity with his definition of legality. His approach is reminiscent of his insistence that Article 6 of the Constitution could be abolished only by the Party, not by the Congress of Peoples Deputies or the Supreme Soviet. We should recall that Gorbachev is a lawyer by education, and that he is a product of a system in which formal rationality has a significant place.

19.   Radio Liberty Daily Report No. 25, February 5, 1991.

20.   Tatiana Zaslavskaia's suggestion that food would appear after martial law may be correct, but it is difficult to imagine that the situation would last long. Similarly, an end to disruptions by *apparatchiki* might improve the food supply to some major cities, but this, too, would be short lived. The promise to provide every family with a house or apartment by the year 2000 would remain a joke.

21.   See Peter Reddaway, "Empire on the Brink," *New York Review of Books*, January 31, 1991, pp. 7-10; and "The Quality of Gorbachev's Leadership," *Soviet Economy*, Vol. 6, No. 2 (1990), pp. 125-140.

22.   See the discussion of public opinion about the need for a "strong hand" By S. Shpilko, *Izvestiia*, January 18, 1991, p. 5.

23.   O'Donnell and Schmitter, pp. 23-24; 55. Also see Samuel P. Huntington, *Political Order in Changing Societies*, (New Haven: Yale University Press, 1968), particularly pp. 219-237.

24.   See note number 20.

25.   Roman Sporluk has formulated this as the choice between "Gorbazelski and Gorbacescu." Cited in Breslauer, "Evaluating Gorbachev As Leader," p. 331, note 32.

26.   O'Donnell and Schmitter, p. 23.

27.   Jerry Hough, "Soviet Dictators—And Democrats." *Washington Post*, February 17, 1991, p. C1.

28.   Marion J. Levy, Jr., *Modernization and the Structure of Societies: A Setting for International Affairs* (Princeton: Princeton University Press, 1966).

29. The Soviet middle class is doubly disadvantaged in economic terms. Its standard of living is low, and it is not in a position to own property in the manner traditionally associated with the middle class. It is a *professional* rather than an entrepreneurial or mercantile middle class. This concept requires additional formulation. For suggestive lines of investigation see Burton Bledstein, *The Culture of Professionalism: The Middle Class and the Development of Higher Education in America* (New York: W. W. Norton, 1976); and Harold Perkin, *The Rise of Professional Society: England Since 1880* (London: Routledge, 1989).

30. Peter Reddaway, "Waiting for Gorbachcv," *New York Review of Books*, October 10, 1985, p. 5.

31. The USSR is in danger of becoming what Samuel Huntington refers to as a "praetorian" system, lacking institutional mechanisms for dealing with political demands: "In a society without effective political institutions and unable to develop them, the end result of social and economic modernization is political chaos." *Political Order in Changing Society*, p. 198.

32. W. Bruce Lincoln, *The Great Reforms: Autocracy, Bureaucracy and the Politics of Change in Imperial Russia* (DeKalb: Northern Illinois University Press, 1990) pp. 176-191; and Ben Eklof and John Bushnell, eds., *Russia's Great Reforms* (Bloomington: Indiana University Press, forthcoming, 1991).

33. For a recent discussion of the magnitude of the task see Alexander S. Tsipko, *Is Stalinism Really Dead? The Future of Perestroika As A Moral Revolution* (San Francisco: Harper, 1990).

Chronology of Major Events:
March 1985–January 1991

1985

March 11	Mikhail Sergeevich Gorbachev is named general secretary of the Communist Party of the USSR (CPSU), signaling the emergence of a new generation of Soviet leadership.
April 5	Antidrinking and anticorruption campaigns are initiated.
April 17	Moscow sets a unilateral moratorium on nuclear arms testing for August 6.
April 23	CPSU Central Committee (CC) Plenum announces Politburo personnel changes: KGB chief Viktor Chebrikov is promoted from candidate to full member; CC Secretaries Nikolai Ryzhkov and Yegor Ligachev are named full members, and Minister of Defense Sergei Sokolov is named a candidate member.
April 26	Warsaw Pact treaty is renewed by member nations for another twenty years.
May 19	Newspaper article praising Stalin is published.
June 21	*Pravda* article criticizes economic reforms in the socialist bloc.
July 1	CC Plenum again focuses on Politburo personnel changes: Grigorii Romanov is removed, and Eduard Shevardnadze is named a full member.
July 2	The Supreme Soviet approves the nomination of Andrei Gromyko as chairman of the Supreme Soviet Presidium, accompanied by the appointment of Eduard Shevardnadze to replace him as foreign minister.

July 24, 1985   Nikita Khrushchev is shown on Soviet TV.

August 1   Gorbachev is named head of the Defense Council.

September 14   USSR expels Britons accused of spying.

September 27   Nikolai Tikhonov resigns as chairman of the Council of
                       Ministers and is replaced by Nikolai Ryzhkov.

October 23   USSR proposes freeze on intermediate-range missile
                       deployments.

November 4   *Izvestiia* publishes interview with Ronald Reagan.

November 19-21   Geneva summit with Ronald Reagan establishes "personal
                       diplomacy," which will come to characterize future summits.
                       A joint statement sets basis for regular summit meetings and
                       broader scientific, educational, and cultural ties.

November 22   Announcement of merging of agricultural and industrial
                       administration in "Agro-industrial complex."

December 7   The existence of AIDS in the USSR is officially acknowl-
                       edged by the head of the Institute of Viruses.

December 24   Boris Eltsin replaces Viktor Grishin as first secretary of the
                       Moscow City Party Committee.

1986

February 10   Natan Sharansky is "permitted" to leave the Soviet Union.

February 25   Twenty-seventh CPSU Party Congress begins (to continue
                       through March 6). Perestroika is formally adopted. Person-
                       nel changes are made in the Politburo: Lev Zaikov becomes
                       a full member, Iurii Solov'ev and Nikolai Sliunkov are named
                       candidate members, and Vasilii Kuznetsov and Boris
                       Ponomarev retire.

April 1-3   A small brawl in Yakutsk leads to a demonstration by
                       several hundred Yakut University students. They protest
                       police handling of the brawl and agitate in favor of local
                       perestroika.

April 19, 1986	Experiment allowing Soviet theater greater autonomy is announced.
April 20	Vladimir Horowitz plays a concert in Moscow for the first time in 60 years.
April 28	The first reports of the Chernobyl nuclear reactor disaster reach the West. Official acknowledgment of the disaster is not made until May 2.
May 13-15	The Fifth Congress of the Filmmakers Union is held, during which the Union initiates change in the cultural establishment by voting out the old guard leadership and replacing it with progressive film artists. Film director Elem Klimov is elected as its first secretary.
May 17	Klimov creates the Conflicts Commission, which subsequently releases many previously banned films.
May 29	Viktor Louis states that Andrei Sakharov is not likely to be permitted to return to Moscow.
June	Beginning with the June 1986 issue, the weekly magazine *Ogonek* is transformed by its new editor, Vitalii Korotich, into a locomotive of glasnost and investigative journalism.
July 2	Viacheslav Molotov, one of Stalin's closest associates and a "non-person" since the defeat of the "anti-Party" group in 1957, gives an interview to TASS.
	Soviet television shows a film about Nikolai Vavilov, a geneticist who perished in the Lysenko era.
August 16	Siberian River diversion project is officially shelved.
August 23	Soviet UN employee Gennadii Zakharov is arrested in New York for spying.
August 26	A short story by Valdimir Nabokov is published in the Soviet Union.
August 30	The KGB detains American journalist Nicholas Daniloff in Moscow.
September 7	Nicholas Daniloff is formally charged with espionage.

September 17, 1986   The U.S. orders the expulsion of twenty-five Soviet diplomats at the UN for espionage activities.

September 29   Daniloff is released, as is Zakharov.

September 30   Reykjavik summit is announced.

October 5   Prisoner of conscience Yurii Orlov is permitted to leave the USSR. Despite formal denials, this is assumed to be part of the Daniloff-Zakahrov deal.

October 11-12   Reykjavik summit focuses on the reduction of strategic and medium-range missiles, but Reagan and Gorbachev fail to reach significant agreement.

October 19   U.S. and USSR each expel a group of the other nation's diplomats.

November 16   Tengiz Abuladze's film *Repentance*, a metaphorical indictment of Stalin, is released to the general public.

                     Rioting occurs in the Kazakh city of Alma-Ata in connection with the replacement of Dinmukhamed Kunaev by Gennadii Kol'bin as the first secretary of the Kazakh Republic Communist Party.

November 24   In a speech in Tashkent, Gorbachev demands greater attention to anti-religious activities and atheist propaganda.

December 19   Andrei Sakharov and Yelena Bonner are released from exile in Gorky, following a December 16 phone call from Gorbachev inviting Sakharov to Moscow.

1987

                     Juris Podnieks' film *Is It Easy To Be Young?*, a documentary portraying alienated and disaffected youth, is released.

                     The Moscow Rock Club is formed, reflecting increasing agitation among young Soviets for popular music and youth culture.

                     Excerpts of Anatolii Rybakov's anti-Stalinist novel *Children of the Arbat* are published in *Ogonek*. The heated debate over the novel becomes more intense when it is published in full in *Druzhba narodov* later in the year.

USSR ceases jamming of BBC and most other Western radio stations.

January 1, 1987   New regulations take effect easing travel restrictions for Soviet citizens.

State Acceptance Commission (*Gospriemka*) begins operation.

January 13   Legislation is adopted permitting operation of joint ventures.

January 26   CC Plenum focuses on reform of the electoral system, involving a secret ballot, multicandidate elections, and permitting non-Party candidates in elections for government posts. Politburo changes include Kunaev's retirement and Aleksandr Yakovlev's appointment to candidate membership.

February 4   USSR intensifies jamming of Radio Liberty.

February 11   Resolution published permitting operation of private restaurants and cafes.

February 13   Gorbachev addresses Soviet mass media, instructing journalists and propagandists on goals and limits of glasnost.

May 6   *Pamiat'*, a right-wing nationalist and antisemitic organization, holds a demonstration in Moscow.

May 28   On Border Guards' Day, West German youth Mathias Rust, violates Soviet airspace and lands his Cessna plane in Red Square. The entire Soviet military is embarrassed, especially the leadership. As a result, Commander-in-Chief of the Anti-Aircraft Defense Forces Aleksandr Koldunov, Air Defense Commander Marshal Anatolii Konstantinov, and Minister of Defense Sergei Sokolov are dismissed. Dmitrii Yazov becomes acting Minister of Defense.

June 25   At CC Plenum, Gorbachev outlines plan for reforming the economy according to new economic methods. He also calls for a Party conference to be held next June. In the Politburo, Nikolai Sliunkov and Aleksandr Yakovlev are promoted from candidate to full members, Dmitrii Yazov is named a candidate member, and Sergei Sokolov is retired.

July 1987 | Crimean Tatars demonstrate, demanding the right to return to the homeland from which they were forcibly expelled at the end of World War II.

September 24 | Politburo decrees that individuals and cooperatives may open small shops—the first semiprivate stores allowed since the 1920s.

October 2 | The innovative television program *Vzgliad* debuts, embracing controversy as a principle. This opens the way for greater glasnost in television, manifested in such programs as *600 Seconds* and *Fifth Wheel*.

October 21 | At CC Plenum, Boris Eltsin makes a speech criticizing Gorbachev for the slow pace of reform, and threatens to resign. Geidar Aliev is retired from Politburo.

October 23 | Demonstrations are held in the Baltic republics on the anniversary of the Nazi-Soviet pact.

November 7 | In a speech marking the Seventieth Anniversary of the Bolshevik Revolution, Gorbachev states that Stalin's guilt is "enormous and unforgivable." He announces creation of a commission to review the cases of victims of repression and to revise the history of the CPSU.

November 11 | Boris Eltsin is dismissed as first secretary of the Moscow City Party Committee as a result of both his October plenum speech and his nonadherence to democratic centralism in Party affairs.

December 8-11 | Washington summit marks the first visit of a Soviet leader to the United States since Khrushchev's visit in 1959. Reagan and Gorbachev sign a treaty banning medium-range nuclear missiles.

1988

Mikhail Gorbachev is selected as *Time* magazine's "Man of the Year." This does little to help his popularity in the USSR.

Vasilii Pichul's film *Malenkaia Vera* is released. Billed as a "glasnost film," it is a stark portrayal of the empty life of a Soviet family, sadly familiar to many in the country.

Mikhail Shatrov's play *Onward, Onward, Onward!* is published in *Znamia*. The publication helps inspire an impassioned debate about Stalinism and its consequences.

January 1
New Law on State Enterprises comes into effect. Under the law, 60 percent of enterprises in the industrial sector are to switch to a system of self-accounting and self-financing.

February 4
Ten Old Bolsheviks, including Nikolai Bukharin, are rehabilitated.

January 17
State Environmental Protection Agency (Goskompriroda) is established.

February 11
Nagorno-Karabakh regional council asks that the region become part of the Armenian SSR.

February 27-29
Violence between Azeris and Armenians breaks out in Sumgait, Azerbaidzhan, following two weeks of demonstrations in Armenia demanding control over Nagorno-Karabakh.

March 13
Sovetskaia Rossiia publishes Nina Andreeva's letter, which is perceived as a defense of Stalinism and a conservative attack on the changes produced by perestroika and especially glasnost.

March 24
A group of Christian priests and activists write a letter to the ailing Patriarch Pimen, requesting that he resign.

April 5
Pravda finally prints a response to Andreeva's letter, defending openness and perestroika as integral to democratization and economic reform, and attacking those who defend Stalinist repression and Brezhnevite stagnation.

April 10, 1988   Easter services are broadcast on Soviet television for the
                    first time.

April 14   Geneva accords on settlement of the war in Afghanistan are
                    signed.

April 26   Gorbachev meets with Patriarch Pimen.

May 15   Phased withdrawal of Soviet troops from Afghanistan begins.

May 21   Republic Party leaders of Azerbaidzhan and Armenia are
                    dismissed.

May 25   First official casualty figures from the Afghan War are given
                    as 13,310 dead, 35,478 wounded, and 311 missing.

May 30–June 2   Moscow summit, the fourth summit between Reagan and
                    Gorbachev, is held. The Americans stress human rights and
                    the Soviets emphasize "new realism" in U.S.-Soviet relations.

June 5   Year-long celebration of the millennium of Christianity in
                    Russia begins.

June 10   Amid rethinking of Soviet history, secondary school history
                    exams are canceled.

June 28–July 1   Nineteenth Communist Party Conference–the first since
                    1941–is held. The Conference approves sweeping political
                    reform, promising a shift of power from the Party to the
                    government, and a new legal system.

August 3   Mathias Rust is released from prison after having served one
                    year of his four-year sentence.

August 26   Legislation is announced permitting 50-year leases on
                    farmland.

October 1   Gorbachev is elected chairman of the Supreme Soviet.
                    Constitutional amendments are proposed to make the Su-
                    preme Soviet a full-time legislature and to provide for
                    multicandidate elections.

October 1-2   Founding Congress of Estonian Popular Front.

October 7   Lithuanians receive permission to display their flag.

November 16, 1988   Estonia declares sovereignty.

December 7   Reagan and Gorbachev meet in New York. Although no major results are announced, the talks help establish the precedent of regular face-to-face contact.

A devastating earthquake strikes Armenia, killing approximately 25,000 people and injuring thousands, and leaving tens of thousands homeless.

December 8   Gorbachev addresses UN General Assembly, outlining a new agenda of common global issues and pledging unilateral cuts of 500,000 troops. He then cuts short his trip to return home and deal with the consequences of the Armenian earthquake.

1989

January   George Orwell's *1984* is published in the USSR.

January 12   The Presidium of the Supreme Soviet rules that Nagorno-Karabakh Autonomous Republic will remain part of Azerbaidzhan, but will be placed under a "special form of administration."

February 7   Shamsidin Babakhanov ibn Zeyudin, head of the Central Asian Islamic Directorate, resigns four days after Tashkent demonstrators demand his removal. He is soon replaced by Muhammad-Sadik Muhammad Yusuf.

March 6   Speaking on Hungarian television, Soviet Foreign Ministry spokesman Gennadii Gerasimov says that every East European country's future "is in its own hands," thereby renouncing the Brezhnev doctrine. On June 11, Soviet officials in Bonn reiterate this policy.

March 26   First multicandidate elections to the Congress of People's Deputies are held, resulting in humiliating defeats for scores of Communists. Elections and runoffs continue throughout the spring in various republics.

April 9   At least 19 people are killed in Tbilisi, Soviet Georgia, when special forces troops attack a crowd of peaceful demonstrators. Soviet Interior Ministry refuses to reveal to medical personnel the composition of gas used on some victims.

April 25, 1989   CC Plenum meets and accepts resignations from 110 members of the CC and the Central Auditing Commission, thereby ridding the CC of most of its "dead souls."

May 2   Hungary begins dismantling the barbed-wire fence along its border with Austria, becoming the first Soviet-bloc country to open a border with Western Europe.

May 18   Lithuania declares sovereignty.

May 25-June 9   At the first session of the national Congress of People's Deputies, delegates enthrall the nation with critical speeches carried live on television. Factory production drops 20 percent during Congress's session.

June 4   Violence breaks out between Uzbeks and Meskhetian Turks in the Fergana oblast of Uzbekistan.

                    In Poland, the Communist Party suffers defeat when Solidarity-endorsed candidates win all 161 contested seats in the lower house of parliament and 99 of 100 seats in the Senate.

June 21   Nursultan Nazarbaev is elected CP first secretary in Kazakhstan, returning the position to a Kazakh and launching Nazarbaev on a prominent political career.

June 26   Live coverage of the Supreme Soviet proceedings is canceled as a result of the drop in industrial output. However, night-time rebroadcast is retained, changing many peoples' sleep patterns.

July 11   Kuzbass coal miners go on strike, followed by miners in the Donbass on July 19. Strikes also spread to Siberian coal mines.

July 27-28   Inter-Regional Group of deputies, a parliamentary faction uniting a loose coalition of progressives, is formed.

July 29   Latvia follows the lead of Estonia and Lithuania in declaring sovereignty.

August-November   Solzhenitsyn's *Gulag Archipelago* is serialized in *Novyi Mir*.

August 24   In Poland, Solidarity adviser Tadeusz Mazowiecki is confirmed as the new prime minister, representing the first democratic transfer of power away from the Communists.

September 1989   Azerbaidzhan institutes rail blockade of Armenia.

September 9   Founding Congress of the Ukrainian popular front movement *Rukh* is held in Kiev.

September 10   Hungary opens its border with Austria to East Germans, suspending a 1968 agreement with East Berlin that required Hungary to block travel of East Germans to a third country.

September 11-14   More than 13,000 East Germans leave Hungary for West Germany, via Austria, in the largest East German exodus to the West since the Berlin Wall was built in 1961.

September 23   Azerbaidzhan declares sovereignty.

September 28   Brezhnev holdover Vladimir Shcherbitskii is retired from the post of Communist Party First Secretary of the Ukraine.

September 30–
October 3   More than 17,000 East Germans emigrate to West Germany via Czechoslovakia and Poland with the permission of the East German government.

October 7   In Hungary, the Communist Party abandons Leninism, renaming itself the Hungarian Socialist Party.

October 9   The Supreme Soviet recognizes the right to strike.

October 13   In a closed meeting with leading Soviet editors and cultural figures, Gorbachev criticizes the mass media for exploiting glasnost and allowing publicity harmful to the goals of perestroika and national morale. *Argumenty i fakty* chief editor Vladislav Starkov is singled out and pressured to resign. Despite a virtual ultimatum from Gorbachev, Starkov, with the support of his staff, refuses to go. Shortly thereafter, Viktor Afanas'ev resigns as *Pravda* editor and Ivan Frolov is appointed to replace him.

October 16   About 100,000 people join in a pro-democracy demonstration in Leipzig, East Germany–the largest unauthorized demonstration in the country since 1953.

October 17   The Soviet psychiatric organization is readmitted to the World Psychiatric Association.

October 18, 1989   East German leader Erich Honecker is forced to resign. He is replaced by Egon Krenz.

October 23   Kuzbass miners stage a warning strike, and Vorkuta miners join them on October 25.

Hungary proclaims itself a free republic.

October 27   The Warsaw Pact nations issue a statement endorsing the right of each member country to seek its own political doctrine, followed by a statement on October 28 by Evgenii Primakov that member states are free to leave the alliance.

November 1   Strikes begin anew in the Donbass and continue in Vorkuta.

November 9   The East German government opens the Berlin Wall to its citizens.

November 10   Bulgarian leader Todor Zhivkov is ousted after thirty-five years of rule and is replaced by the moderate Foreign Minister Petar Mladenov.

November 19   More than 10,000 people rally in Prague. The reform movement Civic Forum is founded.

November 24   Czechoslovak Communist Party General Secretary Milos Jakes resigns. Former Party chief Alexander Dubcek addresses 250,000 demonstrators in Prague.

November 27   The Supreme Soviet approves a law granting economic autonomy to the Baltic republics.

December 1   Gorbachev and Pope John Paul II meet at the Vatican.

In East Germany, the parliament votes to eliminate the Party's monopoly on power.

December 2-3   Malta summit is held. President Bush's first summit with Gorbachev is characterized by the U.S. administration as a "get-to-know-each-other" meeting. They discuss the new structure of international relations following the collapse of East European communist regimes. Gorbachev gives Bush a frank assessment of Soviet domestic problems.

December 10   In Czechoslovakia, a new government is sworn in, with non-

Communist ministers in the majority for the first time since 1948. President Gustav Husak resigns.

December 11   CC resolves to create a separate RSFSR Communist Party bureau. Vladimir Ivashko is promoted to full member of the Politburo.

December 12   Second session of the Congress of People's Deputies begins.

December 14   Andrei Sakharov, the "conscience" of the Soviet people, dies of a heart attack at age 68 in Moscow.

December 15-17   In Romania, protestors ring a church in the city of Timisoara, where authorities seek to evict a pastor who championed the rights of ethnic Hungarians, and thousands riot when officials try to remove him.

December 20   The Lithuanian Communist Party breaks with Moscow.

December 23   Romanian dictator Nicolai Ceausescu is overthrown.

December 25   Ceausescu is tried before a military tribunal and is found guilty and executed.

December 29   Dissident playwright Vaclav Havel becomes Czechoslovakia's first non-Communist president in more than forty years.

1990

The documentary film *This Is No Way to Live* debuts. It is a brutal depiction and indictment of life under Soviet communism.

January   Serialization of Solzhenitsyn's *The First Circle* begins in *Novyi Mir*.

January 19   A state of emergency is declared in Baku following anti-Armenian pogroms and an escalation in fighting between Azerbaidzhanis and Armenians in Nagorno-Karabakh. Soviet troops enter Baku to restore order and to prevent the possibility of a coup by the Azerbaidzhani Popular Front.

February 4   On the eve of the CPSU CC Plenum, more than 100,000

Muscovites march to the Kremlin demanding democratic reforms in the largest demonstration since the Bolshevik Revolution.

February 7   The CC approves the renunciation of the CPSU's constitutionally guaranteed monopoly on power, encoded in Article 6 of the Soviet Constitution, and endorses Gorbachev's proposal to create a presidential system.

February 12   Riots break out in Dushanbe, Tadzhikistan due to ethnic-based tensions over housing, leaving 37 people dead.

February 13   Ottawa meeting of foreign ministers of the four major World War II allies and East and West Germany. The "two plus four" framework for negotiating the reunification of Germany is established.

February 25   Nationwide prodemocracy rallies draw more than 1 million demonstrators.

February 24   Lithuanian Popular Front group Sajudis wins a landslide victory in Lithuanian parliamentary elections.

March-May   Elections are held for republican congresses of people's deputies, and for local governments. Reformers win power in Moscow, Leningrad and many other cities.

March 4   First elections are held to the newly created Congress of People's Deputies of the Russian Republic; reformers make political inroads, but conservatives are also well-represented.

March 6   Gorbachev says that NATO membership for a united Germany is "absolutely out of the question."

March 11   The Lithuanian Supreme Soviet issues a declaration of independence one day before the Congress of People's Deputies meets to adopt secession rules. Sajudis chairman Vytautas Landsbergis is elected Supreme Soviet chairman. A battle of wills between Vilnius and Moscow begins.

March 13-15   The third session of the national Congress of People's Deputies repeals Article 6 of the Constitution, approves the creation of a new executive structure, and legalizes a multiparty system. A new presidential system—consisting of the President of the USSR, a Presidential Council and the

Council of the Federation—is inaugurated. Gorbachev is sworn in as the new president (after running unopposed and being elected by secret ballot). Gorbachev resigns as Supreme Soviet chairman, and Anatolii Lukianov is elected to replace him.

The Congress declares Lithuania's declaration of independence invalid and a violation of the Soviet Constitution.

March 27, 1990   The new Presidential Council, similar in function to the U.S. presidential cabinet, holds its first meeting. Given its composition and proximity to President Gorbachev, there are indications that this organ may become the new locus of decisionmaking.

March 28   Estonian Communist Party votes to split with Moscow.

March 29   Moscow seals Lithuanian borders and orders foreigners to leave the republic, as the standoff between Moscow and Vilnius continues. Demonstrations of support for Lithuania continue in other republics.

March 30   Estonia declares independence.

May 3   Patriarch Pimen dies while still in office.

May 4   Latvia declares independence.

May 16   First RSFSR Congress of People's Deputies opens. The Congress is tasked with the formation of the Russian republic's government and moves to declare Russia's sovereignty.

May 29   After three rounds of balloting, Boris Eltsin is elected Chairman of the RSFSR Supreme Soviet—the closest thing to a president of Russia.

May 31-June 3   Bush-Gorbachev Washington summit focuses on German reunification. Agreements are signed on the reduction of strategic and chemical weapons. Gorbachev travels to Minneapolis and San Francisco urging U.S. businessmen to invest in the Soviet Union, proclaiming it to be a new economic frontier.

June   By secret ballot, Alexei II is elected to be Patriarch of the Orthodox Church.

June 4, 1990   The first of several clashes occurs between Kirghiz and Uzbeks in Kirghizia sparked by local housing shortages. The violence leads to the imposition of a state of emergency and some 200 deaths.

June 8   The Russian Republic declares sovereignty over its territory and resources, challenging the authority of the center.

June 12   Russian Republic declares political sovereignty.

USSR Supreme Soviet passes a Law on the Press, which forbids state censorship.

June 19-23   RSFSR Communist Party Conference designates itself the founding Congress of the newly established Russian Communist Party. The Conference, dominated by conservatives critical of Gorbachev's policies, elects hardliner Ivan Polozkov as Party first secretary.

June 20   Uzbekistan declares sovereignty.

June 24   Moldova declares sovereignty.

July   Ethnic violence breaks out in Tuve, leading to exodus of thousands of Russians.

July 2-14   Twenty-eighth CPSU Party Congress is held. Gorbachev is overwhelmingly reelected general secretary. At the end of the Congress, Boris Eltsin resigns from the Party, followed later by several members of the Democratic Platform. The Congress selects members for a reorganized Politburo, which is to include the first secretaries of the 15 republics.

July 16   Faced with a desperate domestic economic situation and pressure from NATO member countries, the USSR drops its objection to a united Germany's membership in NATO. In exchange the Soviets receive economic assistance from West Germany and assurances from the NATO allies that a united Germany's military will be subject to certain limitations.

Ukrainian Supreme Soviet declares sovereignty.

July 27   Belorussian Supreme Soviet declares sovereignty.

August 2   A presidential decree restoring Soviet citizenship to 23 external exiles, including Alexander Solzhenitsyn and Vladimir Voinovich, is issued.

August 6-31   Academician Stanislav Shatalin leads working group in writing economic reform program to guide the transition to a market-based economy. Called the Shatalin (or 500 Days) Plan, its central features are the right to private enterprise, a voluntary economic union of the republics, and a 500-day schedule. (Meanwhile, a second group formulates a more moderate plan, which is endorsed by the Ryzhkov government.) The RSFSR will later endorse the Shatalin Plan, while the USSR Supreme Soviet will reject it in favor of a compromise plan in October.

August 23   Armenia declares independence.

Turkmenistan declares sovereignty.

August 24   Tajikistan declares sovereignty.

September 23   New Patriarch Alexei celebrates mass in the Uspenskii Cathedral of the Kremlin—the first mass celebrated there since 1918.

September 27   First Congress of Eastern Peoples is held in Moscow.

October 1   The Supreme Soviet passes a new Law on Freedom of Conscience, permitting religious believers greater latitude of worship.

October   Ukrainian student hunger strikes bring down Vitalii Masol, head of the Ukrainian government.

October 13   *Pamiat'* organizer Konstantin Smirnov-Otashvili is found guilty for his role in the groups "action" against Jewish writers.

October 15   Gorbachev is named as recipient of the Nobel Peace Prize.

October 25   Kazakhstan declares sovereignty.

October 28   Elections in Georgia result in victory for a pro-independence government. Following the second round of voting November 11, Zviad Gamsakhurdiia forms a government.

November 13, 1990	Gorbachev meets with more than 1000 soldiers who were elected to various levels of public office, following an often acrimonious discussion of reform by the military personnel.
November 14	Leonid Kravchenko is appointed head of *Gosteleradio*, the state radio and television administration. His restrictive policies lead to a boycott by many liberals.
November 17	In a speech to the Supreme Soviet, Gorbachev announces a major reorganization of the government. The Presidential Council is to be dissolved, and its role in policy is to be assumed by the Council of the Federation. A new post of vice president will be created, and presidential representatives will be appointed to monitor the implementation of decisions.
November 23	Draft of a new Union Treaty is distributed to the USSR Supreme Soviet.
November 30	RSFSR legislature approves private ownership of land.
December 2	Boris Pugo is appointed Minister of Internal Affairs.
December 6	At a meeting of 3500 industrial managers in Moscow, Gorbachev and his policies are subjected to harsh criticism.
December 12	Kirghizia declares sovereignty, becoming the fifteenth of the fifteen union republics to proclaim sovereignty or independence.
December 20	Eduard Shevardnadze announces his resignation, warning of an "impending dictatorship."
	Prime Minister Nikolai Ryzhkov suffers a heart attack, on the eve of his apparent replacement.
December 22	KGB chief Vladimir Kriuchkov gives a speech in which he talks about Western subversion of the USSR.
December 25	Following international expressions of concern about his tone and meaning, Kriuchkov states that his message has been misunderstood.
December 26	Gennadii Yanaev is elected to the new post of Vice President.

December 29, 1990   Secret decree on joint army–police patrols is adopted.

1991

January 2   Soviet MVD troops surround Communist Party headquarters
                   in Vilnius, Lithuania. The following morning MVD special
                   forces occupy and control the main Press Building in Riga,
                   Latvia.

January 6   Christmas is celebrated as an official holiday in parts of the
                   USSR.

January 7   Defense Minister Yazov orders Soviet airborne troops to the
                   Baltics, Armenia, Georgia, Moldova and some areas of
                   Ukraine to enforce military conscription.

January 8   The KGB announces 1990 emigration figures as between
                   440,000 and 460,000 people.

                   The Georgian Supreme Soviet rejects Gorbachev's decree
                   calling for the removal of Georgian armed units from South
                   Ossetia.

January 9   The controversial and popular television program *Vzgliad* is
                   taken off the air, following suppression of several segments.

January 11   The private Interfax news agency is shut down, the staff is
                   expelled from the premises of Gostelradio, and its equip-
                   ment is confiscated. Interfax announces it is reopening in
                   premises made available by the RSRSR government.

January 13   Special forces troops storm the Vilnius TV tower, killing 14
                   people. Around 100,000 Lithuanians surround the parliament
                   building to protect it from military attack. A pro-Moscow
                   National Salvation Committee with connections to the
                   Communist Party claims power in Lithuania.

                   Valentin Pavlov, long associated with the administrative-
                   command system, is named Prime Minister. The appoint-
                   ment inspires little hope for quick moves toward a market
                   economy.

January 20   A demonstration in Moscow opposing repressions in the
                   Baltic region and calling for the resignations of Gorbachev,

Defense Minister Yazov and MVD chief Boris Pugo, draws at least 100,000 people.

January 22
:   A currency reform is announced, withdrawing all 50 and 100 ruble notes from circulation. Officially described as an assault on corruption and unearned income, it creates much panic and confusion.

February 1
:   The Soviet Defense and Internal Affairs Ministries begin joint military-police patrols to maintain public order in major cities. Although seven republics forbid their police to cooperate with the decree, the patrols take place in some 90 cities and involve 12,000 troops.

February 4
:   Representatives of the RSFSR, Ukraine, Belorussia and Kazakhstan meet for the first round of talks on four-way cooperation. The meeting emphasizes bilateral and quadrilateral agreements as an alternative to the Union treaty.

February 10
:   Lithuania conducts a republic-wide poll on independence, pre-empting the scheduled nationwide referendum on the union decreed by Gorbachev. Results show that almost 76 percent of Lithuania's citizens favor independence. Gorbachev declares the poll "legally unsound."

February 12
:   Prime Minister Pavlov justifies the currency reform by accusing vaguely defined Western financial groups of plotting to disrupt the Soviet economy and overthrow Gorbachev. While the statement helps to justify the monetary reform in some circles, it provokes peals of laughter and undermines international confidence in Soviet economic policy.

February 18
:   Gorbachev's four-point peace plan is presented to Iraqi Foreign Minister Tariq Aziz. Viewed with skepticism in the West, it fails to resolve the Gulf crisis.

February 19
:   In an appearance on national television, Boris Eltsin calls for Gorbachev to resign.

February 24
:   Tens of thousands gather near the Kremlin to show support for Boris Eltsin in the wake of conservative machinations to force him from office.

March 2
:   After meeting for nearly six weeks, representatives of nine union and eighteen autonomous republics complete work on

redrafting the Union treaty. The non-participating republics - the Baltics, Moldova, Georgia, and Armenia - schedule their own referenda on independence or secession.

March 3	In plebiscites, 77 percent of those voting in Estonia and 74 percent in Latvia vote for independence
March 7	A new USSR Security Council is established. It is to meet daily and brief the press on defense, economic, foreign policy, security and inter-ethnic issues.
March 17	A nationwide referendum on the preservation of the Union is held. Some republics refuse to participate and others add "local" questions. The results, which show that in the nine republics where voting took place under normal conditions 77 percent voted in favor of preserving the union, are ambiguous due to numerous voting irregularities. Among RSFSR voters, 71 percent favor a Russian presidency.
March 10-18	Clashes in South Ossetia continue. The death toll is now at least 44, including 11 police.
March 19	Miner strikes, begun earlier in the month, spread, with around 300,000 striking by March 19 in the Donbass, Kuzbass, and Vorkuta. Strikers demand better wages, food supplies, living and working conditions, and political changes, including the resignation of Gorbachev and his government and transfer of power to the Federation Council.
March 21	The Supreme Soviet declares that the results of the March 17 referendum will be binding on all 15 Union republics.
March 28	RSFSR Congress of Peoples Deputies, convened at the request of hardline communists seeking to remove Boris Eltsin, the Congress instead passes a resolution suspending Prime Minister Pavlov's ban on demonstrations.
	"Democratic Russia" organizes a pro-Eltsin rally, which is held despite official prohibitions.
March 31	Warsaw Pact military structure is officially dissolved.
April 1	In a republic-wide referendum, 98 percent of Georgian voters choose the restoration of Georgian independence.

April 2   Price increases go into effect throughout the USSR, dou-
                   bling and trebling the cost of some staple foods and consum-
                   er goods. In many cases, these are the first price increases
                   in 30 years.

April 9   President Gorbachev outlines a one-year "Action Program
                   for Leading the Economy Out of Crisis," also known as the
                   "anti-crisis plan." The program is aimed at stabilizing the
                   economy and reimposing some central controls to guide the
                   transition to a market economy. It also includes a moratori-
                   um on strikes and demonstrations during working hours.

                   The Georgian Supreme Soviet, meeting in an emergency
                   session, unanimously declares the Republic of Georgia
                   independent.

April 10   One day after Gorbachev proposes a moratorium on strikes,
                   as many as 100,000 workers fill central Minsk calling for the
                   resignations of the Soviet and Belorussian leaderships and
                   condemning the Communist Party. Strikes are reported in
                   half a dozen other cities.

April 14   The Georgian Supreme Soviet amends the republic's
                   constitution to create a presidency, to which its chairman
                   Zviad Gamsakhurdia is unanimously elected.

April 23   President Gorbachev and representatives of nine Union
                   republics sign a five-point statement on measures to stabilize
                   the crisis situation in the country. Dubbed the "nine plus one
                   agreement," it emphasizes a speedy conclusion of the Union
                   treaty and adoption of the USSR constitution.

April 24-25   At a two-day Central Committee plenum, hardliners hurl
                   harsh criticism at Gorbachev, to which he responds by offer-
                   ing to resign as party general secretary.

April 30   Around 35 people are killed in Armenian-Azeri clashes in
                   the village of Getashen in southwest Azerbaidzhan as Soviet
                   troops and Azeri OMON attempt to evict Armenian resi-
                   dents from the village. A similar number of casualties occur
                   the next day in another village.

May 1   May Day celebrations are visibly subdued throughout the
                   country, and in some republics it is no longer a holiday. In
                   Moscow, about 50,000 people participate in a parade orga-

nized by trade unions, instead of the Communist Party, bearing slogans reflecting the dire economic situation.

May 6   Relief in the miner's strike comes with a USSR-RSFSR agreement to transfer central mines to RSFSR jurisdiction.

May 11   Eltsin says that he now regards Gorbachev as an ally of the democrats, and that he and Gorbachev must combine efforts to keep the Union from falling apart.

May 16   Stating the country is in a crisis, Gorbachev decrees emergency measures to guarantee operation of primary industries in a classic command approach. Jurisdictional questions between the center and republics hamper the program.

May 20   The USSR Supreme Soviet approves the Law on Entry and Exit, easing travel restrictions and phasing out exit visas. The law is to go into effect January 1, 1993.

           MVD officials announce that since the beginning of 1991, 200 civilians and 40 militiamen and MVD troops have been killed in ethnic conflicts. Over the past three years, more than 1,200 people have been killed and 10,000 wounded.

May 21   The RSFSR Congress of Peoples Deputies approves a law establishing a Russian presidency.

May 22   At a press conference, Gorbachev says the Soviet Union needs $100 billion from the West to aid economic reforms.

May 23   Soviet OMON troops attack and burn four border posts in Lithuania and five in Latvia in a series of coordinated assaults on Baltic border and customs offices. Similar assaults occur in the following months in all three Baltic republics.

June 3   At a meeting in the Moscow suburb of Novo-Ogarevo chaired by Gorbachev and attended by leaders of nine republics interested in signing a Union treaty, it is decided to drop the word "socialist" from the name of the USSR and replace it with "sovereign."

June 12   Boris Eltsin is elected as the RSFSR's first president with more than 57 percent of the vote. Reformist mayors of Moscow and Leningrad, Gavril Popov and Anatolii Sobchak, are re-elected.

June 14   President Gorbachev is officially invited to London to meet with the G-7 leaders in mid-July.

June 17   In the USSR Supreme Soviet, Prime Minster Pavlov, supported by the conservative parliamentary faction "Soyuz," openly challenges Gorbachev, demanding expanded powers to bring in the fall harvest and tighten monetary control.

               The Supreme Soviet reviews the final version of the "anti-crisis program," signed by the leaders of the USSR, Belorussia, the Central Asian republics, and Armenia.

June 18   Boris Eltsin arrives in Washington, D.C. at the invitation of the U.S. Congress. During the visit he praises Gorbachev, but also emphasizes a new Russian foreign policy.

June 19   Disclosures are made that Prime Minister Pavlov's proposal for more executive powers was supported by the army, MVD, and KGB.

June 25   The Leningrad city soviet approves restoration of the city's historical name of St. Petersburg, which city voters favored in a non-binding referendum of June 12.

June 26   Gorbachev meets with Grigorii Yavlinsky and American professor Graham Allison to discuss the "grand bargain/window of opportunity" program drawn up by them. Gorbachev says he agrees with 90 percent of the plan, but prefers to stick to his own program.

June 28   In Budapest, representatives of Comecon sign a protocol providing for the organization's disbandment.

July 1   In Prague, representatives of the Warsaw Pact member states sign a protocol dissolving the political and military alliance, which is to be approved later by the signatories' parliaments.

               Leading reformists, including Eduard Shevardnadze and Aleksandr Yakovlev, advocate creating a new "Movement for Democratic Reforms," bringing together all democratic and reformist elements in the country.

July 17   Gorbachev appears before the G-7 leaders in London requesting more consumer goods and support for ruble stabilization.

July 20

Russian President Boris Eltsin issues a decree banning formal political parties from state institutions and enterprises effective August 4. It is a major blow against the Communist Party.

July 29

The RSFSR recognizes Lithuanian independence in a bilateral treaty signed in Moscow.

July 30-31

Presidents Bush and Gorbachev hold a summit in Moscow, during which the long-awaited START Treaty is signed. Bush also meets with Eltsin privately in his Kremlin office, and travels to Kiev where he makes a speech viewed by many as undermining republican self-determination.

During Bush's visit, six Lithuanians are killed at a customs post near the Belorussian border.

August 2

President Gorbachev appears on national television and announces that the RSFSR, Kazakhstan and Uzbekistan will sign the Union Treaty on August 20, with other republics to follow.

August 16

Aleksandr Yakovlev, a close aide to Gorbachev, resigns from the Communist Party. In his resignation statement, he warns that "an influential Stalinist group has formed within the Party's leadership," and is planning a coup.

August 19

A coup d'etat against a vacationing Gorbachev is attempted on the eve of the signing of the Union treaty. Gorbachev and his family are put under house arrest in the Crimea. A State Committee for the State of Emergency, headed by Vice President Gennadii Yanaev, declares that Gorbachev has been removed from his post for reasons of health. The Committee declares a state of emergency, orders tank columns into Moscow, and attempts to control media and communications networks.

August 20-21

The coup unravels in the face of widespread resistance, championed by Boris Eltsin. Military units and top commanders refuse to obey the junta's orders, and attention focuses on protecting the Russian parliament building (white house) and its inhabitants. By some accounts the number of "defenders" exceeds the population of Moscow.

The Estonian Supreme Soviet declares full independence, ending the transition period begun March 30, 1990. The RSFSR swiftly recognizes Estonia's declaration.

August 22 — The coup is pronounced a failure when members of the coup Committee are arrested and Gorbachev returns to Moscow. A mass victory celebration is held in front of the RSFSR parliament building. Eltsin begins to assume powers beyond his post of RSFSR president.

August 22-28 — European and other countries from around the world recognize Estonia, Latvia, and Lithuania as independent states.

August 24 — Gorbachev resigns as Communist Party General Secretary. He calls for the dissolution of the Central Committee, nationalization of Party property, and banning of Party cells in the military, KGB and police.

August 27 — Moldovan parliament votes for the republic's independence from the USSR.

August 30 — USSR Supreme Soviet adopts a resolution suspending the activities of the Communist Party throughout the USSR and freezing its assets.

August 31 — Uzbekistan and Kyrgyzstan Supreme Soviets vote for their republics' independence from the USSR.

USSR State Prosecutor drops charges against investigators Gdlyan and Ivanov.

September 1-5 — USSR Congress of People's Deputies convenes, with ten republics and the center expressing readiness to sign a treaty for a Union of Sovereign States. The Congress approves the creation of a State Council, a new two-chamber Supreme Soviet, and an Inter-republican Economic Council.

September 2 — President Bush announces U.S. recognition of the Baltic states.

September 6 — The State Council holds its first meeting, during which it extends the USSR's recognition of the Baltic states' independence.

September 9 — Tajik Supreme Soviet votes for the republic's independence.

	Several days later, acting President Kadriddin Aslonov bans the Tajik Communist Party and nationalizes its property.

September 10   CSCE admits the Baltic states as full members.

September 18   Baltic states are admitted to the United Nations.

September 21   In Armenia, 95 percent of the electorate votes for secession from the union. The Armenian parliament promptly declares Armenia's independence.

October 5   USSR assumes special associate status with the International Monetary Fund and the World Bank.

October 7   Presidium of the Ukrainian Cabinet of Ministers approves a draft law to create a 450,000-man Ukrainian National Guard and army.

October 11   State Council votes to abolish the central KGB and replace it with a central intelligence service, inter-republican counterintelligence service, and a joint command structure for republican border troops.

October 15   Chechen nationalist leader Dzakhar Dudaev calls on the population of Chechen-Ingushetia to prepare for war, as the struggle with the RSFSR leadership for local authority continues.

October 19   USSR and Israel re-establish diplomatic relations.

October 21   A re-organized USSR Supreme Soviet convenes, with only seven of the 12 republics sending voting deputies. Azerbaidzhan and Moldova send observers, while Armenia, Georgia and Ukraine decide not to send anyone. The economic union agreement is the focal point of this first session.

November 6   Eltsin forms a new RSFSR government in which he will act as Prime Minister.

November 7   Moscow city authorities ban demonstrations on Red Square for the unofficial October Revolution Day. Eltsin bans all-Union and Russian Communist Parties' activities on RSFSR territory. Communist and anti-Communist demonstrations throughout the country are small.

November 8   Eltsin declares a state of emergency in Chechen-Ingushetia
                  and designates an interim administration. Dudaev rejects
                  both acts and declares martial law. Thousands pour into the
                  streets to support Dudaev, while his national guard takes
                  control over MVD troops.

November 11   RSFSR Supreme Soviet rejects Eltsin's state of emergency
                  decree in Chechen-Ingushetia, and calls for a strictly political
                  solution. At the same time, several RSFSR officials accuse
                  the Baltic states of abetting Dudaev in his bid for Chechen
                  independence. The situation is diffused when RSFSR and
                  Chechen officials agree to talks.

November 19   Eduard Shevardnadze agrees to head the new Ministry of
                  External Relations, successor to the Ministry of Foreign
                  Affairs.

November 24   Former Communist leader Rakhmon Nabiyev is elected
                  President in Tajikistan's first presidential elections.

December 1   In Ukraine, 90 percent of the electorate votes to support the
                  August 24 declaration of Ukrainian independence, while 61
                  percent vote for Leonid Kravchuk as president. The vote is
                  quickly followed by Ukraine's annulment of the 1922 treaty
                  that created the USSR.

                  Nursultan Nazarbaev is elected President of Kazakhstan.

December 2-4   Poland, Canada, Czechoslovakia, Russia, the Baltic states,
                  and several West European states indicate they are ready to
                  extend recognition to an independent Ukraine.

December 8   Leaders of Russia, Belorussia and Ukraine announce the
                  establishment of a "Commonwealth of Independent States"
                  and the end of the USSR as a political and geographic
                  entity. The signatories stress that all republics of the former
                  USSR are free to join. Gorbachev says the move is illegal,
                  and calls for an emergency session of the Congress of
                  People's Deputies and a nationwide referendum to decide
                  the matter.

Changes in Leadership Bodies

Changes in Communist Party (CP) Politburo Membership, 1985-1990

Politburo membership when M. S. Gorbachev was elected general secretary in March 1985:

Member	From/To
M.S. Gorbachev	October 1980 - present
G.V. Romanov	March 1976 - July 1985
N.A. Tikhonov	November 1979 - October 1985
V.V. Grishin	April 1971 - February 1986
D.A. Kunaev	April 1971 - January 1987
G.A. Aliyev	November 1982 - October 1987
A.A. Gromyko	April 1973 - September 1988
M.S. Solomentsev	December 1983 - September 1988
V.V. Shcherbitskii	April 1971 - September 1989
V.I. Vorotnikov	December 1983 - July 1990

Candidate Members:

P.N. Demichev	November 1964 - September 1988
V.I. Dolgikh	May 1982 - September 1988
B.N. Ponomarev	May 1972 - February 1986

Politburo Membership Changes Between April 1985 and July 1990:

Full Members

V.M. Chebrikov	April 1985 - September 1989
Ye.K. Ligachev	April 1985 - July 1990
N.I. Ryzhkov	April 1985 - July 1990
E.A. Shevardnadze	July 1985 - July 1990
L.N. Zaikov	March 1986 - July 1990
V.P. Nikonov	June 1987 - September 1989
N.N. Sliunkov	June 1987 - July 1990
A.N. Yakovlev	June 1987 - July 1990
V.A. Medvedev	September 1988 - July 1990
V.A. Kriuchkov	September 1989 - July 1990
Yu.D. Masliukov	September 1989 - July 1990
V.A. Ivashko	December 1989 - present

Candidate Members:

V.V. Kuznetsov	October 1977 - February 1986
S.L. Sokolov	April 1985 - June 1987
B.N. Yeltsin	February 1986 - September 1988
Iu.F. Solov'ev	March 1986 - September 1989
N.N. Sliunkov*	March 1986 - June 1987
A.N. Yakovlev*	January 1987 - June 1987
D.M. Yazov	June 1987 - July 1990
Yu.D. Masliukov*	February 1988 - September 1989
G.P. Razumovskii	February 1988 - July 1990
A.V. Vlasov	September 1988 - July 1990
A.I. Lukianov	September 1988 - July 1990
A.P. Biriukova	September 1988 - July 1990
N.V. Talyzin	October 1988 - September 1989
Ye.M. Primakov	September 1989 - July 1990
B.K. Pugo	September 1989 - July 1990

* Subsequently elevated to full membership.

Politburo, as reorganized at July 1990 Party Plenum:

M.S. Gorbachev
V.A. Ivashko, deputy general secretary
M.M. Burokevichius, First Secretary, Lithuanian CP
G.G. Gumbaridze, First Secretary, Georgian CP
S.I. Gurenko, First Secretary, Ukrainian CP
A.S. Dzasokhov, CC Secretary
I.A. Karimov, First Secretary, Uzbek CP
P.K. Luchinksii, First Secretary, Moldavian CP
A.M. Masaliev, First Secretary, Kyrgyz CP
K. Makhkamov, First Secretary, Tadzhik CP
V.M. Movsisian, First Secretary, Armenian CP
A.N. Mutalibov, First Secretary, Azerbaidzhani CP
N.A. Nazabaev, First Secretary, Kazakh CP
S.A. Niyazov, First Secretary, Turkmen CP
I.K. Polozkov, First Secretary, Russian CP
Iu.A. Prokofi'ev, First Secretary, Moscow City Party Committee
A.P. Rubiks, First Secretary, Latvian CP
G.V. Semenova, CC Secretary
E-A.A. Sillari, First Secretary, Estonian CP
Ye.Ye. Sokolov, First Secretary, Byelorussian CP
Ye.S. Stroev, CC Secretary
I.T. Frolov, Chief Editor of *Pravda*
O.S. Shenin, CC Secretary
G.I. Yanaev, CC Secretary

Changes in the Communist Party Secretariat, 1985-1990

Secretariat membership when M.S. Gorbachev was elected General Secretary *in March 1985:*

Member	From/To
M.S. Gorbachev	November 1978 - present
V.I. Dolgikh	December 1972 - September 1988
M.V. Zimianin	March 1976 - January 1987
I.V. Kapitonov	December 1965 - February 1986
Ye.K. Ligachev	December 1983 - July 1990
B.N. Ponomarev	October 1961 - February 1986
G.V. Romanov	June 1983 - July 1985
K.V. Rusakov	May 1977 - February 1986
N.I. Ryzhkov	November 1982 - October 1985

Membership changes between April 1985 and July 1990:

V.P. Nikonov	April 1985 - September 1989
B.N. Yeltsin	July 1985 - February 1986
L.N. Zaikov	July 1985 - July 1990
A.P. Biriukova	March 1986 - September 1988
A.F. Dobrynin	March 1986 - September 1988
V.A. Medvedev	March 1986 - July 1990
G.P. Razumovskii	March 1986 - July 1990
A.N. Yakovlev	March 1986 - July 1990
A.I. Lukianov	January 1987 - September 1988
N.N. Sliunkov	January 1987 - July 1990
O.D. Baklanov	February 1988 - present
V.M. Chebrikov	September 1988 - September 1989
A.N. Girenko	September 1989 - present
Iu.A. Manaenkov	September 1989 - present
E.S. Stroev	September 1989 - present
G.I. Usmanov	September 1989 - July 1990
I.T. Frolov	December 1989 - July 1990

CC Secretariat, as appointed at July 1990 Party Plenum

M.S. Gorbachev, General Secretary
V.A. Ivashko, Deputy General Secretary
O.D. Baklanov*
B.V. Gidaspov
A.N. Girenko*
A.S. Dzasokhov
V.A. Kuptsov
Iu.A. Manaenkov*
G.V. Semenova
E.S. Stroev*
V.M. Falin
O.S. Shenin
G.I. Yanaev
V.V. Aniskin
V.A. Gayvoronskii
I.I. Melnikov
A.I. Teplenichev
G. Turgunova   *Reappointed to Secretariat

CC Secretariat, as of May 1991:

M.S. Gorbachev, General Secretary
V.A. Ivashko, Deputy General Secretary
V.V. Aniskin
A.S. Dzasokhov
V.M. Falin
V.A. Gaivoronskii
B.V. Gidaspov
A.N. Girenko
V.A. Kuptsov
P.K. Luchinskii
Iu.A. Manaenkov
I.I. Melnikov
G.V. Semenova
O.S. Shenin
Ye.S. Stroev
A.I. Teplenichev
G. Turgunova

USSR Presidential Council (as of April 1990)*

Chingiz Aitmatov, Writer; Chairman, Supreme Soviet Culture Commnission

Vadim Bakatin, Minister of Internal Affairs (MVD)

Valerii Boldin, Chief, CPSU CC General Department

Albert Kauls, Chairman, Latvian Union of Agricultural Workers; Chairman, "Adazhi" Farm Cooperative

Vladimir Kriuchkov, Chairman, Committee for State Security (KGB); Member, CPSU Politburo

Iurii Masliukov, First Deputy Chairman, USSR Council of Ministers; Chairman, State Planning Committee (Gosplan); Member, CPSU Politburo

Iurii Osipian, Vice President, USSR Academy of Sciences; Director, Institute of Solid State Physics, USSR Academy of Sciences

Yevgenii Primakov, Candidate Member, CPSU Politburo

Valentin Rasputin, Writer; Secretary, USSR Writers' Union

Grigorii Revenko, Former First Secretary, Kiev Oblast Party Committee

Nikolai Ryzhkov, Chairman, USSR Council of Ministers; Member, CPSU Politburo

Stanislav Shatalin, Acting Academic Secretary, Economics Department, USSR Academy of Sciences

Eduard Shevardnadze, Minister of Foreign Affairs; Member, CPSU Politburo

Aleksandr Yakovlev, Member, CPSU Politburo; CPSU CC Secretary; Chairman, CPSU CC International Policy Commission

Veniamin Yarin, Co-Chairman, United Russian Workers' Front; Cochairman, "Rossiya" (deputies group)

Dmitrii Yazov, Minister of Defense, Candidate Member, CPSU Politburo

Subsequent additions:

Nikolai Gubenko, Minister of Culture
Vadim Medvedev, former member of Politburo

*The Presidential Council was abolished in December 1990.

Council of the Federation (as of August 19, 1991)

Mikhail Gorbachev, President, USSR
Gennadii Yanaev, Vice President, USSR

Republic Chiefs of State

Levon Ter-Petrosian, Chairman, Supreme Soviet of Armenia
Ayaz Mutalibov, President of Azerbaidzhan; First Secretary, Communist
   Party of Azerbaidzhan
Nikolai Dementei, Chairman, Supreme Soviet of Belorussia
** Arnold Ruutel, Chairman, Supreme Council of Estonia
Zviad Gamsakhurdia, Chairman, President of Georgia
Nursultan Nazarbaev, President of Kazakhstan; First Secretary,
   Communist Party of Kazakhstan
Askar Akaev, President of Kyrgyzstan
** Anatolii Gorbunovs, Chairman, Supreme Council of Latvia
** Vitautas Landsbergis, Chairman, Supreme Council of Lithuania
Mircea Snegur, President of Moldova
Kakhar Makhkamov, President of Tajikistan; First Secretary of
   Communist Party of Tajikistan
Saparmurad Niyazov, President of Turkmenistan; First Secretary of
   Communist Party of Turkmenistan
Leonid Kravchuk, Chairman, Supreme Soviet of Ukraine
Islam Karimov, President of Uzbekistan; First Secretary of Communist
   Party of Uzbekistan
Boris Yeltsin, RSFSR President

*The Council of the Federation was abolished in September 1991, when
the State Council aprroved the creation of a new two-chamber Supreme
Soviet.

**Withdrew immediately after the coup.

Cabinet of Ministers

(established December 1990; membership as of August 19, 1991):

V.S. Pavlov, USSR Prime Minister
V.Kh. Doguzhiev, USS First Deputy Prime Minister
N.P. Laverov, USSR Deputy Prime Minister
Yu.D. Masliukov, USSR Deputy Prime Minister
B. Rakhimova, USSR Deputy Prime Minister
L.D. Ryabev, USSR Deputy Prime Minister
F.P. Sen'ko, USSR Deputy Prime Minister
V.I. Shcherbakov, USSR First Deputy Prime Minister
V.M. Velichko, USSR First Deputy Prime Minister

Security Council

(established March 1991; membership as of August 19, 1991):

M.S. Gorbachev, USSR President
V.V. Bakatin, Chief of Domestic Security
A.A. Bessmertnykh, Foreign Minister
V.A. Kriuchkov, Chief of KGB
V.S. Pavlov, Prime Minister
Ye.M. Primakov, Gorbachev aide
B.K. Pugo, Minister of Internal Affairs (MVD)
G.I. Yanaev, USSR Vice President
D.T. Yazov, Defense Minister

Selected Bibliography

This list provides suggestions for additional reading. Given the explosion of material both in the Soviet Union and in the West, it is impossible to be comprehensive. We have made a particular effort to include materials that would be of interest to students. However, the editor freely admits that chance as well as conscious choice entered into the selection process. There has been no conscious attempt to slight any individual colleagues or publishers.

To avoid a long alphabetical list, the books are divided into broad categories. The categories are hardly exact, and we would not argue with different groupings.

The list includes only books. The periodical literature is vast and growing rapidly. For a summary see Leigh Sarty and John Wright, *The Soviet Union Under Gorbachev* (Carleton University: Centre for Canadian-Soviet Studies, Bibliographic Series No. 2, June 1990). The journals *Problems of Communism, Soviet Economy*, and *Soviet Studies* have provided broad coverage of the Gorbachev period. Virtually every issue of *Foreign Affairs* and *Foreign Policy* includes one or more articles on Soviet international relations. Many of the articles from these journals are cited in the chapters included in this volume.

Harbingers of Change

Cohen, Stephen F. *Rethinking the Soviet Experience: Politics and History Since 1917.* New York: Oxford University Press, 1985.

Friedgut, Theodore H. *Political Participation in the USSR.* Princeton: Princeton University Press, 1979.

Gustafson, Thane. *Reform in Soviet Politics: Lessons of Recent Policies on Land and Water.* New York: Cambridge University Press, 1981.

Hoffmann, Erik P. and Robbin E. Laird. *Technocratic Socialism: The Soviet Union in the Advanced Industrial Era.* Durham: Duke University Press, 1985.

Hoffmann, Erik P. and Robbin E. Laird. *The Politics of Economic Modernization in the Soviet Union*. Ithaca: Cornell University Press, 1982.

Hough, Jerry F. *Soviet Leadership in Transition*. Washington, DC: The Brookings Institution, 1980.

Hough, Jerry F. *The Soviet Union and Social Science Theory*. Cambridge: Harvard University Press, 1977.

Kerblay, Basile. *Modern Soviet Society*. Translated by Rupert Swyer. New York: Pantheon Books, 1983.

Lewin, Moshe. *Political Undercurrents in Soviet Economic Debates: Bukharin to the Modern Reformers*. Princeton: Princeton University Press, 1974.

Politics

Ali, Tariq. *Revolution From Above: Where is the Soviet Union Going?* London: Hutchinson, 1988.

Bahry, Donna. *Outside Moscow: Power, Politics, and Budgetary Policy in the Soviet Republics*. New York: Columbia University Press, 1987.

Brown, Archie, ed. *Political Leadership in the Soviet Union*. Bloomington: Indiana University Press, 1989.

Colton, Timothy J. *The Dilemma of Reform in the Soviet Union*. New York: Council on Foreign Relations, 2nd edition, 1986.

D'Agostino, Anthony. *Soviet Succession Struggles: Kremlinology and the Russian Question from Lenin to Gorbachev*. Boston: Uniyn Hyman, 1988.

Daniels, Robert J. *Is Russia Reformable? Change and Resistance from Stalin to Gorbachev*. Boulder, CO: Westview Press, 1988.

Eklof, Ben. *Soviet Briefing: Gorbachev and the Reform Period*. Boulder, CO: Westview Press, 1989.

Gorbachev, Mikhail. *The August Coup: The Truth and the Lessons*. New York: Harper Collins, 1991.

Hahn, Jeffrey W. *Soviet Grassroots: Citizen Participation in Local Soviet Government*. Princeton: Princeton University Press, 1988.

Hazan, Baruch A. *Gorbachev's Gamble: The 19th All-Union Party Conference* Boulder, CO: Westview Press, 1990.

Huber, Robert T. and Donald R. Kelly, eds. *Perestroika-Era Politics: The New Soviet Legislature and Gorbachev's Political Reforms*. Armonk: NY: M.E. Sharpe, 1991.

Lapidus, Gail W. *State and Society in the Soviet Union*. Boulder, CO: Westview Press, 1992.

Mann, Dawn. *Paradoxes of Soviet Reform: the Nineteenth Communist Party Conference*. Washington, DC: Center for Strategic and International Studies, 1988.

Medvedev, Roy and Giulietto Chiesa. *Time of Change: An Insider's View of Russia's Transformation*. New York: Pantheon Books, 1989.

Mickiewicz, Ellen. *Split Signals: Television and Politics in the Soviet Union.* New York: Oxford University Press, 1988.

Ra'anan Uri, and Igor Lukes, eds. *Inside the Apparat: Perspectives on the Soviet System From Former Functionaries.* Lexington, MA: Lexington Books, 1990.

Remington, Thomas F. *The Truth of Authority: Ideology and Communication in the Soviet Union.* Pittsburgh: University of Pittsburgh Press, 1988.

Tatu, Michel. *L'URSS: Va t-elle changer?* Paris: Le Centurion, 1988.

Tolz, Vera. *The USSR's Emerging Multiparty System.* New York: Praeger, 1990.

Urban, Michael E. *More Power to the Soviets: The Democratic Revolution in the USSR.* Hampshire, England: Edwar Elgar, 1990.

White, Stephen. *Gorbachev and After.* Cambridge: Cambridge University Press, 1991.

White, Stephen, Alex Pravda,nnnnnnnn and Zvi Gitelman, eds. *Developments in Soviet Politics.* Durham, NC: Duke University Press, 1990.

Economics

Aganbegyan, Abel. *Inside Perestroika: The Future of the Soviet Economy.* New York: Harper and Row, 1989.

Aganbegyan, Abel. *The Economic Challenge of Perestroika.* Bloomington: Indiana University Press, 1988.

Aslund, Anders. *Gorbachev's Struggle for Economic Reform: The Soviet Reform Process, 1985-1988.* Ithaca: Cornell University Press, 1989.

Berliner, Joseph S. *Soviet Industry from Stalin to Gorbachev: Studies in Management and Innovation.* Ithaca: Cornell University Press, 1987.

Collins, Susan M. and Dani Rodrik. *Eastern Europe and the Soviet Union in the World Economy.* Washington, DC: Institute for International Economics, 1991.

Desai, Padma. *Perestroika in Perspective: The Design and Dilemmas of Soviet Reform.* Princeton: Princeton University Press, 1989.

Goldman, Marshall I. *Gorbachev's Challenge: Economic Reform in the Age of High Technology.* New York: W. W. Norton, 1987.

Hewett, Ed A. *Reforming the Soviet Economy: Equality versus Efficiency.* Washington, DC: The Brookings Institution, 1988.

Jones, Anthony and William Moskoff. *Ko-Ops: The Rebirth of Entrepreneurship in the Soivet Union.* Bloomington, IN: Indiana University Press, 1991.

Rumer, Boris Z. *Soviet Central Asia: A "Tragic Experiment".* Boston: Unwin Hyman, 1989.

Shelton, Judy. *The Coming Soviet Crash: Gorbachev's Desperate Pursuit of Credit in Western Financial Markets.* New York: The Free Press, 1989.

The Economy of the USSR: Summary and Recommendations. Washington, DC: The World Bank, 1990.

Spulber, Nicolas. *Restructuring the Soviet Economy: In Search of the Market.* Ann Arbor, MI: University of Michigan Press, 1991.

Timofeyev, Lev, ed. *The Anti-Communist Manifesto: Whom to Help in Russia.* Bellevue, WA: Free Enterprise Press, 1990.
U.S Congress. Joint Economic Committee. *Gorbachev's Economic Plans* Washington, DC: USGPO, 1987, 2 vols.

Nationalism and Nationality Politics

Bilocerkowycz, Jaroslaw. *Soviet Ukrainian Dissent: A Study of Political Alienation.* Boulder, CO: Westview Press, 1988.
Furtado, Charles F. and Andrea Chandler, eds. *Perestroika in the Soviet Republics: Documents on the National Question.* Boulder, CO: Westview Press, 1991.
Hajda, Lubomyr and Mark Beissinger, eds. *The Nationalities Factor in Soviet Politics and Society.* Boulder, CO: Westview Press, 1990.
Hauner, Milan. *What Is Asia to Us? Russia's Asian Heartland Yesterday and Today.* Boston: Unwin Hyman, 1990.
Motyl, Alexander J. *Sovietology, Rationality, Nationality: Coming to Grips with Nationalism in the USSR.* New York: Columbia University Press, 1990.
Nahaylo, Bohdan and Victor Swoboda. *Soviet Disunion: A History of the Nationalities Problem in the USSR.* New York: The Free Press, 1990.
Ra'anan, Uri. *The Soviet Empire: The Challenge of National and Democratic Movements.* Lexington: Lexington Books, 1990.
Rywkin, Michael. *Moscow's Muslim Challenge: Soviet Central Asia.* New York: M. E. Sharpe, Inc., 1990.
Senn, Alfred Erich. *Lithuania Awakening.* Berkeley: University of California Press, 1990.
Simon, Gerhard. *Nationalism and Policy Toward the Nationalities in the Soviet Union.* Boulder, CO: Westview Press, 1991.

Society and Social Issues

Attwood, Lynne. *The New Soviet Man and Woman: Sex-role Socialization in the USSR.* Bloomington: Indiana University Press, 1990.
Bridger, Susan. *Women in the Soviet Countryside: Women's Roles in Rural Development in the Soviet Union.* New York: Cambridge University Press, 1989.
Buckley, Mary. *Women and Ideology in the Soviet Union.* Ann Arbor: University of Michigan Press, 1989.
du Plessix-Gray, Francine. *Soviet Women: Walking the Tightrope.* New York: Doubleday, 1989.
Forest, Jim. *Religion in the New Russia: The Impact of Perestroika on the Varieties of Religious Life in the Soviet Union.* New York: Crossroad, 1990.
Friedberg, Maurice and Heyward Isham, eds. *Soviet Society Under Gorbachev: Current Trends and the Prospects for Reform.* Armonk, NY: M. E. Sharpe, 1987.

Jones, Anthony, Walter D. Connor and David E. Powell, eds. *Soviet Social Problems*. Boulder, CO: Westview Press, 1991.

Lane, David. *Soviet Society under Perestroika*. Boston: Unwin Hyman, 1990.

Mamonova, Tatyana. *Russian Women's Studies: Essays on Sexism in Soviet Culture*. New York: Pergamon Press, 1989.

Marples, David R. *The Social Impact of the Chernobyl Disaster*. New York: St. Martin's Press, 1988.

Medvedev, Zhores. *The Legacy of Chernobyl*. New York: W. W. Norton, 1990.

Pushkarev, Sergei, Vladimir Rusak and Gleb Yakunin. *Christianity and Government in Russia and the Soviet Union: Reflections on the Millennium*. Boulder, CO: Westview Press, 1989.

Ramet, Pedro, ed. *Religion and Nationalism in Soviet and East European Politics*. Durham: Duke University Press, 1989.

Ramet, Sabrina P., ed. *Religious Policy in the Soviet Union*. New York: Cambridge University Press, forthcoming, 1991.

Riordan, Jim, ed. *Soviet Youth Culture*. Bloomington: Indiana University Press, 1989.

Rywkin, Michael. *Soviet Society Today*. Armonk, NY: M. E. Sharpe, 1989.

Sacks, Michael Paul and Jerry G. Pankhurst, eds. *Understanding Soviet Society*. Boston: Unwin Hyman, 1988.

Singleton, Fred, ed. *Environmental Problems in the Soviet Union and Eastern Europe*. Boulder, CO and London: Lynne Rienner, 1987.

Traver, Nancy. *Kife: The Lives and Dreams of Soviet Youth*. New York: St. Martin's Press, 1989.

U.S. Helsinki Watch. *Nyeformaly: Civil Society in the USSR*. Washington, DC: February 1990.

Zaslavskaya, Tatyana. *The Second Socialist Revolution: An Alternative Soviet Strategy*. Bloomington: Indiana University Press, 1990.

International Relations

Braun, Aurel, ed. *The Soviet-East European Relationship in the Gorbachev Era: The Prospects for Adaptation*. Boulder, CO: Westview Press, 1990.

Dawisha, Karen. *Eastern Europe, Gorbachev and Reform: The Great Challenge*. New York: Cambridge University Press, 2nd edition, 1990.

Dibb, Paul. *The Soviet Union: The Incomplete Superpower*. Chicago: University of Illinois Press, 1986.

Flynn, Gregory, ed. *The West and the Soviet Union: Politics and Policy*. New York: St. Martin's Press, 1990.

Gati, Charles. *The Bloc That Failed: Soviet-East European Relations in Transition*. Bloomington: Indiana University Press, 1990.

Griffith, William E., ed., *Central and Eastern Europe: The Opening Curtain?* Boulder, CO: Westview Press, 1989.

Hough, Jerry. *Russia and the West: Gorbachev and the Politics of Reform*. New York: Simon and Schuster, 1990.

Horelick, Arnold J., ed. *U.S.-Soviet Relations: The Next Phase*. Ithaca: Cornell University Press, 1987.

Jacobsen, Carl G., ed. *Soviet Foreign Policy: New Dynamics, New Themes*. London: Macmillan, 1989.

Kelley, Donald R. and Purvis, Hoyt, eds. *Old Myths and New Realities in United States-Soviet Relations*. New York: Praeger, 1990.

Legvold, Robert. *The New Thinking and Gorbachev's Foreign Policy*. New York: Institute for East-West Security Studies, July 1987.

Lynch, Allen. *The Soviet Study of International Relations*. New York: Cambridge University Press, 1987.

Saivetz, Carol R. ed. *The Soviet Union in the Third World*. Boulder, CO: Westview Press, 1989.

Simons, Thomas W. *The End of the Cold War?* New York: St. Martin's Press, 1989.

Zacek, Jane Shapiro, ed. *The Gorbachev Generation: Issues in Soviet Foreign Policy*. New York: Paragon, 1989.

Military and Security Issues

Colton, Timothy J. and Thane Gustafson, eds. *Soldiers and the Soviet State*. Princeton: Princeton University Press, 1990.

Garthoff, Raymond L. *Deterrence and the Revolution in Soviet Military Doctrine*. Washington, DC: The Brookings Institution, 1990.

Green, William C. and Theodore Karasik, eds. *Gorbachev and His Generals*. Boulder, CO: Westview Press, 1990.

Herspring, Dale R. *The Soviet High Command, 1967-1989: Personalities and Politics*. Princeton: Princeton University Press, 1990.

MccGwire, Michael. *Perestroika and Soviet National Security*. Washington, DC: The Brookings Institution, 1991.

Parrott, Bruce, ed. *The Dynamics of Soviet Defense Policy*. Washington, DC: The Wilson Center Press, 1990.

Schweitzer, Carl-Christophe, ed. *The Changing Western Analysis of the Soviet Threat*. New York: St. Martin's Press, 1990.

Sherr, Alan B. *The Other Side of Arms Control: Soviet Objectives in the Gorbachev Era*. Winchester, MA: Unwin Hyman, 1988.

Gorbachev and Perestroika

Doder, Dusko and Louise Branson. *Gorbachev: Heretic in the Kremlin*. New York: Viking, 1990.

Gorbachev, Mikhail. *Perestroika: New Thinking for Our Country and the World*. New York: Harper and Row, 1987.

Hill, Ronald J. and Jan A. Dellenbrant. *Gorbachev and Perestroika: Towards A New Socialism?* Brookfield, VT: Edward Elgar, 1989.
Hosking, Geoffrey. *The Awakening of the Soviet Union.* Cambridge, MA: Harvard University Press, 1990.
Kagarlitsky, Boris. *Farewell Perestroika: A Soviet Chronicle.* London and New York: Verso, 1990.
Kerblay, Basile. *Gorbachev's Russia.* Translated by Rupert Swyer. New York: Pantheon Books, 1989.
Laqueur, Walter. *The Long Road to Freedom: Russia and Glasnost.* New York: Collier Books, 1989.
Lewin, Moshe. *The Gorbachev Phenomenon: A Historical Interpretation..* Berkeley, CA: University of California Press, 1988.
Medvedev, Zhores A. *Gorbachev.* New York: W. W. Norton, 1986.
Sakharov, Andrei. *Moscow and Beyond, 1986 to 1989.* New York: Alfred A. Knopf, 1991.
Smith, Hedrick. *The New Russians.* New York: Random House, 1990.
Tsipko, Alexander S. *Is Stalinism Really Dead?.* Translated by E.A. Tichina and S., V. Nikheev. San Francisco: Harper, 1990.
Walker, Martin. *The Waking Giant: Gorbachev's Russia.* New York: Pantheon Books, 1988.
Yeltsin, Boris. *Against the Grain: An Autobiography.* Translated by Michael Glenny, New York: Summit Books, 1990.

Literature and Culture

Bushnell, John. *Moscow Graffiti: Language and Subculture.* Boston: Unwin Hyman, 1990).
Davies, R. W. *Soviet History in the Gorbachev Revolution.* Bloomington: Indiana University Press, 1989.
Garrard, John and Carol. *Inside the Soviet Writers' Union.* New York: The Free Press, 1990.
Goscilo, Helena, ed., *Balancing Acts: Contemporary Stories by Russian Women.* Bloomington: Indiana University Press, 1989.
Goscilo, Helena and Byron Lindsey, eds. *Glasnost: An Anthology of Russian Literature Under Gorbachev.* Ann Arbor, MI: Ardis, 1990.
Gould, Daniel, ed. *Post New Wave Cinema in the Soviet Union and Eastern Europe.* Bloomington: Indiana University Press, 1989.
Nove, Alec. *Glasnost in Action: Cultural Renaissance in Russia.* Winchester, MA: Unwin Hyman Inc., 1989.
Ryback, Timothy. *Rock Around the Bloc: A History of Rock Music in Eastern Europe and the Soviet Union.* New York: 1990.
Sinyavsky, Andrei. *Soviet Civilization: A Cultural History.* Translated by Joanne Turnbull. New York: Arcade Publishing, 1990.

Stites, Richard. *Soviet Popular Culture: Entertainment and Society in Russia Since 1900*. New York: Cambridge University Press, forthcoming, 1991.

Edited Collections Covering Multiple Disciplines

Bialer, Seweryn, ed. *Politics, Society and Nationality Inside Gorbachev's Russia*. Boulder, CO: Westview Press, 1989.

Bialer, Seweryn and Michael Mandelbaum, eds. *Gorbachev's Russia and American Foreign Policy*. Boulder, CO: Westview Press, 1988.

Brumberg, Abraham, ed. *Chronicle of A Revolution: A Western-Soviet Inquiry into Perestroika*. New York: Pantheon Books, 1990.

Breslauer, George W., ed. *Can Gorbachev's Reforms Succeed?* Berkeley: University of California, Berkeley-Stanford Program in Soviet Studies, 1990.

Cohen, Stephen and Katrina vanden Heuvel, eds., *Voices of Glasnost: Interviews with Gorbachev's Reformers* (New York: W. W. Norton and Co., 1989).

Hasegawa, Tsuyoshi and Alex Pravda, eds. *Perestroika: Soviet Domestic and Foreign Policies*. London: Sage Publications, 1990.

Laqueur, Walter, ed. *Soviet Union 2000: Reform or Revolution?* New York: St. Martin's Press, 1990.

McCauley, Martin, ed. *The Soviet Union Under Gorbachev*. London: Macmillan, 1987.

Millar, James R., ed. *Politics, Work and Daily Life in the USSR: A Survey of Former Soviet Citizens*. New York: Cambridge University Press, 1987.

Rieber, Alfred J. and Alvin Z. Rubinstein, eds. *Perestroika at the Crossroads*. Armonk, NY: M. E. Sharpe, 1991.

Zacek, Jane Shapiro, ed. *The Gorbachev Generation: Issues in Soviet Domestic Policy*. New York: Paragon House, 1989.

Collections of Readings and Documents

Cerf, Christopher and Marina Albee, eds. *Small Fires: Letters from the Soviet People to Ogonyok Magazine, 1987-1990*. New York: Summit Books, 1990.

Eisen, Jonathan, ed. *The Glasnost Reader*. New York: New American Library, 1990.

Mann, Dawn, Robert Monyak, and Elizabeth Teague. *The Supreme Soviet: A Biographical Dictionary*. Washington, DC: Center for Strategic and International Studies, 1989.

Melville, Andrei and Gail W. Lapidus. *The Glasnost Papers: Voices on Reform from Moscow*. Boulder, CO: Westview Press, 1990.

Tarasulo, Isaac J., ed. *Gorbachev and Glasnost: Viewpoints from the Soviet Press*. Wilmington: SR Books, 1989.

Contributors

Harley D. Balzer is Director of the Russian Area Studies Program at Georgetown University.

Murray Feshbach is Research Professor of Demography at Georgetown University.

Paul Goble is Special Advisor on Soviet Nationality Problems to the Assistant Secretary for European Affairs and Desk Officer for Estonia, Latvia and Lithuania, U.S. Department of State.

Helena Goscilo is Professor of Russian at the University of Pittsburgh.

Jerry F. Hough is Director of the Center on East-West Trade, Investment and Communications at Duke University and a senior fellow at the Brookings Institution.

Robert T. Huber is Director of the Soviet Program at the Social Science Research Council. He previously worked for ten years as a Professional Staff Member of the U.S. House Committee on Foreign Affairs.

Blair A. Ruble is Director of the Kennan Institute for Advanced Russian Study of the Woodrow Wilson International Center for Scholars.

Gertrude Schroeder is Professor of Economics, University of Virginia.

Galina V. Starovoitova is an ethnosociologist at the USSR Academy of Science Institute of Ethnography in Moscow. She is a USSR Peoples Deputy from Armenia, and represents part of Leningrad and Karelia in the Russian Republic Congress of People's Deputies.

Angela Stent is Associate Professor of Government at Georgetown University.

Josephine Woll is Associate Professor of Russian at Howard University.

Index